MARRY YOUR BEST FRIEND

How to Successfully Date,

Connect with Your Life Mate and

Keep It Going Forever

DANIELLE COULANGES

Praise for Marry Your Best Friend

"Insightful guide!" - *Camille*
"Thought-provoking!" - *Jade*
"Engaging and relatable!" - *Sheba*

From helping readers clarify what kind of relationship they're seeking to exploring contemporary dating perils to offering straightforward solutions for building a successful marriage and sustaining happiness, Coulanges offers eager insight into the challenges and joys of not just marriage itself, but the journey leading up to it. Coulanges's humor puts readers at ease… Her practical solutions and encouraging insights transform the often-daunting prospect of finding long-term love into something exciting and achievable."
– *BookLife – Publisher's Weekly*

Throughout the book, Coulanges does a great job of blending personal and anecdotal experiences with hard facts from studies and other sources. She presents it all with just the right amount of theology as to connect with a Christian readership without turning off anyone outside that category, a truly commendable achievement. Particularly insightful are the chapters "Are There Solutions to Dating Difficulties," "Know Thyself and To Thyself Be True," and "Suggested Tips for a Successful Marriage." – *Judge, 33rd Annual Writer's Digest Self-Published Book Awards*

www.daniellecoulanges.com

CONTENTS

FOREWORD ix

INTRODUCTION xiv

PART 1: WHAT IS A RELATIONSHIP? 1

Relationship - What Is It? 2
Relationship 101 10
Relationship Why? 14
Do You Want A Relationship? 19
Dating Is Difficult 22
Are There Solutions To Dating Difficulties? 34

PART II : PREPARE FOR PARTNERSHIP 61

Ready For A Relationship? 62
Preparing For A Relationship 71
Know Thyself – And To Thyself Be True 73
Know What You Want 99

PART III : MAKING THE CONNECTION 109

Seek And You Will Find 110
Identifying A Candidate 115
Equally Yoked 123
Initial Challenges And Growing Pain 140

Challenges of Options   145

Increase The Odds For Success   158

The Fantastic Island   162

PART IV : PARTNERING FOR LIFE   170

The Chosen Mate   171

Blueprint For   A Successful Marriage   176

Suggested Tips For A Successful Marriage 185

Married Life   204

Tests And Crises   213

How To Keep It Going   239

Tricks And Tools For Success   244

PART V : FOREVER IS A GOOD THING   253

Make It Last A Lifetime   254

Always And Forever   260

ACKNOWLEDGEMENTS   264

REFERENCED SOURCES   271

SPECIAL GIFT GIVEAWAY   278

ABOUT THE AUTHOR   280

MARRY YOUR BEST FRIEND

Dating and romantic relationships can sometimes feel like a scary zipline run. You jump off with great trepidation, but if you can conquer your fear, adopt the required posture, and hang on, it is an exhilarating experience!

In 2022, this adventurous sixty-something senior ziplined in Punta Cana, Dominican Republic.

FOREWORD

My Why

This book was inspired by all those who have fulfilled the role of "my children" in my life, including my former students, but most particularly, my nieces and nephews, my daughters-in-love, and my godchildren. You have allowed me to love you, counsel you, guide you, create beautiful memories with you and on occasions, even admonish you, or spoil you, just like a parent would their child. You have trusted me with your secret dreams and sought my help with practical direction, counsel, and prayers when you encountered life challenges. Most importantly, you embraced me as your wise elder and have shown me so much love in expression and in deeds. My heart expanded and created a new, dedicated chamber for each one of you that is forever yours.

I have prayed over your health, your finances, your careers, your crises, and your successes. What I've never acknowledged to you until now, is that I continuously pray over your love life as well. I ask God to prepare you for the companion He has designed for you, so that when you meet at the proper time, everything will fall into place. I've asked Him to bless the relationships that are already in place, to protect and guide you. I want to see you all in a loving, fulfilling partnership where the awesome individual you are is fully appreciated and cherished. I wish to see you and your significant other gathered around my dinner table, feasting on meals I've joyfully whipped up to celebrate you. I am looking forward to having young ones putter around the garden with me or invite me to attend their concerts or games.

I hope Henri and I demonstrated by our own example what marriage and a successful domestic partnership look like. I pray that disclosing the recipes for our success will provide you the guidance to make your dream of a partnership a reality or strengthen the relationship you are now in. I dedicate this book to you.

One of my greatest blessings has been to live up to the title you affectionately bestow upon me, that of Auntie. For that, my beloved, I thank you and love you forever!

"God bless you and keep you… God lift up his face toward you and give you peace." – (Numbers 6:24-26) But most of all, may The Lord grant you a perfect LOVE!

Aunt D.

WHAT THE BELOVED ARE SAYING

Danielle wrote this book with the very best of intentions and wishes. She truly wants these things for everyone; love and happiness, not for a moment, but for always. *"Marry your best friend"* is a testament to her well lived life, her *beliefs,* and her love of others. **The practicality of this book will ground you and may put the happily ever after you've been seeking within your reach.**

I highly recommend it.

Karen A., age 54 – 1ˢᵗ Niece – Managing Director of HR

Becoming a better version of yourself should be a continuous life objective, whether you are in a relationship or not.

When you lose sight of that, you leave an open space for someone else to define who you are or what you should become and that in a relationship, is the beginning of the end. Key insights from this book for me!

Jeffrey K., age 45 – nephew – Finance Manager

Your partner will never see things precisely the same way you do. And that won't and shouldn't change throughout your journey with them.

You have to be humble enough, curious enough, open minded enough, to welcome and **consider this divergent point of view in order to grow and be a better human being.**

Nadia K., age 43 – niece – Attorney

Aunt Danielle's book intrigued me from the cover design. The image beautifully captures the parallel between the complexities of mazes and the intricacies of relationships. Mazes can be tricky, in that they pose challenges and are designed with several ways in and out and multiple paths to the center, just like relationships. Just as each maze presents a different experience to those who enter it, every relationship offers a distinctive path towards a common goal. You are likely to meet someone who has a different way of doing things, comes from a different background and upbringing, but **so long as you are both trying to get to the same place (the center) how you get there doesn't necessarily matter.** Your path is unique just like the other person's. There isn't a "wrong way," only diverse approaches.

Danielle I., age 39 – niece/goddaughter – Marketing Specialist

This is what the cover of this book conveys to me: You do not fall in love. **Love is not something you "fall" into. Love is something that you "grow" into.** A relationship is not a destination but rather a journey with your best friend. Going through trials and tribulations (the maze) but doing it together through thick and thin. Not just during good times.

Camille J., age 31 – niece – Make-up Artist/Entrepreneur

First off, I love the symbolism on the cover. To me, it symbolizes that the journey of finding your soulmate is not linear. There are twist and turns, but ultimately in the end, if you stick to it, you find each other. And in the shape of a heart; how appropriate: the heart is at the center of it all!

I am excited to continue reading the book. I do think that it's important to evaluate myself, because like you said somewhere in a passage, **you find the person that you're energetically connected to**! Which is so true. Dating is not at the forefront of my mind, but I am excited to start putting more thought into it and being more intentional and strategic when it comes to finding my person.

If I could describe the previewed passage in two words, it would be **"thought provoking"** ...

Jade J., age 25 – niece – Aesthetician/Entrepreneur

My relationship with Aunt Danielle operates highest on a spiritual level. My aunt could see early on that while I possessed good morals and integrity, I struggled a great deal with having faith. Faith in others, faith in myself, and faith in the higher power. When we would have our talks about life and pursuit of career goals, she made it clear to me that until I can surrender myself to the higher power, things won't manifest or come to fruition. **You have to believe in things you can't see or hear while understanding you can talk to and build your own relationship with God.** Aunt Danielle does a great job of not being preachy but more so offering a perspective from her past experiences.

Learning my aunt had booty call situations makes me realize your elders had many lives before they became the evolved version you got to know and love. Would have never thought Aunt Danielle tried casual dating. She's always seemed like a woman who always required and deserved commitment. I guess at some point, everybody has to experience something they don't want, so they know exactly how to pursue something they desire. - I love you and I'm so proud to have you as my Auntie.

Nick Alexander, 32 – grand-nephew – Comedian/Actor

The book captured me from the cover. To me the maze symbolizes the complex and interconnected journey of relationships, experiences, and navigating personal challenges.

As a daughter of immigrant parents, your reflection on balancing cultural expectations with personal aspirations deeply resonated with me, highlighting the struggle I and others like me face in relationships.

I learned about the significant impact of the importance of finding

a balance between personal desires and expectations and your candid sharing of personal experiences and growth made me want to delve deeper to learn more about your insights.

This book is **insightful and relatable!** The reading was **engaging and thought-provoking.**

Bathsheba L., age 38 – daughter-in-love – Educator

My aunt has always been there for me as a mentor. But she is also an auntie who makes you breakfast and takes you on fun activities around the city whenever I am in town. She demonstrates love and makes you feel loved.

Watching my uncle and my aunt in their marriage, I understood the benefits of a united front and the importance of knowing your mate. Those two are the best example of a loving couple I've ever seen.

I am excited to read my aunt's book. The title and the picture both convey love, peace, and make you curious to read the book and find out more. And I really love my aunt!

Emmanuel B. age 47 – nephew-in-love – IT Entrepreneur

My dearest mother-in-love! Congratulations on this exciting chapter in your life. I am so happy to see **you attract the love you deserve.** I am a better woman because of the example of strength, beauty, and love you demonstrated while I was growing up and now the world is going to be a better place if they embrace **"auntie's wisdom!" Embracing this wisdom will definitely help many to attract a healthy relationship and marry their best friend.** Wish you love!

Camille S. age 56 – daughter-in-love

– "The Healthy Love Coach"

INTRODUCTION

Dating. Relationships! Ugh! The frustration and confusion are overwhelming. This process has always been challenging, even when I was single decades ago. Today however, finding a life partner feels like a perilous journey of misadventures, where only a few manage to achieve the coveted status of being coupled or married.

This auntie is here to help you.

In 2010 I published *Cads, Princes and Best Friends,* a memoir in which I shared the journey of self-discovery that followed the break-up of a decade long love relationship when I was in my mid-thirties, and my subsequent attempts to find love again.

During the time expressed in that story, I had been inexperienced at dating even as an adult. I had a lot of questions and made a lot of mistakes. My interactions with men while searching for a mate were "learn by trial and error." After falling off the bike too many times and left with numerous bruises, I eventually found my road partner and we successfully rode off into the sunset together.

I wish there had been a sage or wise elder to counsel me through and explain how to go about gaining a healthy relationship, and further, how to keep it going strong when I did get one. This book, *Marry Your Best Friend*, is that wise elder. It is about how you can find, successfully date, and connect with a life partner and maintain a forever love relationship in the era of disposable everything, currently 2024.

It is based on life lessons learned from my personal experiences, interviews with other individuals, celebrity quotes, and research done using an online survey I conducted in October 2023, *Dating & Relationships in the*

2020s. The survey provided insights from 110 respondents, that included 30 single men, 40 single women and 42 married or committed couples of various age groups ranging from 25 to 55+.

What this book offers:

This book is not intended to be an extensive manual for everything dating or marriage. What it does offer is:

- An informative and realistic guide on the full story.
- **A "reel" on how to do this relationship thing right, at all the various phases:**
  - **from dating**
  - **to courtship**
  - **and eventually a committed, partnered, or married life.**

Who should read this book:

A must-read for:

- Men and women
- between the ages of 25 and 55 plus.
- If you are **single** and seeking a committed relationship.
- If you are **in a serious relationship** and contemplating taking the next step.
- If you are **married** and seek to secure the health of your relationship and keep things exciting and vibrant.

The situations analyzed in this book and my observations are based on romantic relationships between men and women, because that is what I know, believe in, and wish to speak about. Nevertheless, the premise of human relationships carries universal truths that apply to all personal interactions and connection between people.

Marry Your Best Friend provides practical advice to support the guidance given and offers various tools you can use to:

- Know what a relationship is.
- Understand the current dating climate.
- Examine your true self to know who you are and what you want.
- Do the necessary work to prepare yourself for a shared life.
- Determine what you want in a relationship and have the courage to claim it.
- Recognize that there are challenges to surmount and how to equip yourself accordingly.
- And once you are connected to your dream partner, how to maintain the vibrancy of an ongoing successful partnership.

The views expressed in this text are my personal beliefs and where noted, those of the individuals interviewed. I presented the facts as objectively as I could. However, I am a born-again Christian, and that perspective is often reflected in my discussions. In every case, my opinions are shared to inform, not to impose.

This is an open conversation, where secular terms, expressions, and experiences taken from contemporary culture, as well as the occasional biblical references make appearances. This is real life as best expressed by someone who has lived, and continues to live a full life and is not afraid to talk about it.

Read this book with an open mind. Do not miss the opportunity to reap the benefits of the wisdom and lessons offered here.

Mothers and fathers, aunties and uncles, grandmas, and grandpas, share this book with the younger generation who are of dating age. Let it be a conversation starter to tell them your story and add your own wisdom to the relationship narrative.

I am a hope filled romantic who loves the concept of true love. I have been blessed it found me, I claimed it, and have maintained my love story going strong for 26 years, counting the years of pre-marital dating. My wish is that everyone would find their person and pair up for a happy, productive, long life together.

If it is true that love conquers all, then LET THERE BE LOVE!

Enjoy this explorative journey. May it strengthen your spirit and leave you confidently equipped to navigate the dating and relationship waters, ultimately leading you to a marvelous destination!

Blessings!

Danielle – aka D'Auntie

Fall 1995 photo shoot – I was "Dee La Cool" fashion designer. Modeling one of my creations with the New York City skyline in the background.

I appear confident, don't I? And why shouldn't I be? I am beautiful, glamorous, and talented. But, yet…

This tongue-in-cheek picture taken with one of my male models in a way depicts my true state of mind at that time.

On the dating front, I was insecure and needy. I was desperate for somebody to love me.

PART I

WHAT IS A RELATIONSHIP?

Regardless of how much perceptions and beliefs have changed over time, one universal truth remains: human connection, especially the romantic kind, helps us move from the "not good" of being alone to the "very good."

RELATIONSHIP
WHAT IS IT?

Relationship is one of those topics that prompts most people's ears to perk up and listen. Humans are wired to desire relationships with others, starting with the familial, then with friends and business associates and ultimately, with a romantic partner.

Most single people profess to want to be in a romantic relationship of their own, and preferably a long lasting, fulfilling one. People are looking for genuine connections. The survey, *Dating & Relationships in the 2020s*, revealed some interesting facts, as shown by the responses from single men and women:

- 72% of women and 90% of men said they were ready for a serious long-term partnership or marriage.
- 73% of women and 43% of men based their readiness on their desire for a long-term partnership.
- 66% of women and 47% of men wanted personal connection.

Respondents were also asked of their preference, given a choice of dating situations for the rest of their life.

- 46% of women and 22% of men chose casual dating with different people.
- 89% of women and 79% of men picked serious long-term relationship with a life mate.

It is to be noted that some people were open to both casual and serious dating, although most respondents felt ready for a serious relationship, fueled by the desire to achieve long-term partnership or marriage. A big surprise for me was that the percentages for men on those items were as high as they were.

Does this reveal an underlying misconception or a commonly uninformed assumption that men are non-committal and just want to remain casual? These answers seem to suggest otherwise.

We've discovered a common ground between men and women: irrespective of gender, individuals seek long-term relationships that offer personal fulfillment.

◊ ◊ ◊

How can you acquire that coveted treasure known as a relationship? Is it merely luck, where the perfect one falls in your lap, or is there a method to improve your chances of attaining and sustaining a joyful and fulfilling partnership with a significant other?

While the pathways and the approaches used may be different for everyone, there are some basic and fundamental strategies that universally ensure success for a love relationship.

What is a relationship?

The first thing to know about anything you want to get involved in is, what is it? What are you getting into? What, exactly is a "relationship?"

There seems to be a serious lack of knowledge among the younger generation as to what that is. During a conversation about the upcoming book with my good friend Charles F* a married man in his fifties, he found this generation "cognitively challenged" when it came to understanding true relationships. - I used my own euphemism instead of repeating the real (R) word he used, to be politically correct. In any case, a good number of people, especially millennials, who are used to adjusting their ubiquitous selfies to desired effect, fail to realize a few things:

- Life and people are not perfect.
- You cannot edit people or situations to your liking in a relationship.
- It's not all about you. There are two souls involved in a relationship.
- You may not get the perfect shot for your reel, but you choose the best picture among the lot that is suitable for the situation.

I wrote a blog in October of 2023, when I came back from a vacation in Cancun, Mexico, titled, *"Look At me! – The Perils of Self-Absorption."* In it I discussed what I saw as an alarming trend of people so absorbed in taking selfies that they paid no attention to the beautiful scenery that surrounded them. Their objective was solely to find a spot that *showcased* them. A background that made them look good. Mother Nature got no flowers for her works. God received no glory for his creation. The gorgeous views were not even acknowledged with a second glance.

A lot of that self-absorption goes on in relationships today. The partner is overlooked and viewed solely as a backdrop to make one look good. People fail to see that a relationship is an exchange of emotions with everything that it entails. The self-analysis, the give and take, the compromises, the what is best for us, and the occasional "you come first."

In the dating phase, there is the discovery of each other that is fundamental in determining whether a relationship is viable or not. Some people are so focused on themselves that they sabotage any chances of something developing between them and the prospect.

When I was working on this section of the book, in October 2023, news of a TikTok post by an Atlanta influencer flooded the internet. This woman being pursued by a suitor had finally agreed to meet him for drinks. But once at the restaurant, she proceeded to order 48 oysters that she slurped down while filming herself. By the time she ordered an additional potatoes and crab cakes entree, the date had left the building under the guise of going to the restroom. When she texted him later, offended that she was left stuck with the high bill, he offered to Cashapp her the total for the drinks he had originally offered.

The whole thing went viral: her post voicing her outrage at the date for walking out on her and the public reposting the incident in crowded discussion boards. As expected, the comments from men were mostly derogatory toward her, with some feeling it was outrageous to even eat that much of anything, to exhibit bad manners for slurping or act that way on a first date. There were the women who felt that a guy should never walk out on a bill.

I have a few issues with this whole scenario.

- Being an influencer can be a good thing when someone uses their platform to promote a cause: save the whales, abolish genital mutilation, save the planet; share inspiring or meaningful messages. However, too many employ their position of influence to showcase themselves, even when it is in bad taste. "See me here. See me there."

- What are you doing filming yourself during a first date when you should be engaging the other person to get to know each other? This is that self-absorbed malady I referred to in my blog *Look at Me!* The date became a backdrop to showcase herself, instead of an exercise in making a genuine connection.

- If your objective is to make this man spend on you when you don't even know his financial capabilities, how do you think that projects? Are you going to spend the bills money on designer shoes and expect him to just deal with it?

- If you cannot give this person your full attention for the few minutes that you are on a date, how can he depend on you for conversations, for togetherness, for support?

I could go on about what was wrong with that picture. Public opinion was vocal about it. A man wanting some arm candy or a chance to showcase himself might associate with such a woman to be in the limelight with her. But if one is looking for genuine connection and a true relationship, they will do like that guy.

Skedaddle. Skip out. Get out of town. RUN!

Let me put on my teacher hat for a minute.

To get a better understanding of a word meaning or application, it is helpful to look at its given definition. The *Merriam Webster Dictionary* has several definitions for the word "relationship."

- *The state of being related or interrelated* – as in a relationship between weather patterns and global warming.
- *The relation connecting or binding participants in a relationship* – such as kinship or familial connections.
- *A state of affairs existing between those having relations or dealings* – a business connection or diplomatic interaction between countries, for example.
- *A romantic or passionate attachment* – the kind that most people associate with the word relationship.

When it comes to dating or marriage, the default definition is commonly number four: a romantic attachment. However, all of *Webster*'s definitions fit the premise of a romantic relationship, as all those elements come into play.

Indulge me if you will, while I break it down a bit.

1. The state of being related or interrelated – In a relationship, what happens to one affects the other. For example, if one snores, the other risks having a sleepless night! Believe me, I know. I have woken up to my husband upside down on the bed because I was snoring in his face. Go figure! The man will chance a foot kicking his chest, but at least he might get some sleep that night.

Real Talk: Seriously now, being in a relationship means that everything about one person has a reaction on the other. This could be a positive effect or negative one. Relationships do not exist in a vacuum.

2. The relation connecting or binding participants in a relationship – In a familial relationship you know exactly where character traits come from and everyone is accepted as kin even when their name is prefaced with the word "crazy."

Real Talk: A romantic relationship inherently requires that two people accept each other as is and adopt each other as kin.

3. A state of affairs existing between those having relations or dealings – A lot of dealings goes on in a love relationship, as in "deal with it." In dating and in marriage there is a lot of give and take that most people do not foresee or choose to ignore. The expression "state of affairs" could not be more appropriate to describe the status or process. Dating and marriage are akin to a business endeavor!

Since when is romance a business, you may ask?

Yes, it is! A romantic relationship should be looked at as a merger of two individuals, with the expectations, discussions, and compromises that come with establishing the ground work for the successful joining of separate entities.

Dating, marriage, and business have a lot in common. Stay with me for a minute and you'll see how all three situations have similar components.

When you are seeking a job, you are the suitor. You prepare a resume that lists your qualifications and education, your experiences and what you are looking for. The employer (the pursued) prepares their own list of what they are looking for and what they are offering (salary, benefits, growth, etc.)

The applicant/suitor goes into an interview, eager to impress the pursued, to convince them that they are a good match for the position. When a decision is made to hire, terms are agreed upon including duration (part-time, full-time, contract, at will, etc.)

In both business and diplomatic interactions, all involved parties conduct thorough investigations before coming to the table to negotiate agreements that are mutually advantageous and beneficial.

<u>Real Talk:</u> When two individuals recognize that romantic relationships share similarities with diplomatic or business negotiations, and actively engage in meaningful dialogues to establish mutually beneficial terms, they embark on the path toward a successful relationship.

4. A romantic or passionate attachment – Ah! L' Amour! Amor! Amore! L'Anmou! Okay, I am showing off. That is "Love" for you in French, Spanish, Italian and Creole.

The beautiful thing is, whatever language you say it in, it means the same everywhere: that fuzzy feeling you get for someone, where you would do anything to be with them and call them your own. Love: the subject of poems and songs for centuries. Some people want it at any cost, even when the roses come with thorns. Kingdoms have been lost over this thing! – Look at recent history with British Prince Harry, married to American actress Meghan Markle, forfeiting any chances to the royal throne.

That elusive thing called love remains at the top of the chart as one of the things most people desire. In *A Therapist shares the 9 things people want most in life...*, a CNBC online article published in July 2023, Charlotte Fox Weber, a psychotherapist, and author of *"What We Want: A Journey Through 12 of Our Deepest Desires,"* provides a list of nine things that she found most people want in life. This was based on her ten years of practice in the field. The number one item on her list was "To be Loved."

A loving relationship is greatly desired. It could be as simple as two people meeting, liking each other, and deciding to be together for the rest of their lives. It has happened.

However, in today's enlightened environment, human connections have gotten a little more complicated.

<u>Real Talk:</u> Discovering and maintaining a fulfilling romantic relationship seldom occurs by chance. It requires individual and collective effort to nurture its growth and ensure its continuous flourishing.

I believe as we continue this exploration, you will find some navigation tools you can use to identify and recognize your person or true love when you find it, and make a successful and sustainable connection.

Now that you know what relationship is, are you ready to learn more?

Okay. Sit tight. Here we go.

RELATIONSHIP 101

A relationship between two human beings is like a plant. It is a breathing, living thing. As such, it shares a lot of the characteristics of its counterpart. It begins as a seed or cell that germinates, but it needs air and light to grow, nutrition and care to develop.

To flourish, a relationship must be maintained in its most organic state with the proper nutrients and hydration. Its base must remain free of weeds and pests, and it also needs regular application of fertilizer in the form of <u>T</u>ender <u>L</u>oving <u>C</u>are to keep it fresh, vibrant, and thriving.

Depending on the quality of care it receives, a relationship may wither away and die, or it may blossom into something wonderful and long-lasting, that blesses the people involved in it.

If you are an avid gardener, like I am, this analogy will make perfect sense to you. If you are not familiar with plants, a few quick pointers may be helpful:

- Avoid selecting a plant solely based on its appearance.
- Be sure to conduct research on the plant, or at the very least, read the accompanying card or sticker for essential information.
- Do you have the ideal location and conditions for it? Full sun, part-sun, shade, sandy soil, loose soil. Every species of plants has different

requirements.

- Are you willing to take care of it? Are you committed?
- Will you feed it, water it, clean it up, treat it, trim it when appropriate?

Oh, were you under the impression that you simply plop it on a window sill and forget about it?

Just like a live plant, a relationship must be nourished with healthy air and the light of love and positive energy. The weeds – drama of all kind- must be pulled out, and pests of negativity eliminated. It must be nurtured with acts of kindness and positive reinforcement.

A neglected plant is a sorry sight. But a thriving one bursting with blossoms or laden with fresh fruits? Aah! What a delight.

That is what you should look for and strive for in a relationship. DELIGHT!

Given the significant time investment this journey of love demands – potentially a lifetime – it is wise to ensure it is both enjoyable and fulfilling.

◊ ◊ ◊

A Best Friend

Somewhere between the mundane adage "dog is a man's best friend," and the sublime biblical revelation that "the God of the universe calls his followers friends," lies the beautiful phenomenon of having someone you can call a best friend.

The three referenced relationships share common attributes, such as:

- Acceptance
- Caring
- Dependability or faithfulness
- Familiarity/intimate knowledge

- Protection and safety
- Pleasure derived from spending time together

Kudos to you if you have a Fido or Fifi dog companion as a best friend. I had one in my teens who literally shredded/ate my homework. Now, I honestly cannot see myself picking up dog poop on the regular, so no, I do not have a dog.

Those familiar with the bible know Jesus called his followers "friends." There is an old-fashioned hymn *"Oh, what a Friend We Have in Jesus,"* and Israel Houghton, a contemporary gospel artist, released the popular *"I am a friend of God"* in 2004.

Regardless of one's pet ownership status or one's spiritual belief, everyone is familiar with the term "best friend" as a good thing. Fortunate indeed is one who has cherished and continues to reap the benefits of a lifelong friendship.

A best friend is that ride or die partner who is always there for you, knows your history and shortcomings, accepts you for who you are, enjoys being with you, and it is reciprocal.

The *Merriam Webster Dictionary* defines the term as "a person's closest and dearest friend" or "a person's most desirable or valuable resource."

There is a current trend in romance circles, where people are referring to their spouses or significant other as their "best friends." In a July 25, 2023 AARP interview by Harriette Cole, Emmy winning actress Sheryl Lee Ralph of *Abbott Elementary* fame, talks about her bicoastal marriage (her in Los Angeles, California and her husband in Philadelphia, PA). She shares two of the things that make it work: complete trust and a lot of time talking to each other. She concluded that segment with, "I married the man who has become my best friend."

A best friend is the greatest person to have around. A best friend is a gem!

Wouldn't it be ideal if you married your best friend? Of course!

Well easier said than done. My best friend happens to be a female, so that was out of the question for me; and I was not attracted to my male best friend. So, what does the God I believe in do? He arranged for me to meet a wonderful guy I fell in love with, who I eventually married, and he became and remains to this day, my best friend.

It can happen for you too, but this dream come true is not an event. It is a process. The initial encounter may be by chance or providence, as was mine, but a lot of preparation, adjustment and work had to be done to bring two souls to the altar and keep a good thing going for the twenty-two years we have been married.

Finding the love of your life is a journey that begins with an initial connection, or in the case of an existing friendship, the realization that there is something deeper developing. As you discover interesting and likable things about each other, there is a gradual build-up of emotions that eventually leads to falling in love. Then begins the process of establishing a long-term relationship, and consideration for a permanent union.

How do you connect with a romantic partner, who is or will become your best friend, and form a long lasting, satisfying, and successful relationship?

Go ahead, pull up a chair and lean in. Let's talk about love, baby!

RELATIONSHIP WHY?

I notice that whenever a group of women are together, inevitably the topic of relationships pops up and stimulates a lively discussion. When I would mention that I was writing a book on the topic, their responses made me realize how important a subject it is, especially among women over the age of thirty-five.

"Do I have stories to tell you!" some would exclaim.

"Oh, the games that men play!" others say in exasperation.

"I am so tired of it!" bemoan others.

Men do not easily talk about this as women do, but when they do, they often also complain.

"These women out there are out to get you!" some say.

"You can't trust them!" others grumble.

"They just want to hook a husband!" a lot of them gripe.

When it comes to millennials, there is much confusion in the mix that further complicates ages old issues of expectations, gender roles, the art of compromise and misplaced or conflicting values. The larger issue and a troubling question regarding this generation is: who is teaching them about relationships?

Unfortunately, a resounding answer to that is: social media!

Unsettling, when you consider the misinformation and situations making the rounds on the various social media platforms. Apparently, young people do not even know how to date nowadays. Maybe there is also an indifference or lack of interest because members of this generation tend to be too self-absorbed to bother spending their energy on making relationships work.

Previous generations had a clearer understanding of what a relationship was and a more structured path toward connecting with a romantic partner. There was a general social code that informed a family lifestyle and fostered a predisposition to follow the steps that would ensure achieving that state.

Regardless of which generation you belong to, some guidance is needed to preserve that most necessary component of human relations, that of connecting and relating to another on a personal level.

We could certainly use some sort of manual to navigate this thing and there are countless books written on the topic. One considered the definitive authority by Christians everywhere, is the bible. – Hold on! I am not about to preach. Just want to illustrate a point with a quick story you probably heard before, with my own spin added to it. Bear with me.

The good book reports that at the very beginning of creation, God stated "It is not good for man to be alone." His solution was to create a "helpmate comparable to him" for them to manage the affairs of the garden. God knew man would need somebody to give him directions to where things were in the garden every time he asked, "Where is my…?" – I added that last part.

You may or may not believe in creation. But the fact is that man and woman have different attributes that balance and complement each other. We were made to be attracted to and by each other, if for one obvious reason, to assure the survival of the specie.

Regardless of how much perceptions and beliefs have changed over time, one universal truth remains: human connection, especially the romantic kind, helps us move from the "not good" of being alone to the "very good."

Do not get me wrong, I am not saying that being alone is inherently bad.

Some people are perfectly fine being alone. Further, everyone needs time alone to get to know their own self. There are also periods in one's life, where being free of the responsibilities of a partner or a spouse allows a person to devote time to further a career or be available for ministry. However, a romantic partnership develops in us some attributes designed to make us better humans.

Pastor and author, Scott LaPierre, writes in his book, *Your Marriage God's Way*:

God accomplishes much of the work He wants to do in our lives through marriage. After Scripture and the Holy Spirit, marriage is the greatest way God teaches us forgiveness, sacrifice, patience, dying to self, and more. When people remain single, they are more vulnerable to selfishness as they get used to living only for themselves. A married person has the obligation to care for their spouse, and this is wonderfully sanctifying.

I am particularly intrigued by the qualities mentioned: forgiveness, sacrifice, patience, dying to self; all things that are of utmost importance in maintaining good human relations. **In essence, partnering with another human being in a loving relationship is supposed to make each one a better person.**

How much better can the world be, if we all practice those qualities? How much more enjoyable life can be, if we use them to elevate the integrity of our interactions with a mate?

Love still makes the world go around, to borrow an old cliché. It is okay to want it. It is fine to desire the intimacy shared with a mate. It is perfectly acceptable to wish for a steadfast companion for social interactions, mental connection, and emotional support.

Good relationships, great partnerships and successful marriages are necessary to the welfare of mankind.

People are generally concerned about the high probability of divorce. An inherent percentage of failure accompanies most situations or experiments.

There is a misguided, commonly accepted statistic that the national divorce rate is 50%, the high it reached in the 1970s, when perhaps society adjusted to the sexual revolution and women entering the work force in droves. But that is no longer true in the 2000s. The rate has steadily declined to the twenty percentiles in the 1980s and 2010s, and more recently to the teens. But the myth persisted; fueling the fear of marriage that currently pervades relationships.

The 2021 national divorce average posted by the United States Census Bureau was 6.9%; while some states such as Idaho and Arkansas posted as high as 11%. A more recent study by Bowling Green State University's *National Center for Family and Marriage*, indicates that in 2022, there were 14.56 divorces out of 1000 marriages.

The statistics may appear scary, but I prefer to look at the favorable probabilities. If you do the math, even at 14.56% divorce out of 1000, there are 854 marriages out of the 1000 that remain viable. In my view, those are excellent odds.

This computation shows that a great number of individuals have managed to meet someone, date successfully and establish and maintain long-term relationships. *Yes Virginia, there is a Santa Claus*. It is possible!

How do you get there?

This book will examine three phases of romantic partnering:

- The search for and meeting of a potential candidate

– the dating

- The process of learning about and assessing whether an individual is a viable candidate

– the connection

- The progression of establishing, building, and maintaining the committed relationship

– partnering for life

We will accomplish this by using several approaches:

- Review what a relationship entails.
- Look at the mindset and experiences of people who are or have dated.
- Examine these constructs through the wisdom of those who are married or in long term relationships.
- Analyze relationships through the viewpoint of the writer as well as that of experts or authority on the subject, to gain insight into what some of the challenges are, and become familiar with the tools or resources couples have used to successfully "do life" together.

A lot of people have expressed being tired or discouraged when it comes to finding a mate. It is difficult, it is complicated. The fact is life is made of challenges. You win some, you lose some. No championship game has been won without a certain amount of preparation and work. So, it might not be easy, but it is worth every effort when the prize is that coveted cup: a meaningful, loving, working relationship.

So, don't give up on love. Embrace it; it is a beautiful aspect of life. Let's explore together how you can enhance your ability to give and receive love, and foster deeper connections in a one-on-one relationship.

DO YOU WANT A RELATIONSHIP?

I repeat, do you really want a relationship?

What kind of questions is that, Missy? I am reading this book. Ain't I?

Well, just want to make sure you are on the right bus. We are about to go up and down them hills looking for clues on how to do this thing correctly. Observe. Listen. Take notes. Most of all keep an open mind to get as much out of this journey as you can carry with you.

We first looked at the definition of the word "relationship" in the previous pages. Next you want to make sure you know what kind of relationship you want. What are you looking for?

In some cultures, today, as it was in centuries past, marriages are arranged by families to primarily provide that someone will be taken care of, usually the woman. This has also been done as alliances to ensure that kingdoms, businesses, or possessions remain in certain hands. These relationships were forged to further family or empire interests and not necessarily that of the spouses. People were lucky if they developed a liking and eventually a love for that spouse. One could see examples of these unions if you ever saw the Netflix series, *Bridgerton*.

In certain circles, families used a professional matchmaker to insure matrimony for their children. In the Amazon series *The Wonderful Mrs. Maisel,* the protagonist's mother was a matchmaker for the New York's well-heeled Jewish community. The tools used were like those in contemporary matchmaking television shows like *Married at First Sight.* A version of profile analysis worked to pair up people of similar backgrounds and upbringing. In some cases, love developed, but in most, the union at least remained a working partnership to nurture children and maintain a family unit.

My mother and father met and started a family in the 1950's when the expectations for a successful marriage were simpler and followed the model established centuries before. The primary objective was to create a family. You were to marry by a certain age, have your children and raise them to adulthood. Relationships had longevity, given the basic premise of commitment and family. A lot of them lasted based on obligation, even when a personal connection never existed or no longer was.

Today's generation fights for full autonomy on their choice of a life mate. The objective in most romantic relationships remains one where two individuals do life together. Nowadays, contemporary customs allow the ultimate choice in partnering with a mate, and the emphasis is on personal happiness. It is not sufficient just to have someone around, we also seek personal connection and an uplifting and fulfilling experience.

That is where the complications of contemporary dating and marrying come in. More is required of both parties. Not only do you want a relationship, but you want to be happy AND fulfilled in it. Personal happiness is a modern-day mantra.

And why wouldn't you subscribe to that! The pursuit of happiness is a constitutional given right that is very possible and attainable, if you lay the ground work and have the right components. It is like a recipe. All the ingredients in proper measures, used correctly, create a delectable dessert. One missing ingredient can destroy something you have slaved over for hours. Happens to me all the time when I try to adjust recipes for my diabetes.

My sister Bee chides me on my occasional fails. "Sis, keep the recipe as is, don't experiment on us, okay."

She is right. Somebody already experimented with the formula to write the final recipe. They know a little something, something about it. As for my most recent fail, all I will say is: do not try to make lemonade with dark brown sugar. All you get is tasteless dirty water.

◊ ◊ ◊

In a recipe for successful baking, you must start with the right mix of ingredients. However, factors like oven temperature and baking time also significantly impact the resulting product.

Similarly, successful dating involves numerous variables and influences that can complicate or undermine an initial connection.

DATING IS DIFFICULT

In January 2024 the internet exploded with articles about TV personality Gayle King's appearance on the popular *The Pivot Podcast*. In it, the 69-year-old King expressed having dating difficulties when she was asked about her romantic life. In particular, she reports that men find her intimidating.

If you are a woman and you are in Ms. King's income bracket or are a high earning professional, that is a valid dilemma. The reality is if a man is secure in who he is and has valuable qualities to offer, this should not be a problem. Often, there are issues associated with income status or lifestyle that do not translate well in real life.

Regardless of one's financial status, the consensus is that dating in today's environment is difficult for a variety of reasons.

Things are different from what they once were in the dating world. While the end goal is the same – to find love or a romantic partner – making connections is more complex, and the expectations are more complicated. People dating nowadays are caught in the in-between – filtering their choices and assumptions based on their parents or grandparents' definition of relationships, and trying to navigate the challenges and realities of modern-day dating. This can cause one to feel like my friend Charles F. said, "cognitively challenged," when it comes to understanding what a relationship is or should be.

When I was a young adult in the 1980's, people still dated with the intentions of becoming a couple. Boy met girl, liked each other, and became boyfriend/girlfriend. If everything lined up and over time they developed love for each other, they might eventually get engaged and get married.

By the time I became a single adult after a breakup from a ten-year relationship in the mid 1990's, I experienced the dating difficulties that people still face today. I couldn't find a compatible mate. I wanted a serious long-term partnership. The men I encountered were pursuing casual relationships.

In the 2020s, single people have a lot more to contend with. According to the survey, *Dating & Relationships in the 2020s*, single men and women respondents blamed "social influences" as the top culprit for the complications associated with dating. They also chose additional factors that affect the dating terrain.

Difficulty Factors	**Women**	**Men**
Social influences	66%	79%
Narrowed Pool	66%	25%
Complicated lifestyle	29%	36%
Fear of Commitment	60%	50%
Other	3%	32%

We will first examine each factor in detail in the following pages, and subsequently explore potential solutions to address the challenges inherent to the process.

Social Influences

In the science of sociology, social influence refers to how people's feelings and behaviors are associated with their social world, which results in a tendency to follow trends, and move in tandem with the crowd.

<u>Real Talk:</u> In this era of social media and ready public access, there are a lot of voices shouting in the desert, and very few of them are genuine prophets.

Currently, most people get their information from some online platform, be it news, research, motivation, advice, etc. If it is on the internet, it must true, right? Well. It ain't necessarily so.

The internet opened a community of immense proportion where ideas, thoughts, and events are instantaneously shared with an enormous number of people when an item goes viral. However, does the suggested information align with your personal beliefs, character, or goals? Should you follow it simply because everyone else is? Do you feel pressured to conform in order to be accepted?

At one time, public exposure of domestic issues was the domain of celebrities whose private lives were fodder for the gossip columns. Now, personal relationships, just like everything else in a contemporary individual's life, unfold in the public eye on social media. That gives everybody an opportunity to chime in and render their opinion on what you should or should not do. Your personal affairs become a *Reddit* thread.

With all the ideas and beliefs floating around, how do you identify the right thing to do? How do you know the right thing to say to resolve issues or work out the kinks in a relationship. One must be discerning in choosing who and what to follow, and what you let play in your hearing. When interacting or dealing with a potential mate, a degree of wisdom is necessary to look at yourself and them objectively, on the merit of your individual selves, not on what public media says about you or your situation.

<u>Auntie Wisdom:</u> While an understanding of the social influences that motivate your behaviors or actions is a necessary tool to functioning in your world, I recommend a more genuine, individualistic approach to dealing with a prospective partner. We

will talk about this in later chapters.

Narrowed Pool

When it came to "narrow pool" as a reason for difficulties in dating, I was not surprised that, 66% of single women found it to be an issue, whereas only 25% of the men did. According to a CDC National Center of Health Statistics report released in 2005, since 1940, more boys are being born than girls - a sex ratio that stabilized around 1050 boys for every 1000 girls. So, what happened?

Among other things, various historical and social factors have narrowed the pool of available men in the dating world.

- We have lost men to war. As of October 2022, the U. S. Army demographic report shows 84.3% of enlisted soldiers were males and 15.7% females.

- The sexual revolution of the last half century has resulted in homosexuality being more acceptable and open. With a lot of men opting to be their authentic selves, the available bucket of men for women has been further reduced.

- In the African American population, the scarcity of available men is exacerbated by incarceration and violence that remove a large number of them from the dating pool.

- In addition, a good number of African American men are choosing to date or marry other races, further reducing the availability pool for the sisters.

A bountiful basket of offering for the fellows to choose from. More competition for the ladies to contend with since the pickings are few.

Complicated Lifestyle

In discussing the elements that caused difficulties in dating with my research team, the term "complicated lifestyle" came up. It is a phrase that is often used, but hard to define. I once again defer to my default authority on words, good 'ole *Webster*. The definition offered for the word "complicated" is as follows:

"Consisting of many interconnecting parts or elements; intricate"

In essence, a complicated lifestyle is one that consists of many interconnecting parts. If you are of dating age, you've already experienced living. You have baggage. You and everybody else are standing at an airport carousel picking up your luggage.

Yours is tailor-made. It is packed with your things and your responsibilities. What are you carrying around with you? Past traumas, a broken heart, chattered dreams, family issues, dramas with uncooperative co-parent of your child, unhealthy attachments, substance abuse, etc.

You claim that stuff and carry it along with you, bringing everything to your destination where they form the package you present and operate with. Some stuff should be discarded. These beat up shoes should go. They are too heavy, out of style, uncomfortable and really don't match anything you currently own.

Toss them. They are taking space and unnecessarily causing excessive baggage weight that can become costly fees. Streamline. Update your wardrobe with a brand-new pair that makes sense. In other words, get a new attitude.

Fear of Commitment

When it comes to "fear of commitment" being an issue, both sides appear equally concerned, with 60% of women citing it as a roadblock and 50% of men agreeing. My personal experience in dating had shown the word commitment to be akin to a four-letter word that is feared and avoided. If you want to see a man pull a quick disappearing act, mention the "C" word early in the relationship.

You might as well have said, "I died last week, but I could not transition. You are talking to my ghost right now." - *This chick crazy! I'mma pedal right outta here.*

In all fairness a lot of women also harbor a fear of commitment. They'll stay in a relationship as long as both parties keep it light. But they are ready to bounce if the partner even hints at upping the ante to a committed level.

I was curious as to why commitment is such a big issue. "Enquiring minds want to know," as the tabloid *The National Enquirer* used to say. In particular, I wanted to hear what the men were thinking.

My follow up question to the men then, was this:

It has been said that today's men are afraid of commitment. Is that true for you? If so, what are your concerns?

Here are their answer choices.

Loss of freedom	48%
Inability/unwillingness to be faithful	24%
Fear of responsibility	24%
Concern that spouse may change once married	20%
Fear of being inadequate	32%
Other	20%

Mon Dieu – My God! Gentlemen, thank you for being candid!

Ladies, we wanted to know. They spoke. We seek to understand so we can in turn be understood.

When the ladies were asked whether they also feared commitment in a follow up survey, several of them acknowledged having issues as well.

However, the reasons cited were mostly fear the person might change or feelings of inadequacies.

Gentlemen, I hope you are listening.

To gain a better understanding of this dilemma, a thorough examination of each of these categories, their potential significance, and how they are interpreted by both parties could provide us with some clues.

Lost Freedom

Numerous songs have been written about freedom; independence of nations, liberty of a people, or the autonomy to be oneself. the concept of freedom itself transcends time.

In 1967 jazz legend and activist Nina Simone sang *"I Wish I Knew How It Would Feel To Be Free."* In her 1977 song, *Free,* R & B singer Deniece Williams, expresses her desire to be free to be, with an emphasis on the self, "Me." That song became an anthem of sort for the era. In 2008 R & B and hip-hop singer Ultra Naté suggested in her song *"Free"* that one should "Do what you want to do, you've got to live your life." Pop songwriter/performer Christina Aguilera echoed that sentiment in her 2012 song *"Soar"* when she sings "Find a path that is your own." In more recent times, pianist and R & B crooner John Legend's 2022 song *"Free"* refers to the "Freedom to love…to give…to live."

Freedom is important to all human beings, but for black men especially, it is a loaded word that carries connotations of our history and the social issues that black people experience to this day.

Most people, including me, prefer some autonomy in doing what they want to do. Like the song says, feeling unrestricted "to be me." One wants to be their authentic self, and should be able to, to feel whole.

Ironically, when one person pronounces the words: "I don't want to lose my freedom," this is what the other person usually hears.

- I want to be free to date other people.
- I don't need anybody telling me what to do.
- I want the autonomy of doing what I please.

So, here is a reality check, with a few quick points for both sides.

- If you want to see other people, you haven't found your person yet. Keep it light and don't lead the other person on. Better yet, move on and keep looking.
- If you are involved with more than one person at a time, you run the risk of spreading yourself too thin. You cannot be everywhere at once. You are either here or there, with each party getting just a measured portion of your time, a fraction of your attention, and very little of your devotion. - Frankly, the amount of energy it takes to love one person properly…! Concentrate on that. And do it right.

Full disclosure: I personally believe in the one man/one woman arrangement and a traditional Christian marriage.

- Both parties should keep their expectations in check, especially at the beginning, and make no demands on each other. No one should demand proof of affection or caring. Those things should come naturally as a person seeks to please the other and make them happy.
- As a relationship progresses, there is an organic merging of interests that happens, causing two people to do more together. However, this should never eliminate individual pursuit or expression.

Keep both eyes wide open and make sure you understand what the situation has to offer you.

Inability/unwillingness to be faithful

This is a tough one. If someone acknowledges an inability to be faithful, I am sorry to say, they do not intend to or are unwilling to be faithful. Hey, don't get mad at me. I am speaking the truth from my own experience.

I gave ten years of my life to one such man I lived and ran a business with. That roller coaster ride is recounted in my first book, *Cads, Princes & Best Friends*. Early in our relationship, Joe told me plain as day that he wasn't sure he could be faithful to me. We had a fantastic sex life, and he swore he loved me. But for him it was the thrill of the chase. I called him a doggy-pig. It was as if he believed that all women deserved a great sexual experience, and he was going to be the one to give it to them. I eventually left him when I found myself feeling suicidal after witnessing one too many of his flagrant affairs. He remained the same throughout his life. I recently learned that when he became severely ill in his later years and eventually passed, there were several women at the hospital claiming to be his woman.

Fear of responsibility

Every adult person has (or should have) responsibilities. Getting yourself up in the morning is a responsibility. You are accountable for figuring out what you want for your life and preparing for it. We all have a lifetime of responsibilities. Heck, in my family, we train the little ones as soon as they are capable to lift a bag to take the trash out, or grab a broom and a dustpan, or get up on a stool to put the dishes in the sink, or clean their room on a Saturday. My army sergeant sister Bee keeps a running list of chores on her refrigerator. Because of that training, all her children are capable and self-sufficient.

Responsibility is part of life. When a man says he fears responsibilities, it could mean several things.

- He is not ready to take care of a woman and possible children because his income is not where he'd like it to be.
- He may be old school and wants to be able to provide.
- He is concerned about being the one to make the tough decisions and charter the course for a household or family.

- He is afraid the woman is going to dump all emotional and financial responsibilities on him.
- He is concerned about being mentally or financially overburdened beyond his capacity.
- He is still in his personal growth stage (school, career, personal enrichment) and does not want to spend his energy and resources on someone else.

Concern person may change once committed/married

This is not as crazy as it appears. It happens often enough.

I once knew of a couple who lived together for several years and had two small children together. They finally decided to get married and one day had a very nice wedding. The bride's mother was a good friend and neighbor at the time. About a year after the wedding, I asked her how her daughter was doing.

"Oh, her and her husband are separated," she said. "She and the children moved in with me until she can find an apartment."

What happened? Did he or she have an affair? Did he or she change once "the ring was on the finger" in a case of "you my wife now" or "you my husband now?"

I never asked my friend for details, but I remember just feeling puzzled that a union that had worked for several years, could dissolve so quickly after it was made "official."

I've witnessed women lose a ton of weight to look good while dating or to prepare for a wedding, then put on more pounds than before, once the ceremony was over. Hello! He married a size ten, two years later you are 100 pounds heavier! – Caveat: notwithstanding extra pounds a woman gains with child bearing or the ones someone loses because of serious illness. Conversely, a man might prefer and marry a "thick madame" then a year in she decides to go on a non-health related GLP-1 regimen because she wants to be a size 8. That is deception.

I have also known individuals, both women and men, who were solicitous, caring, and charming while dating and engaged, then became neglectful sloth once married; or worse, disrespectful, or abusive. In other words, "I no longer have to impress you or put up any effort, I already got you."

Hunh! No. Nope! Nay. No way! False advertising again. This is the stuff divorce is made of: "irreconcilable differences."

In a lot of cases, one partner puts on a good show of presenting themselves as ideal, then later reveal their true color to the detriment of the other spouse. Serenity* divorced after over fifteen years or marriage had that experience. It left her scarred.

She said: *"It's easy to set up every possible wall to protect self from the pain, caused by the one who made a vow to love, honor, and cherish me all the days of my life; however, their actions for 90% of the union was nothing more than lies, infidelity, and more. Until I master tearing those walls down, I am afraid of commitment."*

Chasity, a Marketing Specialist, confessed, *"Concerned I will be let down again."*

This *after* scenario, is vastly different from the *before* they signed up for.

Fear of Being Inadequate

"You ain't shit!"

"I don't need you."

"I can do bad by myself."

When it comes to gender roles, I cannot speak definitively for the younger generation, but in past generations, there has often been a deeply ingrained sense of confidence associated with feeling adequate, particularly in men. This self-assurance pegged to their feeling of competence, appears coded into their DNA, reinforcing their sense of masculinity. Maybe it is a residue of when he had to chop down trees to build a shelter for his family, go hunting for meat to feed them, and protect his territory from the wild predators to keep them safe. Men like to feel that they are taking care of stuff and are appreciated for it.

We live in a time when the woman can take care of her own. She sometimes earns more than the man, a situation that is common among African Americans. She can provide that shelter, feed herself and the children and protect when necessary.

How do we make sure men feel welcome, needed, and appreciated in this perilous environment?

Let us also admit that feelings of inadequacy are not exclusive to men. I remember the 2007 Tyler Perry movie *Why Did I Get Married?* in which Jill Scott's character Sheila was married to Mike, played by Richard T. Jones. Sheila, who was overweight, was constantly berated by her husband and made to feel inadequate, undesired, and insignificant.

There are also plenty of stories where women found themselves experiencing self-doubt, when their competence or standing as a woman was challenged or in jeopardy.

"I am not good enough!" - "I can't make him happy!

"I can't give him a child!

What do you do to alleviate a partner's concerns? How do you work out the kinks to create an environment where you and your partner feel secure and embrace each other's true value?

ARE THERE SOLUTIONS TO DATING DIFFICULTIES?

People who are looking for a mate must possess a degree of resilience to stay the course. One can meet people daily, but everyone you meet does not necessarily become a friend. In the same way, every prospect you date does not become a partner.

Dating difficulties are here to stay. It is just the world we live in today. However, since the desire for human romantic connection remains strong, we must try to address these concerns. What can we do to alleviate the strain on relationships?

- Pray
- Learn
- Be wise
- Adjust

"Lady, are you joking! Pray?" No, I'm not. The good book, the one that talks about Jesus says to pray about everything. I take that literally, as it happens to work for me. – Sounds simplistic, but of course it's more complex. You first need to know about God and how interaction with Him works. Praying the right way prompts you to learn, teaches you wisdom, and pushes you to

adjust.

You don't believe in that spiritual stuff? No worries. How about some practical scenarios we can examine together, to facilitate your dating endeavors?

ISSUE 1: SOCIAL INFLUENCES

Solution: Different mindset & workable approaches

1. A romantic relationship is between two people. Consequently, what matters is what is important to person A and person B, not what Nene and them think or what is put forth on social media.

2. Stop sharing every detail of your relationships on social media. Work it out with your partner in private. Seek the advice of a wise and trusted friend, if necessary. Better yet, talk to grandma or grandpa, uncle, or auntie. They possess knowledge and insight shaped by lived experiences. I don't mention ma, because often, adult children don't feel comfortable confiding in mom. But the grand-parents and aunties are supposedly full of grace and wisdom. Hey, I am an auntie. We rock!

3. Do you have a solid family foundation to serve as a model or keep you accountable? Use that as your influence.

4. Do you have strong spiritual principles that guide your actions and inform your decisions? – Apply them in your interactions with others and specifically, a potential mate.

5. Seek true knowledge. There are good books written about every topic imaginable, including how to navigate dating or be a good partner. Keep reading, this one is one of those. There is also a wealth of wisdom regarding human interaction in the one called "the bible."

6. Be a better human being. Then find and connect with like-minded

people. Chances are you will find a mate among the lot.

ISSUE 2: NARROWED POOL

Solution: Awareness & acceptance

1. When there is a buffet offering a variety of food, there is a natural tendency to be more selective. Why choose average chicken nuggets when there is filet mignon, shrimp or crab bake.

2. The survey showed the ladies at a disadvantage in this category, but this applies to everyone. – Being aware of the competitive nature of the game, you should learn to put yourself in the best light, by being the best version of you that is possible.

3. Do not be discouraged by the statistics. Just be objective about yourself, what you have to offer, what a potential mate might bring, and what you expect a shared life to look like.

4. Remember that "What is meant for you, is for you." Whether that means finding the right mate or being single for life. If the latter is your fate, make it the best life you possibly can. One that is rich in friendship, adventures, accomplishments, and service.

ISSUE 3: COMPLICATED LIFESTYLE

Solution: Awareness and transparency

Most adults over the age of 35 have experienced some traumatic event in their romantic life, be it a broken heart, a separation or divorce. Some people recover and move on to new relationships or second marriages that are successful. Others are at various stages of their potential recovery or are permanently scarred by their experience. Therefore, be aware of where a person is mentally when it comes to their readiness or willingness to commit.

1. Is a woman talking about her ex every chance she gets, either positively or negatively? She is either not over him or has not yet healed from the wounds he caused. – She needs time to heal and work on herself to be ready and be fully present to receive a partner.

2. Is a man frequently bad mouthing a previous partner and launching about how women are out to get men? Be cautious. You are only hearing one side of the story, his. Later you may find out he did some s… that prompted the treatment. – Tread lightly. *Empathize* with their feelings if they are warranted; but *emphasize* that not every woman is the same.

"Get to know me, who I am, what I believe in and stand for, then you can make your judgement call. But do not lump me in with every bad experience you ever had."

3. You have a lot of situations nowadays where a man is <u>still married</u> <u>and living with his spouse, but they are "separated,"</u> meaning they no longer have a relationship. In most cases there is a complete lack of transparency on the part of these fellows when they go out there seeking to connect with other women. "I am separated," they respond to questions about their marital status, with no further elaboration. Now, for me, when I hear "separated" I am thinking that you are at least physically living somewhere else.

The reality is that even when a relationship is not working, "it is cheaper to keep her." I have known variations on this theme. There are those situations where a marriage is emotionally over.

- "My wife and I don't get along," he would say.
- "Okay. Are you planning on leaving her? Are you still sleeping in the same bed?" I would ask. "Then, you are just going through a reevaluation."
- You also have those arrangements dictated by economic concerns.

Both parties are done but remain under one roof to continue to maintain the lifestyle afforded them by sharing expenses.

- "Does she still cook for you? Do you still function as a couple?" -Let's be real. If a woman feels her man is pulling away, she may redouble her efforts to appear as the good wife. Who would refuse a good meal or clean laundry.

- "Are you still living under the same roof? Is either of you able to creepy crawl into the other's bed if the mood were to strike?" Come on guys, which one of you would pass up free sex? After all, this bootie belongs to you. You are still married.

Are there children? They complicate things even further.

"I do not want to leave my kids."

"I am waiting till they get to a certain age."

- "My kids are my primary concern." – Admirable, but what about us?

Ladies, keep your eyes wide open. Do not be bamboozled by feelings. This man may decide to leave for real to be with you. You will then have to sustain the relationship through his full separation, emotional turmoil, and possible financial setback. At the end of all that, he may decide you are not really who he wants or that he is not ready to jump back into a commitment. Most likely, the position being offered to you is that of a mistress, and that status may have its perks, but is not without perils.

I know a couple in their late forties whose marriage relationship had deteriorated for a variety of reasons. The man had a girlfriend that he would visit at night, but because of some strange personal belief of his, he always came home – in the early morning hours. His wife shared with me how dreadful it was for her. She would lay in bed, half-awake most of the night, knowing where he was. I never inquired whether they still shared the same bedroom or he occupied another. They have a large home and are empty nesters. She eventually moved out to her elderly parents' home to assist with their care.

I knew of the wife's state of mind and feelings of betrayal and abandonment. But I often wondered about the girlfriend. How does it feel to cook for your man, have a good time together, make love and fall asleep together, and see him get up in the wee hours of the morning to say he's going home. *"Isn't home where the heart is?"*

4. Multiple children with a variety of partners should be a red flag. Unless of course, you are Nick Cannon (12 with 6 different women as of 2023), then who cares, right?

- Someone may have had a child in their youth, or was married before. Be careful to detect whether there is a pattern of irresponsibility or immaturity.

- This applies to both sexes. There are some women who erroneously believe that having a man's baby is going to keep them. Sorry. It doesn't work that way. That is why it is imperative to make sure there is a relationship and commitment and a mutual desire for children, before you have them. The reality is there are "accidents," wrong time of the month, busted condoms, birth control pills that fail, etc. Procreation in action. So, protect yourself. – A good basis for no sex before marriage – just me saying it.

"Say what?" I know you are not listening to me on that one. We will explore that whole topic in detail later.

5. To continue talking about the perils of men dealing with previous relationships, very often there are <u>strains on a man's finances</u> (alimony, child support, house payments) that will affect how much is available for a new relationship. It is a HUGE issue. I encountered this scenario with my ex and with my current husband.

- **Ladies, handling these situations requires patience and understanding.** I do not condone a woman supporting a do-nothing man. However, if a man has a lot of responsibilities related to prior children, give him credit for being a responsible parent and work with what he has instead of putting strenuous demands on him. A walk around the park or a latte at Starbucks counts for "time spent together." It does not have to be dinner at Vic and Anthony (Houston) or Momofuku Ko (New York).

- **Gents, be considerate about giving the person you are dating their dues.** Your attention and at times your resources are required in equal measure.

6. Dealing with exes is another big issue: girlfriends that still call, boyfriends on the periphery, on again/off again exes, co-parents from previous relationships. DRAMA!

Did I mention that relationships take patience? Everybody has issues, some way more than others. So, be prepared and ready to deal with what comes with that package of sweetness you are experiencing at the very beginning. Respect and demand respect.

- Understand that there is a history with that previous partner, especially if there are children or unfinished business such as a business enterprise or a home/real estate.
- If there are children, there will always be communication between the parents until the kids are grown.
- Establish the protocol you wish to follow to keep the peace. For example:
- Can you ask your ex not to call my house after 10 p.m.
- Ask her to wait outside when she comes for the kids.
- Don't come in the conversation if I am arguing with my ex.
- I can talk about my ex, but don't you talk bad about the mother of my children (I know…)
- I would appreciate it if you ask your kids' father to meet you downstairs when he comes.

You get my drift. COMMUNICATE! Don't argue. Discuss with a cool head what will work for both parties, respecting each other's boundaries even while trying to establish common ground.

7. A complicated lifestyle sometimes encompasses someone who may be involved in <u>questionable dealings</u> that could be mild enough to frown upon, or sufficiently serious to violate the law or moral codes. In every instance, seek to understand and be understood.

- Is someone pole dancing at the strip club because that is the best avenue they know to pay for their college tuition?
- Is a person engaged in suspicious activities such as trading in stolen goods or illegal substances?
- Is that bodacious beauty posting revealing pictures on Only Fans?

These questions beg for a follow up "why" and "why this?" I am not here to judge and neither should you. People do things because they think that is the only choice they have, or they do not know any better. In a lot of cases, they know exactly what they are doing and do not see anything wrong with it. Be informed.

What is their point of view on their activity? Is this temporary, a no choice situation? Do they intend to make this a career?

COMMUNICATE! If you are interested in the person, a further investigation is warranted to ascertain whether this represents a character flaw that goes against what you believe or will accept in a mate. In the movie *The Best Man*, the character Murch falls for and eventually marries Candy a stripper who performed at the bachelor party. She was a college student at the time using stripping to pay her way. If you cannot accept the person's lifestyle for moral or personal reasons, just walk away. You can try to enlighten them or let them be. Always, be true to yourself. If a lifestyle is objectionable to you or not compatible with your own, do not pursue, or do so at your own peril.

ISSUE 4: FEAR OF COMMITMENT

<u>Solution</u>: This is a complex issue that merits a deep and through analysis. So, we will evaluate in the next section, each of the reasons given by the respondents.

COMMITMENT! What's in a word? Apparently, a lot.

English is not my first language. However, I was an English Literature major when I attended college in the States. Consequently, I always want to confirm that I am using words in their proper context. I frequently find myself checking the dictionary to verify the given meaning or connotation associated with certain words. Commitment is such a word.

What does *Webster* have to say about it?

- the state or quality of being dedicated to a cause, activity, etc. *Example: "the company's commitment to quality"*
- An engagement or obligation that restricts freedom of action. *Example: "business commitments"*

Oy! Vey! My Jewish friend used to say in exasperation. Did the second meaning have to feed right into guys' apprehension? "Obligation that restricts freedom of action." No wonder them dudes run from it. But wait...

The example given is "business commitment." Business is a good thing, right? Men love business. They run toward and into it. They are not afraid of the commitment required there. Ah, ha!

When you accept a job, it is understood that you are not free all the time. It requires your time for at least 8 to 10 hours a day, 5 days a week - often more - for 50 weeks a year if you get two weeks' vacation. In the job, as in business, you sign on for the benefits: the financial payout, the prestige, the accomplishments, the belonging, using it as a platform for greater and better achievements. Any business minded men and women in the house?

I ran my own business for several years. It required my attention 24/7. The obligations of being a small business owner did not afford me much free time. I eventually went back into corporate for a regular paycheck, and subsequently into teaching for more personal fulfillment.

The same mindset you put forth when it comes to a business obligation can transfer to a relationship commitment. The benefits you see in a prospective relationship must outweigh what you perceive as roadblocks. Like all other decisions a human must make, there are always pros, the advantages and cons, the disadvantages. Are there sufficient pros to offset the cons?

In the survey, I purposely put the burden on the men to elaborate on the topic of commitment and the related fear of it. While this sentiment is not exclusive to men a lot of women fear a permanent commitment for a variety of reasons – they are the ones most often accused of exhibiting that trait.

The "fear of commitment" in men is a complex issue. After all, one of the word's definitions is "state of being dedicated to a cause." What if one hitches their wagon to the wrong horse, one that is trained to go west, when you are trying to go east? What if you pledge allegiance to a cause, you thought was to save the *whales,* but come to find out it was save the *eels*? Both sea creatures, right?

Gentlemen, I feel you. I understand your hesitancy. But love is a game of chance. You may believe you know and think you are doing everything correctly, yet it can still come back to bite you unexpectedly.

You are not the only ones. The ladies are weary too. The shenanigans they experience created this atmosphere of distrust that taints their reactions and their interactions with you.

What if we came together to find some workable approaches to help both sides navigate this dating and eventual marriage thing?

Let us analyze each of the reasons given as basis for the fear of the big "C."

Fear of the BIG C #1 - Lost Freedom

Auntie Wisdom: Do not block someone from feeling free to do what pleases them (within reason).

We've often heard the marriage mantra "And the two shall become one." It is a good thing until it becomes stifling. Too many people take that literally and use it to impose on their partner.

A human being remains forever an individual. As such every person is entitled to their own interests, – so long as those don't interfere with the mechanism of the relationship. Discernment and wisdom are required to make a partnership work properly.

A committed relationship is a conscious, social agreement between two people to function together in a certain way. Like all arrangements or transactions, there are some give and take both parties must acknowledge and understand.

- There is a <u>disadvantage</u>: You will lose some of the freedom to come and go as you please.
- The a<u>dvantage</u> is: You gain a companion for the road.

<u>Reality check:</u> During the dating phase, no one needs a play by play of what someone is doing or where they are going, if there is mutual trust. However, there are some DOs and DON'Ts everyone could observe to facilitate smoother interactions and alliances.

Do not question someone's whereabouts or plans, unless they involve you.

- **Do:** Give each other space at the beginning of a relationship, understanding that this person has a life that only partially includes you.
- It is okay to inquire whether the two of you are getting together for the weekend, so you can make your plans.
- It is fine if the person is not available for you then. You don't need to know what they are doing – unless they volunteer the information. If they do, of course, that starts to build mutual trust and respect.

Do not take the person for granted. Once you are confirmed to be an item (steady, engaged, or married), each person should be apprised of what is going on with the other. It is a matter of respect and safety, one prompted by caring and real concern.

- What does your schedule looks like today?
- Will you have time to help me finish this application?
- I may stop by the gym after the meeting. Go ahead and have dinner without me.
- Hey, where you at? I've been trying to reach you for the past couple of hours? You okay?
- Yeah, I'm okay. I had turned my phone down during the meeting and forgot to bring it back up.

Do not interrogate a mate, continuously.

- Instead, communicate and gently discuss or volunteer your plans if they don't involve the other person.
- *Where are you going?*
- *I am meeting my boy to shoot some hoops. (him)*
- *When you coming back?*
- *I'm not sure when I'll be back. But I'll be here in time to finish fixing that shelf for you. (him)*
- *I am having lunch with the girls today. (her)*
- *When will you be back?*
- *I am not sure. You know when we girls get together... Would you like me to order something to bring back for you? (her)*

Do not be arrogant about what you consider "your right" to do what you want. Often individuals choose the selfish route to express their desire to do something that may disturb their mate or even infringe on the health of the relationship.

- You are hanging out with the boys again?
- Yeah. You got a problem with that?
- Well, we haven't spent any time together all week.
- So? That's what I feel like doing today.

Ooh child! Somebody prefers outside company. That is how anyone who cares would interpret these harsh responses. There is a definite problem here!

Here is an example of the freedom to do what pleases, as expressed in my household:

- *I am going to relax. I'll be in front of the TV. (my husband)*

- *Enjoy. I'll be in the bedroom playing music. (me)*

- *Hey babe, I am going to the gym. Want to come?*

- Sure. I exercised to YouTube yesterday. A work out on the machines will do me good.

This is a simple interaction between couples that demonstrates acknowledgment of the <u>he things,</u> <u>she things</u> and <u>we things</u>.

There will be times when the freedom to be self is more costly or serious.

- *This is the car I want. I know it's expensive, but I got it. This is not going to interfere with our bill money.*

- *Okay. You've worked for it. Enjoy.*

In every case, communication is key. Everything concerning one affects the other. You share your dreams or desires with your partner. Explain why these things are important to you. Discuss the ramifications, and how this will affect your interactions or your shared life. Enlist their acceptance and cooperation. You work it out together, respectfully and with love.

◊ ◊ ◊

Everyone is entitled to a degree of individual autonomy. That includes the prerogative of having strong personal friendships in your life, outside of the relationship you share with a partner. Two people can be extremely close, like I am with my husband, but it's always beneficial to have your own friendships.

I maintain a circle of friends, including a couple of men, who share my various interests or background: church, teaching, music, corporate work, etc. Among them are close supportive friends. Likewise, my husband has a large group of friends, some of them women, people he grew up with who stay in constant contact with him. They have long conversations on the phone in Creole, talking about their childhood, the current situation in Haiti or catching up about other friends.

Frankly, there are things I enjoy that my husband would easily pass on, like a symphony concert for example. Would I go with a male friend. Absolutely not! I invite my sister, my nieces, or a female friend with similar tastes.

Being a couple doesn't mean the individual ceases to exist. Each person supports their partner's ideas, friendships, and pursuits; while being respectful of the marriage or partnership and those activities are compatible with the common goals.

Do not question every outside relationship.

- In the beginning phases of a relationship a lot of unknowns may cause suspicion. Allow each other the necessary time to resolve any issues and to settle into a sense of security within your relationship.

- Once you know each other well, each side is aware of the family connections and dynamics, including exes, co-parents of your children, as well as best friends.

- Who you talking to?

- Jake. Jake from State Farms.

- Oh yeah. Is she wearing a negligee?

Couldn't pass that one up.

My point is that someone can talk to a person or friend of the opposite sex without causing World War III. Of course, people must remember to always be respectful.

If you are at that beginning level where you are still talking to other people, have the decency to be discreet. Reserve those calls for when you are by yourself.

Then once a relationship is established with someone, even more so when it becomes engagement, living together and marriage, be respectful and brave enough to get rid of other romantic interests. Concentrate on the work at hand. That of making your partner happy and keeping the relationship successful.

- **Do not assume the worst, unless you were given reasons to.**

Give a person the benefit of the doubt if they show they have your best interest at heart. Do everything you can to **build** trust and to **give** trust.

- Hey, I want this to work. Just want to make sure we are on the same page.

It also helps to put yourself in the other person's shoes.

- How would you feel if you were in my place?

Always be objective about your situation. Remember that trust is earned. Period.

Fear of the Big C #2 – Unwillingness to be faithful

A man's candor about this limitation could indicate a mild concern or a severe issue. Unfortunately, this is one of those things that you do not know until you know. The best one can do is be objective enough to have a strategy on how to deal with any potential issue. My suggestion for the men:

Choose right - Men are genetically more visual. When you decide to be exclusive with someone or marry them, make sure you are getting what you like. I mean, if a sizable bust makes you light up, why you marry a flat chested woman? Then before you know it, you running after Jessica the secretary, size 42D. Just saying.

Do not promise something you cannot give - There are men who enjoy the chasing and conquering more than the reliability and comfort of a steady relationship. It will be all hot and heavy initially, but once they've conquered, they are ready for the next chase. – I am thinking of two individuals I personally know, one of who was married once. They both have several children resulting from the bouncing about, each time the woman thinking she'll be the one to turn him around. I once was one of those women.

Ladies, do not waste your time. But, if you decide to try, go in with both eyes wide open. You have 2 choices. A) be ready to take it on the chin, and walk away when the infidelities begin; or B) you stay, just to say you have a man or there is a kid, and risk getting suicidal because the emotional suffering is too much.

Be honest with yourself & your partner - Ladies. If a man tells you point blank, he is not sure he can be faithful, believe what he says. If that is an issue for you, be wary and proceed with caution.

Gents. If you know yourself to be a chaser, do not give the woman false hope. Unless she is just game for the romp anyway.

Prevent infidelity - Know your partner well, in every way, so they enjoy your company.

- Entertain a friendship to enjoy their company.
- Communicate your needs and preferences.
- Accommodate their needs and preferences.
- Keep the courtship and the friendship going.

CHOOSE to be faithful because you like and enjoy what you have and do not want to jeopardize it.

If you have all of that and still cannot say no to a booty offer, you are just thirsty!

Forgive but cannot forget – Okay, you two had a little rough patch and somebody thought it a good idea to have some third party lick their wounds.

- It happens, but understand that infidelity leaves a dark stain in the heart of the person betrayed.
- It takes time and a whole lot of remedial efforts to gain a person's trust again.
- Even then, it is one of those things that is hard to forget. The person fears it may happen again.
- Worst case scenario, they do not want to continue the relationship

or try again.

So be wise about your actions. Don't be impulsive. You do so at your own risk and jeopardize a relationship that could have been the most beneficial for you.

Fear of the Big C #3 – Fear of Responsibility

Going back to creation – for those who believe in the bible – man has traditionally been the provider for the family, while the woman took care of the household and child rearing. Most people still believe in that model today, even though most women are out in the workforce and often earn more than the men.

Being responsible is required of all adults to be successful in life. It is a rite of passage. However, men get a double portion in that they are expected to care for a wife and family as well. I hear you fellows. It can feel like a burden.

This conundrum requires that we take a more objective look at how we define gender roles in the 21st century. When brute strength was required to tame the wild and subdue large game or predators, it made more sense for the physically stronger sex to handle the getting and providing. This formula continued to apply when most work involved heavy machinery. Today, however, work is mostly light weight and intellectual, accomplished through mental processes using a computer. Society also became aware that men do have a soft side and can be caregivers as well. The roles became interchangeable where the job, the household and the caregiving can be comfortably handled by a man or a woman.

If the traditional set up works for you and you can afford it, great. The man works while the woman runs the household. Couples who can manage it, do that. For the rest of us, we must be realistic: in most cases, two incomes are necessary.

Unlike the traditional model with defined gender roles, the enlightened household functions on what is best for the unit. In today's economy that means both parties are providers, and sometimes swap being the higher income earner. Consequently, the man should not be required or expected to be the sole or primary provider. Unfortunately, a lot of women feel that way.

"Oh, he better take care of me. That's what a man's supposed to do!"

"Hey, Sis. You work too. You make as much money as he does, don't you? How about, you take care of each other?"

Men should not have to fear responsibilities if they can be assured everyone will carry their own weight and contribute to the lifestyle in a manner commensurate to their earning. Likewise, women should not have to worry that running the household and the care of the children is her sole responsibility when she works as well.

Further, be real in this as with everything else in life, BE INTENTIONAL!

- If you are not ready for or do not want kids, make every effort to avoid getting a woman pregnant. The law makes you pay for that for at least eighteen years.
- And don't tell me it's the woman's job to protect her body. It takes two to tango.
- Be selective about who you get involved with. Make sure you know their view on everything that is important to you, even as it relates to a relationship going south.

My personal view is that all responsibilities should be shared by the two partners. I explore that topic in depth in the later section on Financial Discussions for couples.

A relationship is still a beautiful thing. Do not let the thorns scare you away from enjoying the roses.

Fear of the Big C #4 – Concern person may change once committed/married

I have witnessed that phenomenon of a person finally showing their true colors once married. A slim figure who, a year later, is a thick madame. A stylish dresser who now lives in a bathrobe and bonnet. A sweet-talking lady who is now disrespectful…the list goes on.

And men, you can be horrible too. How about when you take the woman for granted, feeling that you no longer need to try, because you already got her? How about going from solicitous to demanding, like she is your servant? Or you do your thing and let her be home as "the wife" or mother?

"Oh, this is not what you signed up for? You got lured into this beautiful mirage?

DID YOU INVESTIGATE? Did you make a solid effort to get to know the person for who they really are, what they believe in, how they function? Or did you just see this gorgeous package and decided right then that was what you wanted to wake up to everyday?

She doesn't cook? She doesn't keep house? She does not like your family? She doesn't respect you? She is a spendthrift? She quit her job since you make good money – now you feel all responsibilities are on you? She doesn't take your feelings into consideration? Did you say she gets on your nerves?

I am not making this up! All the above questions pertain to one man and his two marriages. I happen to have a conversation about him with a common friend the day before this writing, which made this topic timely and relevant. He was at the "I can't stand my wife" stage.

Both times he married a gorgeous younger woman. Makes you wonder. Did he take the time to find out if he and the women were truly compatible; or he got carried away the moment he eyed that Brazilian lifted booty. Twice! – Fool. Did you learn anything?

So, yes. People do change, but they also remain true to their core. If you don't take the time to look below the surface beforehand, you get exactly what you deserve: **the obvious beautiful image that was projected to you and the ugly truth you didn't bother to look for.**

Fear of the Big C #5 – Fear of being inadequate

This is another big one, so remember this:

<u>Auntie Wisdom:</u> In every instance, you can certainly **be decisive,** but never **<u>dismissive.</u>**

My friend Annie, a native Ethiopian, experienced how the traditional and the modern collide. She went to school in the States and was well established in her career when she decided to visit back home. While there, she reconnected with her childhood sweetheart and they became engaged by the time she left. He eventually emigrated to the States and they got married. He worked part time for a while. When they had their first baby, they decided that he should go to school for a degree in the medical field. He stopped working to concentrate on his studies and became the stay-at-home dad caring for the then toddler.

My friend's mother who until then had lived with one of the other siblings, came to live with them at that time. She was an elderly African woman, non-English speaker, who'd only been in the States for a couple of years. My friend began to share with me how awfully her mother treated her husband. She was constantly throwing angry and disparaging remarks at him. In her view, a man provided for his family. But what she saw was her daughter up at the crack of dawn every day for a one-and-a-half-hour commute that included a car ride, the railroad, then two different trains on the New York subway, while the husband was home feeding a child. She did not respect him. She ignored the fact that he was taking care of the baby and even teaching the toddler how to read. She didn't understand when he sat for hours at his desk with the big medical textbooks. In her mind, this man was a loser. Thankfully for my friend, her husband was extremely patient and respectful to his mother-in-law. Although from the old world, he understood the new concept of reversing roles when necessary.

He eventually earned his degree and found a position in his field at a hospital where he worked while attending school. His salary jumped to a professional level, on par with his wife.

They worked it out and are a couple still doing life together after over twenty years.

Everyone has insecurities. With men, when it comes to their finances and their ability to please a woman sexually, there are plenty of soft spots. If a woman is not sensitive to that fact, a callous remark or attitude can carve deep and sometimes fatal wounds.

I recall a family member in his late forties who relocated from New York to Florida to marry a childhood friend he had reconnected with. He left a high paying job, gave up his apartment to move in with her since she already owned a home. When we visited them a few days before the wedding, I picked up that this woman was very bossy, set in her ways, and showy. Like she knew better and could do it all better. The fiancé, a strong personality himself, kept calm however, perhaps viewing her attitude as an effect of wedding jitters.

Several months after the wedding, the wife decided to sell the house so that she could move to a newer, more chichi neighborhood. He shared with us that when they discussed the financing, he offered to give her a sum of money which was all he had available, considering he had just spent everything a few months back to relocate, and now had a much lower salary down south. She derisively told him: "You can keep your <u>little</u> money."

Were this a cartoon, I picture a guy standing tall, chest poking out, handing a wad of dollar bills. That sarcastic phrase dropped out of the wife's mouth in a dark cloud that blew in the guy's face. He immediately shrunk down to a little pee-wee figure with the bills scattered at his feet.

For a man, that remark was indication that:

- You do not value what I have to offer.
- You do not respect me enough to see that I want to do my part as a provider by contributing my fair share.
- You think I am inadequate.

If the roles were reversed and it had been the man who told the woman to keep her money, she would have probably responded, "Oh, really! You want to cover the whole thing? Cool." – I personally would add, "No problem, as long as my name is also on the deed."

Men are not the only ones feeling fearful. Women are also concerned about situations where they would experience feelings of inadequacy. A lot is expected of women, things like, catering to and pleasing their partner, maintaining a household, and taking care of children all while trying to take care of themselves, working a job, and sometimes going to school. Women often feel they are not doing enough or they are not good enough. If a woman is paired to an uncaring partner who devalues her, like the character Mike in the movie *Why Did I Get Married*, (referred to in an earlier discussion of feelings of inadequacy), that can eat away at her soul.

So, ladies and gentlemen, handle your partner carefully. Practice empathy and understanding from the onset. Make it an integral part of your interactions on an ongoing basis. Be decisive, but never dismissive,

Always think, *"Would I like this said or done to me in that situation?"*

Other Fears

We all agree that dating is indeed difficult in the 2020s. In addition to the prompts provided by the survey, a few participants provided additional comments that are worth giving a listen to.

James, a manager in Houston, offered that, *"Women's expectations are not reasonable."*

Dom, an educator living in Houston, believes it is *"money."*

Redbone, a Houston barber says, *"Women are confused."*

Anthony, an anesthesiologist in Houston blames the difficulties on *"cell phones."*

Emma, a Houston high school teacher spoke this paragraph: *"Men have now reached a point where they want the woman to be their care givers. They want the woman to court them and put up a chase. I'm not saying it cannot be a chase, but it could be reciprocated. The old-fashioned way of dating is just not the same as my parents."*

Jake, an auto parts seller in Houston states: *"People don't know how to communicate, everything is over text and usually short 1 to 5-word responses."*

Nick, a comedian out of Los Angeles blames it all on *"surfacy connections."*

Nick's notion was also endorsed by Austin, a store manager in the Houston area. *"The majority of people are incredibly shallow,"* he said.

Rico, a maintenance technician from Houston added an extra component to his list of fears.

"Honestly," he said, *"the idea of committing to a person that is not truly committed to me."*

CONFUSION! FEAR! SHALLOWNESS! DISTRUST! DISCONNECT!

Those sentiments are all over the survey answers. Like Emma said, "The old-fashioned way of dating is just not the same as my parents."

No, it is not. Prior generations had spiritual and moral codes that guided courtship, dating and marriage. What do we have today?

This is the age of the internet, social media, and cell phones; all of which I consider to be "**Weapons of Mass Distraction**."

I confess to being old school when it comes to social media. I feel that people are losing the art of genuine connection. The machine is guiding human interactions. The younger generation does not engage in voice communication anymore. You call them, they text back. If at all.

People sit at a restaurant and everyone is on their ubiquitous cell phone.

Coming down the hallways at the high school, at an event, walking the mall, all eyes are on the rectangular shield. If you are blocking your face by being fully engaged with your device, how can you make eye contact with another human and maybe make a connection?

If all your interactions are postings to a public audience, "friends" or "followers", are you capable of entertaining a personal connection with one individual?

That was certainly an issue with the girl who ate the 48 oysters. Remember her? She was not engaging her date at all, but rather interacting with her device to post on TikTok.

When was the last time you had a meaningful verbal conversation with another human being? In person?

The disconnect that a lot of people are experiencing could be the result of all this machine-oriented way of communicating. We are becoming the "bots" in the way we function, but the heart still has human emotions that it desires to fulfil.

Old solutions for new problems

Looking at the concerns expressed by the survey participants prompted me to remember an old-fashioned relationship concept that is no longer recognized by current generations, that of "courtship."

What is courting? is an article that appeared on Thrivewoks.com, on September 30, 2013. In it, Joe Negroni describes the word as:

"...the systematic process of pursuing the other person. It's the romance of long and intimate conversations (as well as time) spent with a person before you decide to let them in. It's the idea of being intimate friends with someone before becoming an intimate lover."

Basically, it is the time spent learning about each other to determine whether you are compatible to pursue a relationship. Often physical intimacy occurs before the parties had a chance to really know about the other, fooling the parties into feeling that there is implied commitment.

Another article posted on eharmony.com on November 22, 2023, *Courtship vs Dating...* elaborates on the definition of courtship:

"According to the dictionary, a courtship is the 'act, period, or art of seeking the love of someone with intent to marry'. When it comes to courting vs dating, one of the major things that sets courting apart is its seriousness. As a general rule, courting is more formal than dating. It's also more intentional – everyone involved knows what the final step is."

The article further clarifies the difference between dating and courting:

"When you date someone, it's much more casual, and there are fewer rules. Depending on the relationship, it can be fine to date multiple people at once. There's no expectation of marriage at the beginning, or even of a serious relationship like there is when you're courting someone."

I believe the eHarmony editorial team hit the nail on the head with that one.

The biggest difference between dating and courting is the intent.
- Dating is casual: go out with someone and have fun.
- Courting is intentional: seeking a serious relationship or potential life mate and going through the interview or discovery process.

My suggestion is that people interested in connecting with a potential mate re-acquaint themselves with the concept of courtship. Go out, date, get to know people and have fun. But if your goal is to find a life partner, be intentional about it. Be selective and invest the time and energy to get to know the person and ascertain that you are compatible in your values, desired lifestyle, and your standards and future goals are in alignment.

This is the accountability part that most people, women in particular, don't do. Have a standard and make it known.

Spring 1997 – modeling one of my "Dee La Cool" creations - Jersey City, NJ.

This time around, my apparent self-confidence is authentic. I have done the work on myself to know fully who I am.

A client for whom I made the bride's wedding gown and the groom's tuxedo, invited me to attend their wedding.

Nobody can tell this bodacious vixen that she's not all that!

I know what I have to offer and I know what I want.

PART II

PREPARING FOR PARTNERSHIP

When it comes to finding a life mate, it is helpful to have a clear picture of what you want in a partner, the lifestyle you prefer and the values you seek to match with your own.

READY FOR A RELATIONSHIP?

In the 2020s we are several decades past the sexual revolution of the sixties. Society has accepted the new norm, where freedom reigns and the pursuit of personal satisfaction has in instances created a game of instant gratification. A lot of people pursue casual relationships as a matter of course or preference; while others use it as a place holder – until something better comes along.

In some circles, especially in religious culture, dating still follows the model of prior generations of courting as a precursor to marriage. You court someone you like or are attracted to, with the ultimate objective of settling down in blessed matrimony.

Regardless of personal beliefs, human beings are wired to connect with others, more specifically a particular other. Consequently, people keep hoping for and looking for that special someone to be "their person."

The first questions to ask oneself then are these:

- What do *I want* in a relationship?
- What *kind* of relationship do I want?

For our discussion, we will examine two basic categories:

1. A casual relationship where I can call this person when I feel like being with someone and vice versa. A short-term event, just a hook up or escort when needed.

2. A serious, committed relationship where we are each other's person for physical, emotional, and social support. Add to that, something long term with the possibilities of marriage.

Once you identify which type of relationship you want, you should be honest with yourself and the prospective mate as to what your expectations are somewhere around the beginning of the relationship. Most importantly, be prepared to accept the person's perspectives. If it is not what you wanted to hear, make a conscious decision to pursue at your own risk or halt the relationship before it advances too far when hearts can be broken.

When we explored that topic in the section "Relationship – What is it?" respondents stated their preferences for a choice of dating situations for the rest of their lives. Participants of both genders admitted to being open to casual dating; but the majority of them professed to wanting one serious long-term relationship.

CASUAL RELATIONSHIPS

When I separated from Joe, a live in partner and became single around the age of 35, I wanted to get back into a committed relationship. I was raised conservative and by personality have always preferred a one-on-one, we-are-doing-this-together kind of thing.

At the time I was an entrepreneur and fashion designer in New York City. I was meeting new people every day but had difficulties getting dates because I was looking to connect with a potential mate. My best friend at the time, Annie, chided me on being too serious. "Just have fun Dani," she told me. "Just go on dates."

I took her advice and began accepting dating offers even if I didn't really view the person as a potential boyfriend. There were some great first dates where the conversation flowed easily and by all appearance, potential hung in the air. Then I never heard from the guy.

There were others where some dude thought he had hit the lottery for going on a date or two with me, and I, always the diva, felt like I had downsized to a less than desirable companion.

I was never a fan of dating, this searching, trying out, getting to know you, hoping that this might work; then watching it fizzle out before it even had a chance to germinate. I was tired of the games, threw caution to the wind and decided to join the game. I would try casual relationships so that I would at least have a semblance of a love life.

On one occasion I met this man at a professional party. He had his own business as a promoter or something. He traveled a lot between Los Angeles and New York. He called me the day after our first date and admitted that he liked me a lot and that I was the type of woman he was looking for. Then he proceeded to propose an arrangement.

"I'm a very busy man," he said. "I'm looking for a woman I can call on when I'm in town."

He was a good looking, successful man, and good company. I agreed to give it a try. Then when I thought about it later, it dawned on me. *Danielle, that is not what you want! This man is looking for a booty on call when he's in town, a mistress.*

I called him the next day, admitted that I could not be what he wanted. I was looking for a committed one-on-one relationship.

The next time, I tried a different approach to casual dating with someone else. This man was a good conversationalist, educated and he had a good job working for the City of New York in a professional capacity. Physically not really my type, but the deal was to stop being hung up on type and try the person for who they were.

One thing kept bothering me. On several occasions he would mention the fact that "he liked to do what he likes to do with no interference." The deal was that he parked himself in front of the television during football season and watched games after games simultaneously, using the window view feature on his set. He alluded to the fact of being alone so that he would not be told what to do. A little red flag popped up in my head, *"Caution, this one is set in their ways."*

We went out to dinner a couple of times, then one evening he invited me to his apartment. At that time, even though I was conservative compared to my peers, it was still standard operation to sleep with the person after a few dates.

I will always remember that feeling of emptiness the next morning when I looked at this man that I had been so intimate with hours before and saw an absolute stranger. I did not like him any more than I did prior to the deed and apparently, he did not fall in love with me either. That was the turning point for me to completely veer to serious relationship mode going forward.

We had breakfast and I left and never called him back until months later. When I became a born-again Christian, one of the lessons was to examine ourselves and look at past behaviors and see how they would have to be different going forward. I realized that back then, I had expressed the same callous attitude that I would bemoan of men in the dating game.

I called the guy and apologized for my disappearing act. He chided me, "You found religion or something?"

"As a matter of fact, I did," I replied. "I want to live my life differently."

I had made peace with myself, but we never reconnected.

SERIOUS RELATIONSHIPS

That short-lived encounter with this man marked the turning point for me. I knew for sure I did not want casual relationships. I desired a committed relationship that could possibly become long-term or permanent. That's what most people say they desire. Wanting it is one thing. Understanding what it is, and finding it, is another.

A serious, committed relationship scares many people and from my experience, men in particular. For some reason, some people like to keep their options open in case something better comes along. Then that tells you right there that this person you are currently with is not the one for you. While it may feel nice to have a person around, you are not being fair to them for leading them on. I am pretty sure no one seeing someone on a regular basis has ever honestly made the following confession:

"Well, I am just hanging with you. The minute I meet the man/woman of my dreams, I am out of here. So, let's just enjoy this for the moment."

Here comes the pot of hot grits, right upside your callous head!

If you are a Tyler Perry fan you know that scene from the movie *Madea's Family Reunion*.

So dumb-dumb, here comes the hot grits for being so careless and uncaring. Be careful, some might even use a hammer or a gun if they ever hear those words come out of your mouth.

I have known male friends to date a woman for years and when asked what's up, they are like, "I am not sure that's the woman for me." Or they might say, "I'm not sure I want to marry her."

I could slap them over the head – if I would not be charged with assault!

Anytime you are seeing someone for a subjectively long time (for some six months, others five years), it can be interpretated as a desire to make this long term or permanent.

People develop feelings. They become attached. They could be vesting their emotions when there is no buy-in from the other party.

In my single days, a co-worker friend introduced me to a young man she thought I would hit it off with. My friend was a New York City Jew who had a very diverse circle of creative friends. I believe she looked at me and must have thought:

"Danielle is black and she is very nice. My friend Patrick is black and very nice. They are perfect for each other!"

When I met Patrick, I was not attracted to him at all. But he was a nice person. We went on a few dates and he was good company. But, the more I hung out with him, the more I realized that I was not into him and we did not have a lot in common. He, on the other hand, started to develop feelings for me. It all came to a head when he invited me to visit his parents' home with him for the Thanksgiving holiday.

"My mom will like you," he said. He was already thinking of us as a couple.

I had to come clean that I did not feel the same way about him. He was devastated. I felt bad for breaking his heart.

The reverse of that is that I had my heart broken too when someone I was seeing decided I was not the one for them. Dates were cancelled, phone calls not returned. I was ghosted. Finally, he told me straight out that he no longer wanted to pursue the relationship.

All of which made me realize that there is no easy way to end a relationship, regardless of its duration. Whether you are casually dating or deeply committed, if you feel in your heart that the situation is not right or things aren't aligning with your desires, a break-up may be a necessary step to take.

Singer and entertainer Ciara appeared in an episode of the *Call Her Daddy* podcast in 2023, where she shared some things about her past relationship with rapper Future to whom she was engaged and had a child with. She recalled when she knew it was time to end the relationship.

"It's almost like your taste buds change," she told host Alex Cooper.

Clean Your Slate

Realizing that a situation isn't right for you can be a bitter pill to swallow. Sometimes this realization comes early on, while other times it occurs much later. That is why it is crucial to understand your true desires and not allow yourself to be swept away by fleeting emotions or the desire to simply be with someone.

According to my survey, most people have experienced a break-up. Some have been on the receiving end of various methods of breaking off relationships or they have themselves dished out various means of letting go. Participants were allowed to choose more than one response.

Methods Used to Break Up	Men	Women
Straight forward calm conversation	67%	76%
Ghosting	30%	59%
Start an argument	0%	32%
Sabotage	0%	12%
Other	7%	0%

I couldn't help notice that the men in the survey chose not to use argument or sabotage to break up. Based on the stories a lot of women shared with me, I am wondering how truthful they were.

Just remember to be gentle, whichever method you employ. Avoid the bad karma of threshing on someone's heart and the possible *Fatal Attraction* scenarios.

On the opposite end of the spectrum are those who don't have the heart or the honesty to let go after they've realized that the situation they are in is not for them. I asked respondents to consider why they keep going anyway, if it's not working. Here are their honest answers, choosing more than one.

Reasons for staying	Men	Women
Fear of loneliness	12%	26%
Insecurity	32%	24%
Something in the meantime	8%	15%
Selfishness	12%	9%
Other	36%	26%

When I look at this information, this is what stands out to me. Someone could be in an ongoing relationship, anticipating that things are going to progress, and not be aware that, in fact, the other person is there for any of the above reason, and not for love or the desire to go permanent.

It is imperative that you study a person's interactions with you, in words and actions. Learn about them, their desires, preferences, and plans, to see if you fit in their mold. Communicate often and deeply to gauge whether you are both on the same page.

I recommend that if it is not exactly what you want, and you know for sure **there is no possibility of anything stronger developing, then you must wipe your slate clean, clear the clutter. Make room for your blessing.**

Here are some additional comments provided by the respondents regarding why they stayed in relationships that were not working. The ladies said:

"Because I'm tired" – Kristen

"Comfortability" – Amber

The guys were a bit more eloquent.

"Worried about hurting the other person. Especially if they are a good person and didn't do anything wrong" – Charles Z.*

"Bored, dry spell" – Anthony

"I hate hurting other people, so if I had to ensure a little bit to make them happy, I'll gladly do so" – Jake

"Open minded to the possibility of amazingness" – All Day*

When you acknowledge to yourself that you want a committed relationship, you must accept that it comes with a set of criteria.

A committed relationship is sometimes also referred to as serious.

It is identified as serious for a reason. It requires

both parties to form a one-on-one bond that is taken seriously.

You are mutually agreeing – (should not assume) – that you are exclusive.

You show your commitment by genuinely caring about one another's welfare and happiness and being there for each other.

That physical, emotional, and even financial support of each other is what doing life together as a couple involves. Dating long term in a committed relationship, is in a way, the trial period to officially coupling or marriage.

Regardless of whether it takes several months or you know from day one that someone is the one, a serious relationship does not happen overnight. It develops over time, even when there is an early connection.

PREPARING FOR
A RELATIONSHIP

Auntie Wisdom: A relationship requires work. Just as we previously analyzed the intricacies of a new business partnership, it is essential to address any issues that arise. **Your personal challenges should ideally be resolved before entering this cooperative arrangement, allowing your focus to be on refining the merger without distractions.**

You have taken the time to analyze what a relationship is and you determined that you do want a serious or committed, long-term one and are ready for it. Once you make that decision, there are some steps that you must take to make sure you are prepared, and fully equipped to enter a romantic partnership.

When you are seeking a job, you make sure to acquire the required skills and prepare by updating your resume. When you have a prospect, you do your research on the company, practice with mock interviews, lay out your best business attire, and make sure you are on time, etc. If you are planning to run a marathon, you do your drills, sprints, and daily runs to get your body into shape. A boxer hits the gym to get into shape before a match. A lawyer researches case laws and works on their brief before appearing in court… You get my drift.

It is said that "luck is when opportunity meets preparation."

It is no different in seeking a long-term mate. Your preparation is to develop the best version of self you can muster, and build confidence in who you are and what you want. Then the odds are more favorable when the opportunity presents itself to connect with a potential mate. I agree that there is a degree of randomness that comes in meeting someone. I choose to call it God's blessings and plans in action. But ultimately, what solidifies an initial connection is when both parties are in sync mentally and emotionally.

There are several components that create the ideal setting for a serious relationship. Be on the lookout for them and analyze each as you encounter them.

Each party must know themselves fully and know what they are looking for.

- There must be some form of initial connection.
- Each person must be ready to consider a serious relationship.
- The timing must be right for both parties.
- The getting to know you must progress in a positive direction.
- Red flags are analyzed and evaluated.
- Beige flags are evaluated and deemed not a deal breaker.
- They must be able to overcome some sort of challenge or test together, and the successful resolution of it should solidify their choice.

KNOW THYSELF – AND TO THYSELF BE TRUE

<u>untie Wisdom:</u> If you do not know who you are as a full human being, including your gifts, your core values, and your personal beliefs, you risk leaving it open for someone else to come in and write their own narrative for your life.

An essential tool for leading a fulfilling life and fostering successful relationships is self-awareness. When you truly understand yourself, you become conscious of what aligns with your values and what doesn't.

If not, someone else might impose their desires and preferences on you, leading you to lose your true essence. Conversely, you must be willing to adjust where necessary to accommodate compatibility with a potential mate.

In early June of 2024, I had a chance to talk directly to Houston radio personality, KG Smooth, and asked him if he had one thing to say about relationships, what would it be. His answer came without hesitation, and summed up perfectly the viewpoint I propose in this section of the book.

"When it comes to relationships," he said, "everybody wants a great partner; until it requires them to be a better person."

In a relationship, it is imperative to know yourself: what you want, what you like, what you bring to the table, how you function, etc. Each party will have to examine their package and see if they are compatible, regardless of feelings.

In the survey *Dating & Relationships in the 2020s* that I conducted to prepare for this book, I asked respondents whether they had done the work on themselves to prepare for the person they seek. The question was formulated as follows:

What work have you done on yourself to be more compatible with and attract your desired potential mate? In other words, what would a person like the one you want, be looking for in a mate of their own?

They were given the following answer choices:

- *Make improvements to personality*
- *Work on physical appearance*
- *Therapy - Increase self-awareness*
- *Further education*
- *Faith investigation or renewal*
- *Adjust expectations*
- *Other*

These choices among others, are various methods you can use to prepare for a relationship. We will examine them one by one, to see how they can assist in creating a better version of yourself.

And listen. No shade. Nobody is perfect. You may believe that you are the "bomb.com," but there is always room for improvement. Especially when you are targeting a particular goal.

Take a Selfie – aka -Hold a Mirror to Self

A self-assessment is not an easy thing to do. You must be able to look at who you are objectively. Who are you? How do you feel about certain things?

What makes you feel good about yourself or life? What unnerves or derails you? What do you like to be surrounded by? What matters to you?
What is the sum of you?

A business proposition would involve an analysis of a company's operations and a review of their profit and loss statements. This information lets the prospect know whether this would be a profitable merger or acquisition.

In dating or seeking a mate, a person basically puts themselves on the market, offering their goods. Their physical package, their personality, their values, financial position and who they are as an individual.

To be real, we all assess. Men do it and so do women. Sometimes the look hits home for us, other times the personality or financial position does it. Consequently, it makes sense that everyone should take stock of what they have to offer.

Taking selfies is commonplace today. Everyone does it to post to their social media or to memorialize a moment. And when one does, the objective is to show oneself at the best angle and in the best light, even using filters, if necessary, for full effect.

It is advisable to do the same with how you see yourself and how you reflect to others. Especially if the purpose is to meet someone you expect to be with for a long time.

Take an honest look at yourself, literally and figurately, then adjust your angles and filters as necessary.

Improvements to personality

Several respondents to the *Dating* survey indicated making improvements to their personality in preparation to seek or attract a mate. I did not ask them to elaborate, but I can imagine they ran the gamut from shy to outgoing, from brash to caring, from boastful to humble, from snotty to friendly, from lazy to motivated, and on and on.

When I became single in my 30's, part of my self-assessment involved working on my personality.

To see me enter a room today, smiling, and confident and immediately connecting with others, one would never guess that I was once so reserved that people thought I was either shy or snobbish. I have never been shy. I was the talkative one in school, the bold one that was in my element on stage and approached whoever I needed to in business.

Nevertheless, my proper Caribbean upbringing dictated that I'd be reserved and well-mannered. Well, I still have great manners, but the reserved part had to go. Former co-workers, who later became close friends, confided that their initial impression of me was that I was stuck up, a perception that couldn't be further from the truth of who I am.

When it came to romance, I operated under the belief that you waited for the right man to approach you with his good intentions in full display. Consequently, if a guy did not appeal to me, I did not mislead by engaging him. If a man came across too strongly, looking for a good time, I was not interested. And if I liked someone, I didn't know how to show interest without appearing forward. I only smiled in response to a new acquaintance's smile.

Men would literally call out to me on the street, "Hey, smile, pretty lady!" Once a man told me while on the dance floor at a party, that I "was too serious." When the song ended, he walked away. My face betrayed the serious part of me, but in truth, beneath that serious demeanor lived an adventurous and spontaneous spirit that enjoys good, clean, fun. I just was not projecting that.

This stern personality trait caused me to unwittingly miss connecting with great guys who might have been good prospects.

People in your close circle are a great help in holding up a mirror to you when you cannot see what may be wrong with you. If you can trust that they have your best interest at heart, listen to what they say to you.

My friend and hang out partner at the time, Annie, who has always been a buzzing bumble bee, told me "To relax." She said:

"You are too serious Dani. Just date and have fun. You don't have to take every guy for a potential husband."

I started to smile more. I began to engage people in conversation rather than wait to be spoken to. I let it show that I am naturally caring and a true friend. I resolved to accept offers for dates even if the man was not "husband potential," just so that I would become more comfortable around the opposite sex and study them up close.

◊◊◊

Effects of Physical Appearance

<u>Auntie Wisdom:</u> What your eyes see is the first thing that connects you to a person. – Unless your first introduction was a voice over the phone. In that case you need to work on your tone and vocal mannerism.

Appearance does matter. That is what I believe. Apparently, that is what most people subscribe to, if I am to believe the results of my survey where 69% of the women and 93% of the men cited looks and physical appearance as the first thing that attracted them to someone.

What we are going to look at is two-fold: 1) the physical appearance that comprises what God or nature bestowed upon you at birth, and 2) how you choose to project the essence of you.

Growing up on the island of Haiti, I never thought I was pretty. I knew I was not ugly. But in a society where back then, the standards of black beauty were measured in the lightness of your skin and the length of your hair, my bronzed skin nor my short hair qualified me as beautiful. However, I have always had an innate sense of style and a love of fashionable clothes that by my late teens developed into wanting a modeling and acting career. I barely realized that I had blossomed into a beautiful young woman who was desired by the neighborhood boys and approached by men all the time. I was never fazed by it because the childhood self-image in my head kept me humble.

I was around twenty-one when I met Joe, a worldly and sensual man of thirty-three who brought out the sexy in me. Joe was extremely visual. He liked his woman to look sexy and relished making other men envious by showing me off. He was extravagant and a fashion buff himself. We also ran a fashion business together.

Whenever we went out for an occasion, my attire was Instagram worthy, before such a thing existed. A snapshot taken then could very well be from the pages of a fashion magazine.

After we separated, I continued to dress in the same style, especially since I was still involved in the fashion business, on my own this time.

When I started dating again, I noticed that men would focus on my "sexiness." It has always been there, but if it was enhanced or flaunted in the way that I dressed, they immediately picked up on it. That would become the focus of their conversation.

This began to bother me. There I was, looking for a genuine connection and a serious relationship, but apparently, I was not projecting that. I decided to reverse trend and dress conservatively: long skirts, loose clothes, little make up. I met my next date, an MBA graduate, at an event where I was dressed simply as described above. When he saw me naked for the first time, he was surprised that I had such a "beautiful body."

I chose to end the budding relationship after some time because the more I got to know him, the more I realized we were not compatible.

That experience showed me that your appearance _and_ what you project factor in the way a prospective mate sees you.

<u>Auntie Wisdom</u>: Looks are not everything. Appearance is. And there is a difference.

I believe that we are all uniquely and "wonderfully made," and all of God's creatures, including humans have our distinctive looks. However, beauty standards vary by cultural and personal preferences and are as numerous as there are people. Because standards do exist, men who are considered attractive, and women who are deemed beautiful by our society get more attention than others.

Should that stop anyone from feeling worthy of catching the attention of possible mates? No. Is there something you can do to up your chances? Yes.

Someone who is naturally attractive will most likely have an easier time of catching the eyes of prospects, but someone who takes care of their appearance increases their chances as well.

It is like looking in a jewelry store window. The eye is first drawn to the shiny objects: the sparkling diamonds, the glistening emeralds, the glossy gold. Then the more you look, and depending on your taste, you notice the subtle brilliance of the champagne diamond, the gentle glow of the opal, the fiery blue of a lapis lazuli, or the exotic vein of a jade or jasper. Oh! Look at the design on that silver bracelet! That star-shaped ring with the tiger stone!

All jewelry has unique qualities that appeal to individual tastes. When enhanced in the proper setting, with the velvet background and the spotlight shining on it, its beauty is showcased to full effect.

I have seen plain looking women who were so pulled together that they appeared attractive. A neatly dressed man always makes a good impression.

In addition, today with the help of cosmetic enhancements, the looks you are born with are hardly a stumbling block. I do not condone the exaggerated lips, busts or butts that prevail today. But I think minor modifications are perfectly acceptable to enhance your looks. – Just remember when the babies do not look like either of you, you will have some explaining to do.

More so than physical looks however, what comes across to others is how you present yourself and what that reflects about you.

The MBA guy I dated briefly, was a frumpy dresser, while I always was and remain a fashionista who at the time, ran a fashion design business. The contrast in our appearance troubled me. I believe in always looking neat and put together. I throw on a cute top and some lip gloss just to run to the corner store.

This guy stopped by my exhibit booth at a Black Expo at the Jacobs Javits Convention Center, in a tattered college tee-shirt and a too tight plaid short that was probably as old. I was mortified!

Dee La Cool – my fashion moniker at the time – the coolest fashion designer this side of Manhattan, with a date looking this shabby! *Quelle horreure!* – the horror. The times when I rode in his car, I had to clear old newspapers and books off the front seat and floor to sit down. When I visited him, I walked into a messy apartment. All things that confirmed for me what his appearance had announced. He was messy and care not the least about his appearance or surroundings. I am a neat freak. We were on opposite ends of a spectrum.

That was a deal breaker for me when I added other things that did not work for us.

The funny thing is, I ran into him a year later, on the New York subway. He was well dressed in a nice linen shirt and pants. Then I noticed the woman who accompanied him and put it together. *"Oh, she gave him a makeover. Good for him. Good for her!"*

In his case, he was lucky a woman was willing to work with him. He did have potential as an MBA with a good job and was a nice enough guy. He just wasn't right for me.

<u>Auntie Wisdom</u>: Why not be a jewel? In other words, when you remove the poetic imagery - every man and woman should always present themselves in the best possible light. Especially when in the market for a mate.

From my experience and what I have observed, in most situations, it is easier for women to look past looks and investigate other qualities, like the woman did with the frumpy MBA. It is a little harder for men to be as flexible. In general, men are first attracted to looks, in whatever variable that strikes their fancy, and based on their preferences. If there is a later, they will start to notice the other stuff like personality, character, and values.

When I lived in Jersey City, New Jersey, my condo's front door faced a main thoroughfare. From my windows, I could observe people walking the avenue, on their way to or from work in New York City. There was a very attractive, well-dressed man who I ran into several mornings as we made our way to the train station. I wished he would approach me, but he never even looked my way.

My roommate at the time had a sister who stopped by at times in the morning on her way to work. We had similar looks, built and physical shape. However, where I looked plain, dressed corporate and wore minimal make up; "sister girl" had that glamourous look. She showed up at eight in the morning one day in full make up, hair piece in place, leather skirt, and high heels. We both left the house at the same time, right when the guy was coming up the street. He took one look at her, his eyes lit up and he approached her. She snubbed him. She wasn't interested.

There I was; I was interested and a decent prospect, but he did not even notice me. He never got to know that I was educated, was a compliance analyst at a prestigious law department, had a fashion business on the side, was nice, caring, fun loving and a Christian. Had she accepted his advances, he would have found out that her boyfriend was the biggest drug dealer in town and was currently serving a prison sentence. She was not educated. She had this man's child and was rumored to be running the business while the boyfriend was incarcerated.

Feel free to mentally insert your own comments.

I also experienced another version of men responding to looks. When

I ran the fashion business, at one time I worked closely with my friend Annie who was also my business partner. Annie was a gorgeous model, an exotic looking Ethiopian whose bubbly personality made her very likable. Whenever guys came around her, they were immediately smitten. The glint in their eyes and their immediate desire to cater to her betrayed their adoration.

I often had mixers or fashion showcases at the condo, as I used its large loft area as a showroom for my business. Times when we partied, guys would line up to dance with Annie or flirt with her and she reveled in the attention. The whole thing amused me immensely because I knew she was not interested in any of them.

On one occasion it was the same scenario: Annie surrounded by my male guests taking turns dancing with her. A conversation took place where it was revealed that the business was mine and so was this beautiful two-level modern condo in downtown Jersey City. In no time I was surrounded by several solicitous admirers, eager to make conversation.

Annie noticing that all the attention had shifted away from her started to shake her groove thing in a sexy dance move to lure it back. One guy went to her but two stayed with me. When I mentioned that my feet were hurting, one of them dropped to the floor, and took my shoes off to rub my feet – good thing the toes had had a recent pedicure.

Yes, people do naturally first gravitate to looks. However, if you can show your inherent value in other ways, you have just as much of a chance as Beauty Queen or His Handsomeness. Might have to work a little harder to showcase those assets without flaunting.

Auntie Wisdom: Project your Best! Looks are important. Consequently, men and women who are looking to date, make the effort to always look your best.

By best, I don't mean a man in a tuxedo and tie, or a woman, full makeup, and a sequin dress at eight o'clock in the morning. Rather, I'm talking about a neat and well-groomed appearance that indicates you care about what you project about yourself. Shabby tee-shirts work for Simon Cowell (*America's Got Talent* television contest judge), because his position and net assets speak for him. The rest of us need to always make a good first impression.

Advice for the Guys: when meeting a lady for a date, get a haircut, wear a nice shirt or sweater if the weather is cool. It makes you look sophisticated. You can open the top button to show that you work out. And get some breath mint. You don't want her assaulted by the deadly vapors emanating from your mouth!

Caution: Keep it simple. Not too much cologne. You don't want her to suffocate. Clean hands and nails also say a lot in your favor.

Advice for the Ladies: I recommend you have a little something interesting, something that stands out for you. For some it may be lipstick, or a nice hairdo, or manicured nails, a statement pair of earrings or a color that makes your skin tone pop. Just enough on an ordinary day, then you do it up when you are going out on the town or for special occasions.

Caution: Do not overdo it. - Men want to see as much of the natural you as possible; the way you might look when you first wake up in the morning. – I have yet to meet one man, young or old, who likes the one-inch eyelashes a lot of women favor today!

Fresh* a 30 something survey respondent who is a Safety Manager, stated one of his preferences for a future mate as: "I would like for her to be secure in her skin and not feeling like she needs beauty enhancement surgeries or tons of make up to be attractive."

◊◊◊

Increase self-awareness - Therapy

You lady, are sitting in a restaurant, surveying the crowd. A man strides into the room, his whole demeanor so captivating, his mere presence calls you to attention. Celebrity? Basketball player? Actor?

You sir, perched on a bar stool, waiting for your buddies. A woman, not a beauty by any means, walks in, looking so self-assured that magnetism radiates from her. Is she a model? Actress? Influencer?

This is a scene from the movie of your life. You see people like that and wonder what they got going on that creates that aura around them. What do these two strangers in your movie have in common? Self-confidence!

Self-confidence is a very sexy attribute. People tend to gravitate to someone who exhibits that trait, perhaps viewing it as a sign of emotional strength.

The term self-confidence is generally defined as a person's attitude about their skills and abilities. When you know yourself and what you are capable of, you feel more in control of your life. You are braver in pursuing things because you know your strengths. You don't mind taking calculated risks because you know how to use your weaknesses to your advantage. You feel positive and that energy surrounds you and infuses your interactions with others.

My theory is further supported by the following quote from a November 11, 2021 post, *Confidence is Key,* that appeared in a high school publication, the Herriman Telegraph (*herrimantelegraph.org*). In it, Kendall Stables elaborates on the importance of confidence:

The meaning of 'confidence is key' is the ability to <u>see</u> the best version of yourself and to <u>be</u> the best version of yourself.

When you know what you are made of and you are comfortable in your own skin, you exude self-confidence. And the best route to achieving self-confidence is to be self-aware.

What is self-awareness?

According to an article posted in February 27, 2023, on the TSW website a leadership and management training firm in the United Kingdom(*tsw. co.uk*), Andrew Wallbridge, the Head of Leadership & Management, offered the following definition.

Self-awareness is the ability to recognise and understand your own thoughts, feelings, and emotions.

It's a key part of emotional intelligence because knowing yourself and how you impact others will help you maintain strong relationships, build trust, improve communication and a range of other "soft skills."

These definitions support my overarching theory of "knowing thyself."

Your thoughts and emotions play a significant role in shaping your feelings. These feelings, in turn, influence how you engage with and react to others, while your values serve as a compass guiding your actions. Ultimately, these components interplay to shape your interactions with others, thus impacting your relationships.

This self-knowledge exploration often takes the form of professional therapy. Sometimes the brain knows what to do, but the heart is unable to be objective. That's when you need a disinterested party holding up a mirror for you to look at yourself, help you acknowledge your emotions and sort out your feelings.

By the way, let's make one thing clear:

THERE IS NO SHAME in seeking professional therapy!

Some people refuse to consider professional therapy and offer myriad excuses. *"I am okay." "I can handle it." "That's a waste of time."* And the best I have heard among my Caribbean people and in African American culture, *"I am not crazy!"*

Some cultures just do not believe in it. However, if your mental state is so clouded with negative or conflicting emotions, if you tried the traditional methods of prayer, personal interventions, and peer counseling, and you are still dealing with issues, it may be time to consider professional help.

Several respondents in the survey *Dating & Relationships in the 2020s* – (27% of men and 46% of women) – shared that they have used therapy as a means of developing self-awareness.

I've never had professional therapy, but have seen how it helped those who have used it in time of crises. I highly recommend it as a tool for self-assessment and a device for building self-awareness.

When I decided to break off from Joe and subsequently separated from him, I went through some very dark times. My emotions were a mess. I was depressed, lonely, felt lost and was briefly suicidal. My circle of sisters was instrumental in helping me along the path that brought me balance. However, the most impactful method for me, in re-calibrating myself and healing, was journaling and prayers. I had constant conversations with God and I journaled almost daily.

Being a creative person, I live in my head a lot. Thoughts run around in there at warp speed, like a carousel gone awry; and when you are emotional, it becomes overwhelming. The five Ws and the H bounced around in my brain like giddy clowns. **Who** am I? **What** do I want/need? **Where** am I heading in life? **When** will it get better? **Why** did this happen to me? **How** am I going to survive?

Since I've always liked to express myself in writing, I started a journal as my therapy. I gave my imaginary confidante a name, Erma/Mimi. She would be a sounding board for me, my therapist.

Over a period of several years, I opened myself up to this made-up counselor. She could not speak back to me, but I was forced to come face to face with myself and my thoughts. I had to relay the facts, ask the questions, share how I felt about them, and decide what to do about things. I had to examine my personality to understand my natural tendencies. I took a hard look at my upbringing that formed my values, and recalled past experiences that shaped who I was. Most importantly, I had to scrutinize the far recesses of my soul to learn about myself and decide what I ultimately wanted from a relationship and from life in general.

Periodic visits to past journal entries helped me compare my current state to those previous reflections. I was able to recognize the progress made in understanding myself and my behavior.

That journal was the basis for my memoir, *Cads, Princes & Best Friends.*

<u>Auntie Wisdom</u>: Do what you need to do to center yourself. Pray, talk to people who care about you, read, journal, seek professional help and therapy if necessary. Your objective: Be THE BEST VERSION OF YOURSELF that you can be!

◊◊◊

Further education

<u>Auntie Wisdom</u>: Ideally, it is best to do the necessary self-work before you enter a relationship. However, life doesn't always unfold that way. A successful individual is one who continues to evolve, sometimes finding themselves in situations that require change or growth. In an ideal scenario, both partners' visions are compatible, enabling them to support each other in their journey towards a more fulfilling life.

Education is another important component in an individual's package. It factors in how you see yourself, how you view others and how they see you, and how you interact and relate to others. Next to your familial upbringing, education is an experience that shapes your values and affects the way you function in the world.

In some circles, an education prompts an attitude considered "bougie." In other words, one with a college degree should not even consider someone who doesn't have one. That philosophy assumes that the two people are not on the same intellectual or social level, consequently not equally matched.

I experienced being on the short end of that measuring stick at a wedding I attended when I was single. The couple, who was Ethiopian, met while attending Cornell University. Most of their guests were from the same circle, good looking, elegant and educated Ethiopians. At first glance I fitted right in. I had the looks and the elegance.

I eyed a tall, confident, good-looking man among the guests who happened to be seated at my table. We stroke up a conversation. The question "What do you do?" came up. When I mentioned being a paralegal, he replied, "Oh, just a couple of years, you'll be a lawyer." I shrunk inside. At the time I did not even have a bachelor's degree, having stopped college after my second year.

I was attracted to this man and he engaged in conversation with me amiably. If the circumstances lent themselves to an offer to connect, how would his perception of me be affected by the fact that I did not hold a college degree? I can almost guarantee you that there would be no connection. I was not in his league.

In the television series *Suits,* that is getting a new life on Netflix as of this writing, the main character, Mike Ross, encountered a similar experience. Mike is a genius with astounding recall and an immense reservoir of knowledge who happens to be a college dropout. In that episode, he works as a bike messenger but has a side hustle of taking the bar exam for others. The contents of the law books reside in his brain. He meets a law school student who also works at a non-profit. He convinces her to go on a date. When she shared difficulties with a case, he pretended to be a law student as well and helped her figure out the best argument with supporting case studies to win the case. However, when it came to making a court appearance, he could not keep working on the case. He had to acknowledge to the woman that he was not in fact going to law school. She broke it off and honestly told him that she had bigger plans and he did not fit in. All she saw was a bike messenger.

I concede that there is some validity to the attitude that a degreed person should only associate with their kind. Someone's level of education is a contributing factor to their earning potential. In considering a mate, one should consider whether pairing with that person fulfills your expectations for a desired lifestyle. In addition, matching someone's intellectual capacity holds a measure of importance, since it affects how you view life, handle situations, how you discuss issues, and how you go about things. Education is a formative experience that helps put people on the same page.

However, in a lot of cases, it doesn't matter. Some people are self-learners who read books and research information for their own personal growth. For a long time, I was one of those. Others are naturally gifted with wisdom and common sense. A conversation with one of these individuals can be more stimulating than one with a PhD who might just be book smart. You have probably heard the expression, "an educated fool."

When I started dating my husband Henri, I had some hesitation. In my social circles, he didn't come across as sophisticated as I prefer a man. Henri grew up in Haiti, with an education exclusively in French or Creole. When we engaged in intellectual English discussions that centered around the American culture, he struggled to participate. I witnessed him interacting with Haitians when we visited his family, and noticed how articulate and comfortable a speaker he was. I then understood that it was the language and cultural barrier.

As time went on, he became more comfortable expressing himself with me and with my mostly English-speaking friends.

What I have always admired in him is the curious mind that is willing to investigate and learn. But best of all, **he does not stop me from learning** what strikes my fancy and growing.

When you are working on yourself to be who you want to be, it is helpful to be with people who support you. When it comes to a mate, it is imperative that the person also embraces your vision, for your relationship to remain successful.

◊◊◊

Henri and I were already dating seriously when I decided to go back to school to complete my bachelor degree. I had stopped college in my second year because at the time, I chose to concentrate on my singing career.

I also always maintained a corporate job, and worked first as a trained secretary, later obtained a certification to work as a paralegal and eventually became a compliance analyst in the legal department of a Wall Street firm. But as time went by, I felt it necessary to obtain my degree to keep up with the recent graduates flooding the industry. A degree had become the norm for entry level positions, jeopardizing the value of my years of experience.

I am and was an avid reader, a self-learned individual who could hold my own in any conversation from politics, to art, through history, current events, entertainment, philosophy, etc.

When I was introduced to and later joined the non-profit organization, the Haitian American Alliance (HAA) in New York City, I was surrounded by lawyers, doctors, nurses, teachers, urban planners, accountants, HR managers, and PHD candidates. I felt right at home. This was my crowd. They were educated, successful, cultured young Haitian Americans who were giving back to their community. To top it off, they knew how to party! In style! The annual fundraisers we put together brought out large crowds of New York Haitians and American supporters in the arts, music, literature, and politics. Our events were the talk of the town.

This was me! That is still me today. Being a member of that organization embodied everything I am and like: giving back, engaged in community, creative, cultured and a fun-loving social creature. This was where I belonged!

My intellect and character spoke for me. I was nominated and elected to serve on the board of directors. Internally however, this promotion prompted an awakening. Sitting around the table with these educated professionals made me realize that it was not enough that I talked the talk, I wanted to be college educated too.

That, and the threat to my professional career, motivated me to go back to school to complete that degree.

I never dated anyone in the group; they were mostly younger than me. However, being part of them and being engaged in the things we did, raised my confidence to a new level. I knew what I was made of and what I brought to the table in any situation, including dating.

Having a degree did not materially change me. I was the same Danielle in my spirit and in my soul. However, it was such a huge boost to my self-confidence that it affected me in tangible ways. I was able to parlay my newly acquired asset into a better position and higher pay at my job. I no longer had self-esteem issues because I felt on par with the people I interacted with.

When I met Henri, the man who would become my husband, I was full of myself. Not in a bad way. Rather, I knew who I was, what I liked and what I wanted. No more insecurities. No more self-doubt. What you see is what you get, and it is an extremely great deal. You want it, come correct. You are not sure; go figure it out. Some other suitor may come along and recognize this fantastic deal and grab it. Going once… This package may not be available when you get back; you missed your chances.

Furthering your education has a host of benefits that go beyond preparing yourself for a mate. Yes, if the type of people you desire are the degreed professionals, you will have to be one as well, to be viewed as a viable candidate suitable for pairing.

Primarily, whatever you accomplish is for you! It opens you up to new possibilities, it boosts your self-confidence, and makes possible better opportunities for your career.

"Go for it. Claim self-enhancement!" — Check!

◊◊◊

Faith investigation or renewal

Auntie Wisdom: If you are Christian, do not be afraid to embrace your authentic self, and live a life more aligned with God's design. Understand that there will be challenges, but the rewards of doing God's will come in many forms. **A relationship with God is the ultimate connection that guides the one with our fellow humans, including a romantic partner.**

The 2011 movie, *Jumping the Broom* with Paula Patton, Angela Basset, Laz Alonso, and Loretta Devine, presented an instance of faith renewal that was laced with hilarious situations. The film opens with Sabrina (Paula Patton) in bed with Bobby, the previous' night conquest, who is on the phone with another lover. He is so engrossed in sweet talking the person on the phone, that he barely notices when Sabrina, horrified by his callousness, picks up her clothes and rushes out of there. She makes a promise to God that if He got her out of this situation, she would no longer have one-night stands and would only have sex with a future husband.

It's a rom-com. Cue in the chance meeting with a fantastic guy and the foibles of keeping that promise while engaged.

Faith renewal takes on different forms, but it is most often the result of a crisis severe enough to prompt a person to call on their faith, most specifically, God's higher power.

Being a Christian, I subscribe to calling on Jesus for everything that concerns my life. I believe that God has my best interest at heart and He also knows what is best for me. Most Christians believe that, but human beings are naturally disposed to do things their own way. Consequently, even those who know God or know about the required precepts, do not always follow them.

As a single woman dating in the 1990s, the *modus operandi* for me was to sleep with someone after a few dates. That was what the magazines told us and the movies showed us, but that was not who I was. As adventurous a spirit as I am, I was raised a "good girl" who has always preferred to meet the right person and just be with them going forward. But I had bought into the precept that this was what grown people do.

I also had my "Sabrina" moment when I spent the night with a guy and noticed no change in his or my feelings the next morning. Feeling shallow and empty, I also promised God that the next instance of being in bed with a man would be in a serious relationship.

What happened? What crisis brought the change?

In the middle of dealing with my dating woes, my mom passed away from an aggressive cancer. She was in and out of the hospital for a few months, and then gone. She had been a devout Christian, a church-going, serving member who prayed over everything. Even while laying on her death bed, she never lost her faith. Her passing reminded me of the person I was inside, one who had a relationship with God her entire life, even when I was not walking the walk of the faith.

I began to seek a deeper connection to God, attended church regularly and started studying the bible with a church group. My mindset regarding sex and relationships changed. Now faith and the accompanying behavior of my belief would have a major impact on the type of men I wished to connect with and how I would interact with someone I was dating.

Several dates into going out with Henri, one evening he became frisky.

When he became so aggressive, I could barely push him back, I completely freaked out. This, from a woman who, a year or so before, did not hesitate to be the one making advances.

I had changed because of my faith renewal. Consequently, my profile as well as that of any prospective suitor was modified.

For those who may not practice Christianity or any religion at all, there are some fundamental moral codes that are similar to Christian precepts. The topic of this book is not that discussion, but I have seen the benefits of my faith in my life. **You may wish to investigate for yourself what I am talking about.** There are countless resources available.

◊◊◊

Adjust Expectations

In a patriarchal society where (supposedly) men have the upper hand, their specie is more comfortable approaching women who are beyond their reach. I am referring to the mailroom guy who tries to lay his rap on the secretaries or young executives. Or the brick layer who whistles or hollers at the passing beauty who could be the corporate lawyer or vice president of the company. In general, men will try.

I asked some male friends and they explained that a man will take his chances, even if they most likely expect a no. I am picturing a scenario where that young VP turns around and gives her number to that brick layer. In true romantic comedy form, he turns out to be the owner of a construction company covering the day for an absent employee. Hey, I have a wild imagination!

A middle school student once told me very convincingly that Rihanna was his future wife. This while Ms. Thang was on her way to baby number two with ASAP Rocky. (If you need me to explain who they are … Well, her, billionaire entertainer/business mogul; he, famous rapper/music producer.) This young man did not consider that the object of his affections was socially and financially out of his league. What did he have to offer her if he were given a chance to meet her?

Women fantasize out of their reach too. Who would not want the lawyer, the doctor, the successful businessman, the millionaire basketball or football player or the famous artist? Once in a blue moon you get a story like *Maid in Manhattan*, the movie where a New York senator meets Jennifer Lopez's maid character, and they fall in love. Even in movie land they run into myriad challenges. Movies being fiction, they end up together.

The rom-com is guaranteed a happy ending. However, back on *terra ferma*, the real world, things work a little differently. People have clear expectations of what they want but sometimes fail to look at what they realistically have to offer or what circumstances may offer them.

Let us look at a scenario where a woman's ideal mate is attractive, smart, and caring; he has a great career and earns a lot of money. In the movie *Daddy's Little Girls*, Gabrielle Union plays a high-powered attorney who meets and falls for Idris Elba's character, who owns his garage shop and earns enough to support himself and his two daughters. He meets the first half of the requirements, but his career as a mechanic is not in par with hers. This is further complicated by the fact that her bourgie friends do not accept a suitor outside of, and, below their social strata. Big dilemma for Ms. Esquire who must decide:

- Give up this man because of my friends and social circle, and contend with my battery-powered fake human part to keep me company on lonely nights? – He found it in her medicine cabinet when he was looking for aspirins.
- Keep this love thing going with this real man who cares for me and who I care about, adjust, and make allowances for our differences?

I bet you know what she chose, even if you haven't seen the movie.

The survey showed that a lot of people did the self-analysis and remedial work necessary to increase their chances of meeting the person they desired. A consensus was revealed across both genders with only slight differences.

Work Done	Men	Women
Increase self-awareness	77%	66%
Make improvements to personality	65%	57%
Work on physical appearance	46%	57%
Further education	31%	43%
Faith renewal	31%	29%
Adjust expectations	31%	26%
Therapy	27%	46%

In addition to the listed choices, several respondents offered free responses regarding the work they did on themselves.

Ferg, a college career adviser in Houston, thought it best to advance his career before considering a serious relationship.

Edward, a truck driver as well as KP and Redbone, both barbers and Anthony, an anesthesia technician also in Houston, indicated working on their finances.

Van, a public relations executive, chose to heal from past relationships before she felt ready to pursue something new.

Very wise choices, all of them.

I also had to do some work on myself after separating from Joe, before I was mentally and emotionally ready to begin a healthy relationship.

I went through major withdrawal and experienced the usual low self-esteem period that happens when a man cheats on you flagrantly with a much younger woman. – *I am not good enough. I am getting too old. I could not make him happy.* – Then subsequently, there were the failed attempts at capturing an ongoing relationship with a new man. I was needy and fantasized that every man who approached me or that I was attracted to was going to be the one to replace my lost love.

My saving grace was a combination of several of the factors mentioned in the survey, but the major shift happened with the faith renewal.

I was raised Catholic, had always been religious and attended church periodically. When my mother passed away, it had a profound effect on me. She was only in her mid-sixties. At the time I was also struggling with a new business on my own, post-separation, and navigating tumultuous financial waters. I had an epiphany. I was in my early forties.

Danielle, you only have about twenty something years left, if you have your mom's life span. What do you want the rest of your life to be?

The answer did not drop in my spirit immediately, but the changes began to show. I wanted to live a life more reflective of my belief in God and of my mother's faith. I later came to understand that faith was the legacy that she left with me.

Don't freak out about what I am about to say next, dear friends. My fellow Christians will understand. – I literally had a meeting with Jesus!

The sisters from my mom's ministry had asked me if I desired prayers. A week after the funeral, they came to my house for a prayer meeting. As they prayed, I was suddenly struck by this overwhelming force, fell to my knees in tears, hollering and sobbing! I had been touched by the Holy Spirit.

I eventually joined the church and the choir at Christian Cultural Center, Pastor A. R. Bernard's megachurch in Brooklyn.

I strongly desired a life companion. But I also recognized that I wanted a man who appreciated my potential physically, emotionally, financially, and valued everything I had to offer and brought to the table. He would also need to have faith in God and beliefs and values that were close to mine, if not identical.

I felt confident in who I was, had a good circle of like-minded friends, and was enjoying doing things that I liked socially. I had grown used to the idea that I might be alone for the rest of my life and was finally okay with that. I wrote a prayer to God in my journal.

"God, I said, "I am done with this dating business. I am not looking for anybody anymore. If you are going to send me somebody, I literally have to just bump into them."

It was about three years after my break up from Joe when I met Henri. He approached me while we rode an escalator in one of the World Trade Center buildings. We both had been working in the same building, five floors apart, for two years and never crossed paths before that day. I tell the full story in my memoir, *Cads, Princes & Best Friends*.

Note this: I met my life mate when I was <u>READY</u> to receive him. I was looking cute that day, as I always strive to. But I believe the self-confidence that radiated from me, like beams of light, captured his attention. I had done the work on myself to know who I was and what I wanted. I had also adjusted my expectations to truly look at the human being, instead of the labels and the flash and dash I used before, to gauge a man's desirability.

Shout out to my God! I literally did, just bump into my love. Rather, he bumped into me. Even better, since the bible recommends that the man does the finding. Proverbs 18:22 quotes *"He who finds a wife finds a good thing."* I was found. I was chosen!

If that doesn't build someone's faith…

I think I'll smile and take a selfie! Look at gloriously blessed me.

KNOW WHAT YOU WANT

Auntie Wisdom: **Be aware that one's perception of self may be Denzel or Brad Pitt, when you are in fact, Shrek. Consequently, make sure to brush up on your wit.**

I have been one to keep a journal throughout the years since my teens. I also draw lists: daily to do's, semester entertainment lists, movies I want to see on Netflix, house remodeling projects, travel plans, etc. Some people do vision boards, I do lists.

Writing things down is a tool widely recommended to sort out internal conflicts, manage your emotions, gauge where you are, focus on what your dreams are or what or where you wish to be at certain points in your life.

When it comes to finding a life mate, it is helpful to have a clear picture of what you want in a partner, the lifestyle you prefer and the values you seek to match with your own.

In my memoir, *Cads, Princes & Best Friends*, I recount a journal entry discussing what I wanted in a relationship after I had been single for a while.

Ah love! I crave the sharing and caring. I want respect and commitment, a good friend and don't forget, good sex. I wish for a man who looks pleasant enough to appeal to me; one who thinks I am a great woman and would make a great wife; he is smart and emotionally stable; he shares my values concerning life, family, romance; someone interesting or intellectually stimulating; he is adequate in bed (notice I don't demand great), and we have to like each other enough to fall in love and get married!

This list is very specific. While it does not show every single attribute I wished for, it represented the values that were essential to me. Consequently, every time I met someone the checklist would quietly run through my mind.

Everyone has a list of requirements concerning a life mate, even if it is not written down. Most people have a mental list that they check off as they get to know and assess a suitor. In the survey *Dating & Relationships in the 2020s*, participants were asked to first list the three things that attracted them to someone. They could choose any three. The following table shows the results.

First 3 Things that attract you	Men	Women
Looks/physical appearance	93%	69%
Personality/Creativity	68%	71%
Intellect	54%	57%
Charm or Self-Confidence	25%	51%
Attentive/Caring	21%	23%
Position/Title	11%	23%
Instant Connection	11%	17%
Other	7%	0

Both men and woman value the same things when it comes to what attracts them, as shown in the ranges. However, the degrees in which they do, vary among the sexes. Where looks/physical appearance is way off the chart for men, followed by personality/creativity second, then intellect; the ladies place personality/creativity first, then looks, and intellect or charm.

If you are serious about wanting to connect with a mate, take notes and be prepared.

Ladies, we already know that looks and physical appearance are a primary hook for men. While we should all strive to always look good, that carries different connotations for every individual. We can enhance what we have or showcase it in an appealing way. However, most often, it is just a coded preference in a man's brain. Certain shape or size, complexion, height, walk, chest size, nice bottom, etc.

Gentlemen, knowing women value personality/creativity over looks, everyone can remain hopeful.

Next, respondents were asked to identify the traits that characterized their top five preferences compared to their top three deal breakers in a potential mate. I will list for you a few anonymous, random sample responses.

The ladies highlighted the following items:

Preferences

- Steady, suitable income, responsible. Attractive, respectful, honest.
- Must have done the work on themselves… They understand my worth and do not take me for granted.
- Attentive, reciprocal energy, Christian, Smart, funny.
- A steady job, family oriented, Christian, presentable, respectable.
- Someone who is kind, compassionate, and empathetic. – A good sense of humor and the ability to make me laugh – Ambitious and has goals for their future.
- Good communication skills and willingness to openly discuss issues. Similar values and beliefs.
- Emotional availability and intelligence, communication Attentiveness.
- Someone who is respectful and treats me as an equal…
- Intelligent, good hygiene.
- Religion, Race, Career, Hygiene, Values

Deal Breakers

- Unmotivated, boastful, abusive in any aspect.
- Liars, inconsistent, not ready for commitment.

- Bad breath, no job, no personality.
- Substance abuse, addictions, domestic violence.
- Lack of respect and communication in a relationship. Infidelity or dishonesty. Incompatible values or life goals.
- Lack of ambition, emotionally manipulating, lack of self- respect.
- Smoker, Braggers, No Income.
- Unemployed, rude, no family relationships.

Here are samples of what men seek in a female companion:

Preferences

- Financially stable - Belief in God, intelligent, independent/ can provide for self.
- Not too many kids, employed, family oriented, submissive, cooking -THAT'S a MUST
- Woman who listens, hold a conversation, nice teeth, weave, nice hands.
- Loves God, keeps herself up, not selfish, makes me feel wanted, house clean.
- Loyalty and Honesty - A trustworthy partner who can communicate openly with me and not hide anything.
- Sense of humor - I like people who have a sense of humor, they can make me forget about the stress in life and bring me joy.
- Selfless, loyal, ability to communicate effectively, generous, empathetic.
- Being willing to grow as whole. Attractive and well taken care of. Having the ability to support themselves. Willing to try new things. Being drama free as much as possible.
- Intellect, Personality, Emotional Intelligence. Honesty. Loving and caring.
- Kind, considerate, emotional intelligence, emotional management, and supportive.

Deal Breakers

- No income No goals or aspirations. Influenced by social media.
- Lying, untrustworthy, lazy
- Talks too much, not feminine, unhappy.
- She can't be atheist, if she can't get along with my family or friends and I can't have a girl who isn't willing to be loyal.
- Disrespectful/abusive towards others. Failure to take responsibility for one's actions or make necessary changes for growth.
- Lack of respect and communication in a relationship.
- Incompatibility in values and life goals.
- Inconsiderate, overly opinionated, and emotionally, unstable.
- Inconsiderate, overly opinionated, and emotionally unstable.
- A person who is loud and wrong about everything. Not willing to grow. Not being able to handle stressful situations maturely.

I noticed a few recurring themes in these responses. Both men and women want loyalty, trust, sense of humor, kindness, stability, communication, and respect. Take notes of what the opposite sex considers highly desirable traits and what they view as non-negotiables. Remember, "knowledge is power." Now that you have this knowledge, you are in a more powerful position to guide your search for a partner to a successful outcome.

A Profile of Your Person

The last question we asked in that series was: "What would make you consider someone your person?"

This is an individual notion where the responses are as varied as the people who answered them. Here are some random samples for you to gauge. I also include the key thoughts or themes represented in the respondents' answers for our analysis.

I will begin with the ladies speaking their heart's desires.

"If the person I'm with makes me feel safe and at home when I'm with them." Ashlyn – Sales Associate – <u>KEY:</u> SAFETY, COMFORT

"Undeniable connection that can't be explained fully. Someone who understands that even with a deep connection, commitment still takes work and they are ready and willing to."

Maya – Accountant – <u>KEY:</u> CONNECTION, COMMITMENT

"The way that we work well together in all aspects, including problem solving, chemistry, day to day tasks, how much we can laugh and have fun together."

Amber – Educator – <u>KEY:</u> WORK WELL, LAUGHTER, and FUN

"Outgoing, funny, caring personality. Also, intelligent, and well-traveled."Ti Cheri*– Manager – <u>KEY:</u> CARING, CULTURED

"Clarity with their intentions followed by actions. Showing me they care. Making me a priority."

Kristen – Librarian <u>KEY:</u> CLARITY, CARE/PRIORITY

"Same morals & values. Super chemistry towards each other. Same humor. Just a "feeling" that you have with no one else."

Cmillie* – Make-up Artist – <u>KEY:</u> SHARED VALUES, CHEMISTRY, FUN

"They make me laugh and bring positivity into my life."

Harper* - Nutritionist   <u>KEY:</u> LAUGHTER, & POSITIVITY

"If I feel safe and comfortable with him, if I trust that person and if I feel loved and respected."

Ari – Public Relations – <u>KEY:</u> SAFETY, TRUST, LOVE & RESPECT

"I can be my authentic self around them."

Amelia – Criminal Justice Associate – <u>KEY:</u> AUTHENTIC SELF

"We instantly click and learn how to work for and with one another. Feeling like I'm dating my best friend."

Van – PR Executive – <u>KEY:</u> CONNECT, WORK TOGETHER, BEST FRIEND

The fellows also spoke from the heart:

"How people act with you during difficult times. It's easy to be a great person when everything is wonderful, but only a few will stick with you when you are going through a rough pass."

Charles Z* – Marketing Pro – <u>KEY:</u> RELIABILITY, THROUGH THICK & THIN

"Vibe connects. Strong balance between us. Enjoy our passions together. Communicate on all levels."

James – Manager – <u>KEY:</u> BALANCE, CONNECTION, COMMUNICATION

"We can support and inspire each other to grow."

Thomas – Chef – <u>KEY:</u> SUPPORT, GROWTH

"They tolerate my shortcomings and mistakes and help me become a better person."

Joseph – Dentist – <u>KEY:</u> ACCEPTANCE, GROW TOGETHER

"I am a priority to her. I can depend on her."

Fresh* Safety Manager <u>KEY:</u> DEPENDABILITY

"Understanding, knowing how to handle situations, accountability."

Rafiel – Athlete – <u>KEY:</u> ACCOUNTABILITY, BALANCE, SUPPORTIVE

"When I constantly want to be around them and if I am always looking for ways to make them smile or do something for them."

Jay – Cust. Success Mgr. – <u>KEY:</u> ENJOY PRESENCE, RELISH MAKING THEM HAPPY

"The connection we make when we are happy or upset with each other."

Teo – Store Associate – <u>KEY:</u> CONNECTED THROUGH

THE GOOD & BAD

"We feel relaxed and at ease together, without feeling pressured or artificial."

Robert – Doctor – <u>KEY:</u> GENUINE, COMFORTABLE

"They bring me a sense of security and trust."

Sammie – Attorney – <u>KEY:</u> SECURITY & TRUST

"They understand and appreciate my personality and interests."

Brian – Accountant – <u>KEY:</u> THEY <u>SEE</u> ME

"She is a WOMAN! She takes care of me, she's not selfish."

Romello* - Coach – <u>KEY:</u> WOMANLY, CARING, GIVING

The responses may be different, but they all have one thing in common:

Everyone aspires to meet someone with whom they can truly be themselves, feel complete, and enjoy life together.

Making a List and checking it twice

Several respondents noted in their comments that the questions forced them to think about what they wanted. We often discuss various topics and hold opinions about them, but when you take time to analyze your thoughts and feelings, a clear picture emerges of what truly matters to you and why.

Knowing what you are looking for in a mate will help you focus on making connections that matter.

Keep in mind that dating or marriage is a negotiation.

- This is what I bring to the table.

- What do you have to offer me?

- Is there enough synergy for a good alliance?

Concessions might be necessary, as in any arrangements; but it is crucial that both parties find common ground to establish a successful partnership.

Fresh* a Safety Manager in Houston stated: "At the end of the day, we all just want to be with someone who appreciates the qualities we bring to the relationship."

Here is my gift to you: if you would like to receive a copy of the *Relationship Profile Template, Ten Questions to Ask Yourself* personal questionnaire that is based on the survey questions, see the back pages of this book for instructions. That questionnaire is a self-analysis tool, to assist single individuals desiring a mate, in building a profile for the person they wish to connect with.

Sit down with yourself and think carefully about each question before you answer them. The result will be your objective guide to remind you of what you want, and how to recognize it when it comes your way.

<u>Auntie Wisdom</u>: Next time you meet someone and you start dating or hanging out, check your list, and make sure you are heading in the right direction of what is good for your heart, your spirit, and your lifestyle.

Summer 1997 – On a boat party on the Hudson River in Manhattan, NY
This is the night, a couple of months into our dating, that I realized I was
falling in love with Henri. My friend who was my ride back home was
leaving, but I couldn't pull myself away from Henri. I just remember feeling
so at ease with him. I felt at home.

PART III

MAKING THE CONNECTION

*People usually recognize when they see potential in a relationship.
How they proceed from there will determine whether this budding possibility can
develop into a tangible partnership.*

SEEK AND YOU WILL FIND

When asked if "they were ready for a serious/long-term relationship or marriage," 72% of the women and 89% of the men answered YES. Okay then, let's go!

All aboard the fantastic voyage! You are ready to embark on that illustrious quest! Finding your mate. You are fully equipped; having gone through all the steps we talked about to prepare yourself. When and how is it going to happen? What should you do now?

Ask! Pray! Seek! Wait!

Meeting the right partner can be a matter of luck or providence, as well as it could be through active searching or asking. Sometimes it takes deliberate attempts at setting the stage; for others, it happens seemingly out of the blue.

<u>Ask:</u>

- A believer should of course, always ask God. *"Father, if it is your will for my life, please send me the right partner."*

- Some of you may prefer to say, *"put it out there to the universe."* The objective is to open your mind and your heart to receive with wisdom and discernment.

- Ask your friends and family members. They may know a potential candidate. 40% of women and 36% of men from the survey met people they previously dated through friends and 6% of women and

4% of men were introduced by family members.

Pray:

- If you are a praying person, pray for guidance and wisdom.
- Pray that God would place you in the right place at the right time.
- If you don't believe in, or practice prayer, you are on your own, baby.
  – Stay positive.

Seek: (The Meeting Spot)

- **Social Activities** was the top opportunity where respondents met prospective dates, at 82% for men and 60% for women.
- That was followed by **Dating Apps:** 43% for both genders.
- Next came **Bars/Clubs/Parties:** 39% men, 51% for women.
- **Church group or membership organization** was 29% for the men and 31% for the ladies.

For the benefit of everyone reading this book, I will add this little caveat which was not in the survey:

Home, in front of the television Response: an obvious <u>0%.</u>

If sitting in front of the television is what you do all the time on your down time, future mate is not going to ring your door bell. Unless he or she is the neighbor who, in a twist of fate, happens to knock, to return a package delivered to the wrong address. You peek out and notice this Adonis (if you are a woman) or Aphrodite personified (for the guys) standing behind the door. Holler *"Give me one moment please!"* in your best Quiet Storm voice and run to your closet for that top or shirt that shows you in your best light. If the hair is messed up, put on a hat, tie on a pretty scarf, or throw on a casual wig. Should not take more than 90 seconds, top. The person on the other side of the door may legitimately get antsy. – That is why you should never look raggedy, even at home.

Honestly, if you are like most people, you look a mess when at home, chilling. What I would suggest, is to always be ready for the unpredictable, like yours truly, Ms. Fashionista Extraordinaire, does.

When I wrote my first book, *Cads Princes & Best Friends,* I was certain it was going to be a best seller and Oprah was going to call me to appear on her show, which was still on network television at the time. I bought a pair of badass snake skin high heels that I called my Oprah Winfrey shoes. If I got that call, I had the perfect shoes. She never called and I wore my shoes to church.

I also have a Publishers' Clearing House Sweepstakes top. It is a pretty top that adds a touch of sophistication to a pair of black leggings. I occasionally order knick-knacks from the company, and whenever I do, I complete the ubiquitous sweepstakes entries. Well, if one day they were to ring my bell and I see the prize posse outside, I would run to my closet and slip on that top and the black leggings. Two minutes top, and I am camera ready.

This discussion also helps me segue into the topic of readiness. You should be always ready; in case you were to run into a prospect. This author does not leave her house without looking put together. Sometimes the process for a trip to the supermarket is as minor as a nice top or day dress, some flats or sandals and fresh face tamed with some powder and a subtle lipstick or lip gloss. If the outing is an event or party, the wardrobe, make up and accessories are amped up to suit the occasion.

You don't have to be extra like me. However, let me remind you that when you are on the market (and even after you've gotten your prize), you always want to, and should be, looking your best. Chance meetings are a real thing. And first impression is a strong sentiment that affects every connection.

<u>Wait:</u>

<u>Auntie Wisdom</u>: Your waiting should not be stagnant, because it may be long-term or indefinite. Instead, be productive and fruitful while you wait.

After you have asked, prayed and you sought, you just have to wait. Some of you may find it hard to wait gracefully. *"What's taking so long?"* Do not fret.

- You've done your job of preparing yourself for a mate.
- Keep your eyes and ears opened.
- Be opened to possibilities. Sometimes what we seek comes in a different package.
- What is for you is for you and if it is to happen, it will, at the proper time.
- And since none of us knows what is in the cards for us, marriage or not, well, be the best version of your single self as you can.
- Pursue personal interests, and do have a social life.
- Engage in formal ministry at church or give back to your community with personal projects or by joining an organization.

◊◊◊

Hopeful notes

If I were single and looking, I probably would join the large number of people who use dating apps. Of course, it would be one appropriate to my age group and my beliefs as a Christian. Unlike a chance meeting where you need more time to learn about someone, a dating app provides an application or resume for the prospect. You choose to instigate an interview or not. If all parties are being truthful in the information provided, you go in holding some preliminary information. However, I recommend meeting face to face once you've established mutual interest and a desire to learn more about each other. Doctored or old pictures can be problematic.

There is an ongoing debate about who should take the first step in courtship, the man or the woman. In Christian circles, the adage, *"A man who finds him a wife, finds a good thing,"* assumes that the man is doing the seeking and the finding. Nowadays, both sexes are engaging in the finding, especially when it comes to dating apps. Somebody has to swipe to initiate a conversation. Could be either of the sexes.

Olympic gymnast Simone Biles is reported to have met footballer Jonathan Owens on the dating app Raya in 2020. She confessed to swiping first. They married in early 2023.

Various websites recounted the marriage of basketball star Chiney Ogwumike and boxer Rafael Akpejiori in November 2023. They mentioned that the two met on the dating app, Hinge. Here also, Chiney acknowledged making the first move when she asked Rafael out on a date.

Ask. Seek. Pursue

IDENTIFYING A CANDIDATE

Everyone has a type. Our preferences automatically cause us to be attracted to someone who possesses the attributes we like.

We explored in an earlier section, *The Effects of Physical Appearance,* that one of the major things that attracts most people to someone is their looks. We will take another look in reference to identifying a dating candidate.

Seeing that person across the room, or eyeing that picture on the app and finding that your interest is piqued makes the case for physical attraction. Sometimes it unfolds as the real thing, sometimes it is a mirage.

In the 2010 movie *Just Wright,* starring singer Queen Latifah, and Paula Patton, rapper/actor Common plays Scott, a well-known sports figure who meets Latifah (Leslie) first and they hit it off in a buddy kind of way. Paula's character, Morgan is Latifah's godsister. She is beautiful and glamorous, but a true gold digger. She orchestrates a chance meeting with Scott and plays out a rehearsed scenario to capture his attention. Scott is smitten and they are engaged within three months. When he gets injured and at risk of losing his career in basketball, Morgan walks away. Leslie who began working with Scott as a physical therapist starts to develop a relationship with him when they find they have a lot in common. As soon as Morgan hears that Scott is rehabilitated and back in the game, she returns and claims her man, to the detriment of Leslie who had to step away from the burgeoning affair.

Soon, Morgan's true essence is revealed, prompting Scott to re-evaluate what is truly appealing and valuable. He ends up marrying Leslie.

Henri and I met on a random Friday afternoon, going down an escalator at the original World Trade Center in Manhattan, New York where we both worked at the time. He was behind me on the steps and just struck up a conversation. I reluctantly answered his attempt to chat me up, then tried to evade him by crossing the street. He caught up with me and gave me his phone number to set up meeting for lunch.

I once asked him what made him approach me that day. I mean I was looking cute and all, on my way to a meeting at the non-profit organization of which I was a board member, but still why me?

He simply said, "You looked exactly like this girl I saw in my dreams a long time ago."

Whoa! So, I was literally the girl of his dreams!

The reality of it however, was that I was purely the type of woman he was attracted to. When we became a pair and I saw pictures of his ex-wife, the mother of his children, I was not surprised to find we resembled each other. Similar complexion, size, and height.

Some men prefer a full-bodied woman, some woman like a tall guy. One person may like brunettes, another a blonde. Our preferences go through range of colors and physical features as well as personality or character traits. Funny, quirky, quiet, effervescent, talkative, reserved. Every individual has their fondness for particular or specific characteristics in a person.

I am no different from anyone else. I've always liked a man with a certain shade of brown skin and particular features that include thick eyebrows and facial hair. One time I happened to come across old pictures while searching a storage box and had an aha! moment. If you lined up pictures of my first teenage love, my long-term partner Joe and my current husband, they could all pass for cousins. I realized that the men I'd been involved with, were all

Teddy Pendergrass look alike! Pendergrass was a 1980's R & B crooner I used to crush on.

It is human nature to gravitate toward whatever type one prefers. Your type may be good or bad for you depending on the circumstances. However, we all want what truly appeals to our senses or what makes us comfortable. When one is considering long-term relationships, the natural attraction to your type comes in full display.

Do looks matter? Of course!

Looks matter quite a bit, as we saw in the results of the survey. While everyone deserves a chance to show what they offer into a relationship in various other ways, I dare say that if a particular look is important to you, you should give your assessment full consideration. Being able to express feelings and sustain physical attraction for your partner depend a lot on whether you are liking what you see, especially for men. – Hey, don't knock me. They are wired that way.

Looking at this concept deeper and being objective, we also ask ourselves "Is looks everything?"

Absolutely not! But there are some complexities to the question.

First, looks are subjective. What is considered attractive to you, may not be so for me. Second, someone's value should not be based on looks alone. Imagine ladies, meeting someone who is smart, interesting, and intriguing, but he is not six foot tall as listed in your requirements, or you gentlemen, meet a woman who is not as busty as you would prefer. Do you pass up on getting to know that person? No. You might miss out on an otherwise good thing. Given a chance, you might find out that the person's other qualities supersede your missing prerequisite.

I caution you though, be honest with yourself. If a particular look or physical attribute is that important to you, do you. Do not marry personality when you are going to be in bed with looks. You will have to live with what you choose for as long as you are together.

I recently caught an episode of "Queen Charlotte – A Bridgerton Story" the celebrated Netflix series. There was a segment where the queen's confidante, Lady Agatha Danbury, had a flashback of her twenty something self, in bed with a husband three times her age, because of an arranged marriage as it was often the case in the late 1800's.

She was laying facing away from him with a horrified look on her face as you could see a silhouette behind her and hear grunting mixed with the thumping of the shaking bed. Explicit, just like show creator Shonda Rhimes likes her love scenes.

When he exhaled and the camera panned to his face, contorted in ecstasy, I gasped. Goodness! I have never liked to use the word ugly to describe people because I believe no one chooses the way they look at birth. I prefer the gentler "unattractive." Lord Danbury however was old and "Ugh-ly!" In other scenes and conversations, you could tell that Lady Agatha did care for him, but physical attraction? None. Zip. Nada. Whether by mutual agreement or not, he at least spared her having to stare at that face during lovemaking.

In true life, the actor Cyril Nri who plays Lord Danbury is an attractive man. Hollywood make-up artistry turned him into a Shrek for the part.

Someday, somehow, people find their match. Just got to hang in there and be the best version of you that you can be. There is a Haitian proverb that translates to "every bread has its matching cheese." Considering the French are estimated to have at least 1000 varieties of cheese, there should be one for every kind of bread. Even Shrek found his Fiona.

In committing to a mate, looks and physical attraction do play a part. In all relationships each party should find something in the other that pique their interest and will keep their attention. As time goes by, nature follows its course and hair falls out, waistlines thicken (especially if there is childbirth), muscles droop or disappear, etc. The look that was "the bomb" twenty years ago is more like "bombed out territory" down the line.

An example that comes to mind is the actress Jackée Harry, the bombshell neighbor in the television sitcom "227" circa 1990. She played the quintessential sexy femme, bodacious and flirtatious and she had the physique to portray that character. I saw her in a recent movie where she played a grandmother. The woman aged of course, like we all do. She is no longer the sexpot of yore, but the mischievous twinkle in her eyes and that toothy smile were still there.

There it is! That thing! That is what you must find in your partner. That little something that years down the line will make you smile as you recognize the person you fell in love with years before.

My husband and I are both legitimate seniors, late sixties, and I have observed our aging bodies go through changes. We crack jokes about growing bellies (both of us), bald crown (mine) and other insults mother nature chose to inflict upon us.

Despite those changes, we still find that we are attracted to each other. I have experienced instances where I caught a glimpse of his wide shoulders, his hairy chest, or his dimpled smile – all things that I like, and I am prompted to touch him or kiss him.

In turn, there are occasions where I am going about some mundane business around the house and I catch him looking at me. The look is then followed by a "come here."

Oh boy! Let the games begin! We are then forty-five again.

Check Your List – Again

We equated your search for a mate to an explorative voyage. You have made the first of many stops in your journey. You have identified an island to visit based on its charming looks. Next comes the characteristics. Time to pull out your list of preferences and deal breakers. What attractions or tourist sites are you interested in? Will this be a place you want to linger for a while, return to periodically, maybe stay permanently, or move on and never visit again?

Looks helped you glean some basic information about this person you just met or started seeing. You can gauge their style and how they comport themselves. But you are going to have to walk the miles or hop on the jetty to explore this island's features, besides its apparent beauty.

It is okay to be objective regarding something as important as finding a mate. Pull out that list and start assessing. Does this person possess a reasonable number of the attributes you seek? – Reminder that no one is going to come in at 100 percent. – What percentage meets your requirements? 60%, 70%, 80%? Out of your five preferences, do they have at least three? Which one/s are a must? Which are you willing to forego?

What about the deal breakers or non-negotiables? Are they flagrant? Are you noticing any red flags? Is there one you are prepared to negotiate or accept? Is that prudent? Is it a potential hazard that can jeopardize the health of the relationship?

Question, question, question! Better now than later.

Pastor Jerry Martin of my church, Light of the World Christian Fellowship in Humble, TX, preached a sermon for the singles in May 2024 entitled "Signs and Wonders." He explained that this title referred to "What signs to look for in relationships and what you should wonder about." He emphasized that whenever you see a sign, you should always wonder about it. He further elaborated that "Dating is not designed to reveal. It is designed to conceal. Consequently, whenever you see a sign, you should always wonder about it."

When people are dating, they typically present their best selves to impress their potential partner. It's important for you to do your due diligence and identify any behaviors or traits that might not work for you or could become problematic in the future.

As Pastor Jerry said, "Whatever was there before, amplifies after marriage." Consequently, you must:

Question. Analyze and assess.

◊◊◊

Of course, the process of getting to know your partner to determine whether this is a suitable match is not a day trip. It takes time, since deep beliefs and true behaviors unfurl as a slow reveal. That is why it is imperative that you communicate honestly and place yourselves in authentic and organic scenarios so you can observe and learn about each other.

- How much is this person sharing about themselves?
- What are their views on various topics – life, faith, family, children, work, etc.
- Does this individual show any interest in long term relationships or are they adverse to commitment or marriage?
- Do they have any plans for their future lives? What are their goals?
- How do they function in a social setting?
- How is the interaction with their friends or co-workers?
- How are they around your friends?
- How do they relate to or interact with their family members?
- How do their family members regard or treat them?

Conversations will also allow you to pick up on someone's personal beliefs. I am talking about real conversations, where you engage each other; not text messages and hashtags or emojis.

Several of the respondents bemoaned the lack of communication in today's dating scene. Younger people have lost or never developed the art of genuine dialogue, the kind that leads to deep discovery of someone's inner thoughts.

The more you talk and experience things together, the more of someone's internal mechanism is revealed, allowing you a more defined view of their personality and character. That is that courtship period that will help you determine whether to proceed with something more serious.

When I dated Henri, I became increasingly impressed with him, the more opportunities I had to see him interact with friends, co-workers, and family members. Everyone loved him! He was a best buddy, a respected colleague, and a favorite cousin. They recognized in him qualities I had yet to discover. He is caring, funny, friendly, and always ready to help others, even strangers. Each time I witnessed another display of his character, his name etched itself deeper into my heart.

On the flip side, you could also be uncovering some things that give you pause. Be brave. If the beautiful shoreline you saw in the distance turns out to be a bunch of plastic plants, the gorgeous landscape and rock formation, just a giant backdrop, and the aquarium in the lobby just a projected screen, feel free to turn around and get back on the boat. This ain't it.

To quote Pastor Jerry, "Don't be in such a hurry to reach a destination that you ignore the signs."

I will also point out that a lot of people decide to stay on that island anyway. They cited various reasons that we talked about in the earlier section, *"Clean Your Slate"* among them loneliness, selfishness, or insecurity. Stay at your own risk.

Observe. Analyze. Evaluate.

EQUALLY YOKED

Shared core values are fundamental to all successful relationships. Every person has a set of essential beliefs shaped by their culture, family heritage, personality, upbringing, education, religion, and personal experiences. These beliefs define who they are, inform their decisions, guide their choices, and influence how they wish to live their lives. This concept holds true across race, nationalities, and religions, and remains as relevant today as it was in centuries past.

I grew up catholic and nurtured religious beliefs since childhood. However, it wasn't until I was an adult that I experienced "church," black church, the culture of gospel, with its lingo and customs.

Whenever Christians talk about marriage, the expression "equally yoked" always comes up as a must in choosing a mate. I could not help the literal picture that popped in my head of two oxen harnessed to each other, walking in tandem.

The term "equally yoked" comes from the agricultural practice of attaching oxen together with a wooden beam to enable them to work in pairs to till the land or pull a load. For the practice to be effective, the two oxen must be of equal or matching size, weight and gait which enables them to work in synch.

What a spot-on metaphor for romantic partnerships and marriage!

Equally yoked makes perfect sense. When you are doing life together, you are hitched to each other, marching in steps, and hauling the load together.

The equivalent expression in lay terms is "shared values." Whatever your value system is, it must be compatible with your mate's. Otherwise, it would be like a wagon hitched to one horse facing east in front, and another facing west in the back. Once you shout *"Giddy up!"* they each take off in opposite directions, tearing your carriage apart.

It is imperative that you know yourself well and learn everything you can about a prospective mate's character and beliefs, to make sure you are a good match.

I witnessed the "equally yoked" phenomenon in action recently. Violet* a single woman in her forties, joined my church a couple of years back and both her and her young adult daughter immediately began working in ministry. She is blessed with a very feminine, Jessica Rabbit body, always draped in pretty dresses and high heels, and she displays a very sweet disposition.

"Oh, the single men are gonna be all over this," I thought.

Last year an attractive man started coming to the church, apparently at her invitation. He showed up every Sunday and even registered for the biblical classes offered by the ministry. At the time, I was helping with the registration process and talked directly to him. I felt this man discomfort. It was as if he determined to try this woman's way and lifestyle because he really wanted to be with her. But his heart was not really in it. This was not his thing.

After a couple of weeks, he disappeared. The courtship apparently ended. These two did not want the same things.

Several months later, I noticed that after service, Violet would wait for Tom* one of the musicians, and they would leave together. *"Hum, are these two dating?"* I wondered.

Tom is a wonderful brother, dedicated to the church, who has served faithfully for years. He is cool and a laid-back type of guy. I served with him for years when I was on the praise team and always thought highly of him.

On a recent Sunday, Violet came in wearing a white lace dress and as we chatted, she revealed that her and Tom had gotten married the previous day. I rejoiced, with her, and for them! This is a match made in heaven, destined to last. Every Sunday, they come to church together, he goes to his ministry with the band, while she joins hers in hospitality. After service they leave together.

Compatible lifestyle! That is being equally yoked!

The "equal" part of the equation does not necessarily mean identical. I have served in church for years in different capacities: choir member, praise team, greeters, events committee, etc. This has meant church every Sunday, weekday rehearsals or meetings, bible studies or other events. I slowed down over the years as my health demanded that I put less on my plate, but I am still very involved in ministry.

Henri is a believer who prays daily, but he is an occasional church goer. He's never served in ministry; citing being burned by "church people." However, he doesn't stop me from dedicating a lot of time to the church. He also shares my belief in God and in serving others. Nevertheless, I am careful not to let my involvement in ministry affect spending quality time with my husband.

Pastor Jasmine Berry, the eldest daughter of Pastors Jerry and Jackie Martin, preached the sermon "Singleness: The Journey" in May 2024 in which she talked about the journey from singleness to married life. She voiced something that I believe Christians need to hear. While loving and serving God should be primary in every believer's life, those who are married should remember that "When you are married, your first ministry is your family" Pastor Jasmine said.

I have seen married individuals devote so much time to ministry that they neglected their relationship with their partner. **Balance is key in this,**

as in all other aspects of your life.

To continue on the equally yoked vein, I have never been a drinker; and as much as I love to dance, I could not picture going to clubs or bars the only thing I do for entertainment. If two people enjoy doing those things, then they are compatible. If one does, but the other one prefers going to the theater, a concert, or to church; then they are not.

Therefore:

- **Question**
- **Observe**
- **Investigate**
- **Learn**
- **Assess**
- **Make informed decisions**

◊◊◊

Red flags and beige flags

You've finally met someone who likes you, and the feeling is mutual. It's exciting and the air is full of possibilities. You are spending time together, getting to know each other, and learning new things about one another. You are in discovery.

When I worked in law (was a paralegal for years), I encountered the term "discovery" in litigation, as the phase where both sides of a lawsuit are in the process of obtaining evidence, information and testimony relating to the case.

In the discovery period of dating, both sides are observing and learning about each other. Each meeting is an opportunity to uncover what social scientists call "red flags" and "beige flags." They are like dormant medical conditions that may flare up in the future, fully blown. (Forgive the old people metaphor.) They must be monitored and you must have possible treatments at the ready. They are the signs and wonders Pastor Jerry referred to. They must be analyzed and assessed. Therefore, keep a watchful eye, attentive ears, and observant mind.

Red flags are generally those things that are so flagrant, they jolt you, like those strident amber alerts. Beep, Beep, Beep! *"Examine quickly and make a decision."*

Here is an example of a red flag for me. I was in my early twenties at the time, and a guy who was interested in me took me to an *Earth, Wind and Fire* concert at Madison Square Garden. As soon as we got to our seats, he lit a joint, smoked it and as he inhaled his last hit, exclaimed, *"Now, I am ready to enjoy the concert."*

Mortified and horrified, I didn't know what to do! This was in the seventies when smoking marijuana was a covert activity. I sang with a band back then and was accustomed to the guys lighting up occasionally, especially at parties. – Full confession, once at a party with my musician friends, I took my one and only drag on a joint and decided I didn't need anything to help me enjoy a good time.

I just love to party to good music and adore dancing, a Coulanges family trait. I was hyped the moment I got in the car to head to the concert, looking forward to the exceptional show that *Earth, Wind* puts on every time. I was doubly disturbed by my date's behavior.

- Does he need to get high in order to enjoy everything?
- Does he realize that he is being disrespectful to me? We are in public, he is overtly smoking an illegal substance, and people who use marijuana are considered degenerates (This was the late 1970s).

I am an occasional social drinker and do not use other substances. To me, anyone who relies on chemicals to enjoy social or personal interactions lacks integral grit and natural essence. You guessed it. That was a one and only date.

Another example is a man I briefly dated who kept repeating the mantra, *"That is why I prefer to be by myself"* to excuse his addiction to football season on television. Fool, so be by yourself then, you don't need me! Most importantly, I don't want you!

Red flags are unique identifiers of the individuals that generate them or important markers for the person observing them.

A good way to recognize red flags is to remain consciously alert of your deal breakers list. Remember, things like: bad smell, narcissistic, opinionated, disrespectful, liar, etc. You already know what you consider are non-negotiables. Once you see hints of those characteristics in the potential mate, pay attention and determine whether you should cut your losses and move on.

Observe. Assess. Decide.

Beige flags are the subtle idiosyncrasies you must decide whether you can live with for the next few decades. Each one of us has little mannerisms that may make some people laugh while they get on others' nerves. Sometimes, the same quirk can affect the same person differently depending on the circumstances.

I am not a fan of plastic utensils. I use them only when necessary. I buy take out and pull out a regular plate and fork to eat my food when I get home. Henri laughs at me sometimes, but on any given day he might suck his teeth at me with a derisive *"You're too fancy for me"* commentary.

My husband is a very affable, no fuss-guy – until something hits him where it hurts. In particular, he is very sensitive to being taken for granted or feeling disregarded or dismissed. I found out in the early days of us dating, when we stopped for gas and the attendant took his time to pump for him, then exacerbated the situation by dragging his feet to come back for the payment. We were running late for an event. – For those from different states, in New York and New Jersey, at least back then, you sat in your car and an associate pumped the gas and manually took the payment.

Suddenly, this booming voice (he has a deep baritone) chattered my ears with a round of expletives. I was shocked and a bit embarrassed, since there were other patrons within earshot. Shocked, because I was concerned that I was involved with someone with a bad temper. Embarrassed, since a prissy lady like me was with "this loud, foul mouth negro."

By the time we drove off, I expressed my concern about what I had just witnessed.

"I am sorry," he said. "This guy pissed me off. He was ignoring me." His agitation had gone back down to a manageable level.

I had to think about that one. I abhor arguments and cussing. I continued to observe to see whether this was a character flaw or a possible problem. Nothing else happened to support my alarm in subsequent months. – Beige flag!

Henri's temper is like a firecracker, a loud pop that fizzles out immediately and causes no harm. I could live with that.

Sometimes a beige flag may turn out to be fatally serious. I remember a movie where this man was engaged to a woman he considered near perfect. One thing that drove him bananas was the sound of her laughter, a cross between the howling of a hyena and a donkey's braying. He struggled with that constantly. During his bachelor party, when his buddies were doing the ritualistic teasing of "this one woman forever," he realized that he could not listen to this woman's torturous laughter, every day forever. – I feel you, Bro. Let me see? That is possibly, 365 x 40 years = 14,600 days plus a few extras for leap years!

He called off the wedding.

Those beige babies run the spectrum, but, so long as they are not egregious, you should be able to take the good with the bad. Like my college economics professor used to say when discussing the financial markets, *"Ceteris, Paribus"* – everything else remaining equal – just go with the flow if you can safely tolerate them.

Observe. Assess. Decide.

◊◊◊

Investigation required

If I were single today, I would probably run a Google search on anyone I started seeing regularly. While you should not believe everything you see on the internet, there is enough information available to give you an idea of what a person has been up to – where they've lived, who they are related to, where they attended school, and whether they have a criminal history. Some sites even offer credit information, which can reveal judgements or bankruptcies, or on the positive side, ownership in real estate or a business.

Hey, don't bash my curiosity! I am not being a hater. I am being real. Hundred percent. If you worked very hard to maintain a good credit profile, stay out of the legal system, acquire some assets, and be a good citizen; do you want someone, who is supposed to add to your life, come in and mess up your hard-earned financial position? I don't think so!

Where one might overlook a person' inability to contribute financially, based on their circumstances, no one would want to put themselves in a situation where getting together with someone means taking an economic step back.

Assessing a potential partner's earnings or economic position is a valid component of courtship. After all, you are considering a merger. But it is not something that is easy to do.

A March 15, 2024 Yahoo.com article by Donnavan Smoot discussed

"How Gen Z is challenging the taboo of talking about salaries..." In it the writer shares how Gen Zer's are sharing their salaries and investments techniques on social media. They profess full financial transparency, whereas previous generations found it difficult to discuss the topic.

Talking about one's finances is one of those touchy subjects that most people avoid. Nevertheless, it is a necessary conversation once a relationship is deemed to head toward or has become serious. It is part of the *"where are we heading"* and *"how do you handle things"* discovery to ascertain that you are compatible.

Depending on when or how the topic comes up will dictate the proper approach to that sensitive subject.

The question **"How much do you make?"** should **NEVER** be posed in the early stages of a relationship! Most replies would probably be "None of your business" anyway.

Someone's finances should not officially come into play in the initial stages of dating. I say "officially" because the fact is the assessment begins from day one and assumptions are being made. Does the man offer something simple on a first date like meet for drinks or a walk in the park? Is he being cheap or genuinely interested in conversation? Does the woman suggest someplace expensive? The man may view her a gold digger, who has no consideration that this place might be unaffordable for him.

As two people make it past the first couple of dates and continue to get to know each other, there is a tally taking place as each person is evaluating the other. Checking the boxes, if you will. When it comes to the topic of income, there is the impetus to assess whether you both want and can afford compatible lifestyles.

Once you learn of the person's current or future profession, one can gauge a general income bracket for that individual. Is she a high school teacher? $50K to $70K in the state of Texas. Is he a police officer? $50K to $80K in New York. Is she a lawyer in Florida? $64 to $120K. Is he a struggling entrepreneur anywhere? $20K. Is he a successful legal entrepreneur? $250K. You get my drift. Google knows it all and readily shares information for free.

The level of income may skew a person's assessment. If the level is considered too low, they may miss out on the candidate's other inherent qualities. If it is very high, that may obscure a person's judgement. Is a gesture of generosity the evidence of genuine kindness, or is it deep pockets attempting to buy someone's affections?

One must proceed with caution, both eyes wide open when assessing, and look at the full package. Each person must know what they are getting into, especially in the realm of one's finances.

A bit of informal investigation is helpful in uncovering your potential mate's financial profile, in addition to their income. Credit or background checks are available, but this research can be as elementary as observing someone's pattern of behavior to uncover some red flags. **Observe and learn.**

- Are they spendthrift, wasteful with their money?
- Are they always short, even though they are employed?
- Are family members supporting them or supplementing their income?
- Do they have bad credit or maxed out credit cards?
- Do they appear to function on a now basis, with no financial goals or plans?
- Then the big one: do they ask you for money directly or request that you pay a bill for them?

Eventually, as people become committed and more comfortable with each other, they should feel less hesitant about letting the other know how much they earn.

In conclusion, pulling up a general profile that includes location, relatives, education, criminal and financials, will suffice to draw a basic picture of that individual. Begin with that to identify any red flags. A prudent soul re-assesses red flags, just to make sure you are not overreacting. But once confirmed as a major issue, make the healthy choice. Get out of town!

Investigate. Assess. Decide.

In other realms, partners play "show me yours, I'll show you mine." Why not transfer that same concept to your financial status? Start out with a slow reveal where you only exchange basic information such as salaries and basic assets (you own your home for example). As the relationship progresses, you will have to gauge when and if you should expose more, if an increased level of trust supports it.

Be cautious not to flash the goods all in one fell swoop. In many cases, the other party may get intimidated, especially men. Often, if a man feels that he cannot offer a woman more than she already has, he may feel inadequate and bow out. In others, an opportunist will latch on to misappropriate or deplete your assets. There are plenty scams out there of fake love stories, where a man or a woman pretends to love someone and goes as far as marrying them and then absconds with that person's fortune.

Observe. Communicate. Assess before you decide.

◊◊◊

Sex before marriage: All-inclusive resort or pay as you go

This next topic may leave some people uncomfortable, but it needs to be addressed so you know what you stand to encounter at this location. Are you registered for the all-inclusive package, or are you only offered a few select perks? By that, I am talking about the subject of sex before marriage.

Participants in the survey were asked the following question:

"An important consideration for Christian individuals who are dating is the issue of no sex before marriage. Is that important to you and are you willing to go that route?"

Respondents were divided on this one. There were as many "No – No way!" to many "yesses" or "willing to try." For those who do not subscribe to a religious principle, this is a no brainer: first and foremost, you date to have a sex partner. However, what happens in reality is that for most women including myself, the heart wishes for a committed companion or future spouse. But, in practice, we often settle for what is readily available: someone to hang out with and have sex with.

When I was single, thirty years ago, and before I became a born-again Christian, that was how I functioned. I always allowed several dates before I became intimate with someone, but getting to the confirmed "boyfriend/girlfriend" phase was not even a prerequisite. It was acceptable that this was what I could get for now. I already shared with you how I had an epiphany and recoiled at my own callous behavior. I was no "ho" – I still have plenty of folded fingers left when I count my lovers – but I was headed for a weird zone if I had kept going.

In today's culture we are told to go for self-gratification in seeking pleasure. Bar pick-ups, internet hook-ups, sex clubs, etc. People hop in a bed, stretch on a sofa, or meet in a gym's shower in a heartbeat. That is what we see in the movies. Meanwhile, there is a soul yearning to love and be loved.

To sex or not to sex! That is the question. Do you just do it? Do you wait till you are sure this is going somewhere? Do you wait till engagement or marriage?

What you do is ultimately a personal choice based on your beliefs, what your gut tells you, and hopefully, not pure impulse.

The Christian faith dictates that couples wait till marriage. That is a tough challenge for most people. Especially if you are an adult who already had a sex life. It was for me. I was celibate by choice for a good while, having decided that casual encounters were not for me. When Henri and I had been going steady for a few months, we did become intimate. Of course, every time the subject came up in church, I cringed in my seat. Churches are full of people who are sleeping around or living together, unmarried. I am not accusing; this is just an observation. After all, I was one of them. This is real life in our current era.

I became increasingly uncomfortable sharing intimacies with Henri after a couple of years together and no talk of marriage. I did not want a forever boyfriend and I was not shacking up; been there, done that. I had made that clear from the beginning. I took a leap of faith and told him that we would no longer share intimacies unless we were engaged. I was prepared to lose him, if necessary, because if he walked, then he was not the one for me. He remained. We struggled. Long stretches of celibacy, then one of us would break down, mostly him.

See, when you love someone, you want to hold them, touch them, and feel physically connected to them. That is human and natural. The problem is often you do not know what's love and what's just thirst.

I was so glad when that man finally put a ring on my finger! *Oh, what a relief it is!* – That was an old Alka-Selzer commercial.

I do believe that the religious precept has fundamental benefits.

If you are dating with the intention of finding a life partner, you do need to get to know the person, their character, their values, and belief, before you really get involved.

Sex at the onset of a relationship tends to cloud your judgement in the feel-good release of dopamine. In the old days you got to know the person first, secured a commitment, then had sex. Nowadays, the process is reversed. You first have sex, then you are trying to assess whether you are good for each other. The problem is, you probably are not. In the light of day, things often appear very different. You end up with bruised feelings, battered egos or an impression of being used.

There are a lot of situations where a man walked away because they were not willing to do the celibate thing. A young man wanted to rekindle his religious life and started going back to church. He liked the pastor's daughter and began courting. He talked about them going away together on a vacation. She indicated that she did not do that, since that would mean sharing a room together and all that it implies. He was taken back. To him that was one of the things young couples do, travel. He would not be able to do that with her until or unless they were married.

Gone!

Actress Meagan Good chose the celibacy route when she was engaged to DeVon Franklin, a Seventh Day Adventist preacher. They married within a year and were together for a few years. Unfortunately, they divorced ten years later.

One thing too about the wait, people tend to get married quicker. You cannot drag that thing into a four-year engagement. Just saying.

The choice is yours to decide what you want and what works for the both of you. If you want to stand firm on your belief to wait until marriage and the other person is agreeable to that, fine. Beautiful. Just beware of the manipulators. I saw a movie recently where this pastor's assistant refused the advances of his fiancée, under the guise of waiting till their wedding night. Meanwhile he was sleeping around with another church member.

My recommendation is, if you are looking for a long-term or committed relationship, and you value a certain standard about sharing intimacies, wait at least until you are confirmed to be an item. You are going steady. You are officially boyfriend/girlfriend. You feel vested in this relationship and the other person appears to feel the same. Then intimacy becomes another step in the discovery process.

The participants offered additional thoughts on the topic of delaying sex till marriage, and I was personally surprised to see a lot of the fellows willing to wait. Here are some diverse sample responses for you.

"If needed. No problem. If bond created is strong."

James – manager

"It is somewhat important but if our feelings towards each other are so strong that we give in and we know we're in for the long haul, then I wouldn't mind at all but I want to at least try to save ourselves."

Jake – auto parts sales

"It's not important and it's a pretty outdated standard and somewhat unrealistic nowadays."

Charles Z. - arts & marketing exec.*

"Although this path may have challenges, I am willing to work hard to follow God's will."

Brian – electrician

"As a Christian, I believe that marriage is sacred, so I will not consciously make decisions that go against God's will."

Thomas – chef

"I would have loved to experience intimacy before marriage."

Judith – activist

"I understand that it may be difficult to find someone who shares the same view, but I am open to having open and honest conversations about it in a relationship." *Harper* – Nutritionist*

"I believe that waiting until marriage can bring a deeper level of intimacy and trust in a relationship, and I am willing to go this route for the right person." *Amelia* – Criminal Justice*

"It is not a deal breaker for me, but I would prefer to be with someone who shares the same values and beliefs about waiting until marriage."

Elizabeth – Human Resources*

"No, but I can attempt to compromise."

Teo – Store Associate

"I am not opposed to premarital sex but it is also something to consider when dating."   *Romello – Coach*

"It is not a bad thing but it's not for everyone. I would be able to go that route if me and the other person are truly set."

Ralph – Athlete

* Names with an asterisk are aliases or pseudonyms used for publication purposes.

So, what will it be for you, my friend?

1) Everything or nothing? All-inclusive or no go? Or

2) Are you willing to enjoy incremental perks while you wait for the day you earn your VIP status and get the full-access package?

Assess. Evaluate. Choose.

◊◊◊

Timing and common aspirations

When I was single, I remember looking back on men I had met who would have been great companions. At the time, I either did not see it or we weren't on the same page.

One of the first questions asked in my survey, *Dating & Relationships in the 2020s,* is whether the respondent felt ready for a relationship. When everything lines up, a relationship can be very simple. Most of the time, however, there are other factors that come into play that may derail one before it gets a chance to become established.

I recently got hooked on the television series, *Suits,* being shown on Netflix, that features Meghan Markle, before she was married to England's Prince Harry. One of the characters, Louis Litt, is a brilliant attorney, but he is full of quirks and insecurities. He finally met a woman of his caliber (a recruiter for Harvard University lawyers) with whom he shared a love of the arts and adventurous intimacies. When Louis went through a health scare, he realized he is in love with this woman and he proposed to her.

One night they were sitting in domestic bliss, he reading the papers, she reviewing notes on a candidate. The topic of future homes came up. He assumed that she would move from Boston, Massachusetts where Harvard is located. She had no intention to. She asked him if he would move to Boston. No way! New York City was the only place to be for a successful corporate attorney.

The conversation then segued into children. He wanted several. She had "an aversion to anyone under the age of 22" and children were not on her agenda. Period.

Their story ends there, with two broken hearts.

There are some difficult conversations that must be had when you are dating with a purpose. You need to know not only where the person is currently, but also what their future goals are. Do those plans align with yours or can your goals accommodate each other?

In my early twenties I was engaged to a young Haitian medical student who lived in Haiti while I lived in New York. After doing the (very) long distance thing for a couple of years, I came to realize that I wasn't ready for marriage, motherhood and possibly moving to Chicago or Africa where his residency would have taken him. I broke off the engagement. The love was there, but following a spouse across the world was not the life I wanted at the time. I wanted to be in New York City doing my music.

<u>Auntie Wisdom</u>: Sometimes love is not enough. If you are hitching your wagon to somebody else's, you better make sure you are going in the same direction.

INITIAL CHALLENGES AND GROWING PAIN

A new relationship will inevitably test your mettle. This trial may happen early in the courtship, few months in or a few years down the road. It is an integral factor in building a foundation for going to the next level. It is akin to a hurricane hitting that beautiful island while you are there on your temporary stay. Will it survive the storm? Will it be all hands-on deck, in good spirit, to restore things or bring them back to working conditions? Or, are the damages too severe to repair? Is it time to pull up anchor and sail elsewhere?

What I am referring to here, is that crisis that shows up for one person, but reveals things about both parties.

- How does the person act under pressure?
- Do they invite the other to partner in with them in solving this problem?
- Do they shut the other person out?
- How does the unaffected partner respond? Supportive or uncaring?
- Does this crisis unveil a red flag?

Be attentive to pick up invaluable clues in times like these.

I once dated a guy who had split from a woman he was dating, who thought she was the one for him. Things unraveled when she became pregnant while he was in the process of purchasing a home, and he admitted that she was not moving in with him, and he was not marrying her, all while she had been involved in the search and the viewing of prospective homes. Of course, their parting ways was not amicable, especially when there was now a child.

Just a couple of months into our dating, he stopped by one evening, agitated and rattled. He was going through major drama with the woman. He ranted for a bit, then announced he was going to see his mother and sisters. "They know how to soothe me," he said. I was shut out.

Soon after that incident, the phone calls began to dwindle, and eventually, he told me point blank that he was not interested in pursuing the relationship. I was devasted, I had begun to fall for him. In retrospect, I understand that the drama with his ex, re-ignited unresolved issues. He realized he was not ready for a new relationship.

Few pages back, in the section titled *"Identifying a Candidate"* I referenced the movie, *Just Wright*, starring singer Queen Latifah (Leslie), Paula Patton (Morgan), and rapper/actor Common (Scott). Beautiful Morgan sweeps basketball star Scott off his feet. But when he is injured and expects his woman to be by his side, Morgan leaves him, fearing his career may be over. Her unsupportive self is draped in a big old red flag that reads: GOLD DIGGER!

You also hear stories of crises that solidified a burgeoning relationship. The partner that fell ill, was involved in an accident, lost their job, or was tangled in some legal issue. The other person stepped up to the plate and offered advice, help, financial assistance, their time or whatever was necessary to support.

Mine was when my car began dying on me after Henri and I had been dating for about a year. One day it stopped right outside the Holland Tunnel that connects New York and New Jersey. Thankfully I always maintained a AAA membership, and a tow truck came to my rescue. I shuddered at the thought of being stuck in the busy tunnel.

"I need a new car, but my money is short."

Henri offered to give me his income tax refund to put with mine to get another used car.

This man is a true partner. He wants to take care of me. He wants me to be safe. He is meeting me half way. This might be my person!

When someone really cares about another person, they show up, they support, they are consistent.

Observe. Analyze. Evaluate.

◊◊◊

Relationships are also challenged by growing pains. After you have been dating for some time, it is logical for at least one of the parties to consider the next step. In a lot of cases, unfortunately, the longer the person stayed on the island, the more they realized this was not their best choice for a final destination.

Relationships end for a variety of reasons. The survey respondents offered some insight into this by choosing from a range of answers, when asked to name the top reasons why they believed past relationships or marriages did not work out. Here are the results.

Reasons Did Not Work	Men	Women
Grew apart	59%	33%
Immaturity	30%	71%
Abuse	26%	38%
Infidelity	15%	29%

Incompatibility	37%	38%
Finances	15%	21%
Family/social influence	7%	12%
Other	15%	0%

"Growing apart" was the number one reason for men, followed by "Incompatibility." For women, the number one issue was "Immaturity" followed by "Abuse" and "Incompatibility."

Finances came in as a notable factor for both sides. It could have been a lack of it. Or maybe, the concentration required to strengthen someone's economic standing diverted from focusing on the relationship itself. For example, working over-time in excess or holding down two different jobs.

Family and social influences were cited. A prospective mate may not be liked by your family or friends. There are situations where the person does not get along with your people. These conflicts can make it difficult to have a successful relationship. There are cases where a person disconnects themselves from their people so they can be with that mate. That could be considered brave or foolish, depending on what the future reveals.

If conflicts relating to family or friends cannot be resolved, often people choose to walk away, try somewhere else.

<u>Auntie Wisdom:</u> Your family and true friends are significant pillars in the building block of you. A mate should become your primary support beam, but the others are also needed to keep a structurally sound edifice. If things were not to work out between the two of you, who would you turn to, if you burned your bridges with your people?

Sean, a college professor added, "We grew apart because I was more focused on my career." Redbone* a barber acknowledged, "I didn't know myself." Allday* a banking associate, cited "life pressures."

Regardless of the reasons relationships do not work out, people are still hopeful that there is someone out there for them. When asked whether past failed relationships had completely turned them off from considering a serious one or marriage, only 11% of men and 14% of women responded *"Completely."* There are circumstances where an individual might not be opposed from having someone in their lives, but the cause of a breakup was so egregious that they are not willing to risk facing a similar situation.

When I met my ex, Joe, he admitted to not wanting to get married again. He had gone through a contentious divorce and child support debacle that had him in family court surrounded by a woman judge, women attorneys, women social workers, and his ex-wife, all pointing the finger at him. He vowed to never be put in that position again, with women in control of him. My ears heard it, but my heart said, *"I'm gonna love you so good, you will marry me."* WRONG!

Charles Z* an arts and marketing executive, who experienced the painful revelation of ongoing infidelity in his first marriage, confirmed, *"I'm not opposed to long term relationships but will not get married again."* He is trying to protect his heart, like a lot of people. We cannot blame him or anyone else. Rather, we should seek to understand and work with what we are presented with. But always, take the person at their word.

A large majority of people, (48% men and 46% women) answered the question regarding shying away from relationships with *"Not at all,"* while others acknowledged that they were spooked *"Maybe/A little."*

So, do not give up. Continue your quest. Just be wise and objective, navigating safely. The magic island could be a few nautical miles away.

Hope springs eternal…

CHALLENGES OF OPTIONS

A<u>untie Wisdom:</u> **Seize the day! Take a chance on love, even though it might show up in an unexpected packaging or brand.** When we broaden our horizon to date people who are not our usual type or are outside of our racial or cultural sphere, we must prepare for a different set of issues that are inherent to the new territory. Those must be analyzed and addressed to inform whatever decision the parties make.

Dating outside of type

We discussed the important space looks and types occupy in our choice of a mate. We can all agree that finding someone who possesses the characteristics and traits we desire is incredibly beneficial. While it's natural to seek those preferences that we're initially drawn to, considering a broader range of attributes can enhance our chances of finding a compatible mate and fulfilling relationship.

I believe one should investigate if presented with the opportunity to know someone who might not necessarily be your type. I will use the metaphor of my purchasing an automobile to illustrate my point.

I have never liked black cars or white ones. I am innately Caribbean at heart in that I like colors, preferably bright ones. When I was able to afford my first brand new car, my choice was a sparkly maroon Nissan Murano, the year that model was released. When I was ready to replace my aging beauty for too many repair trips, I narrowed my research to three SUV models I was interested in, an Infinity QX50, a Lexus or a Jaguar (if I could stomach the cost).

I was the one to drive the day my husband and I went to the stretch of highway where the dealerships are located. The car reached a corner on the feeder road and the GPS told me to turn right, feet away from an Acura lot.

"Crazy GPS" I told my husband. "The lot is right there. Why is it telling me to turn?"

When I pulled into the parking lot, my eye caught a glimpse of a white, sleek looking car parked on the side row along with a variety of blue, grey, red, and black SUVs. It had contemporary lines with black and chrome trims that accentuated its features.

"What car is that!" I exclaimed to my husband. "I kind of like it."

Once inside the showroom, we were approached by a salesman who offered his help.

"I'd like to see your Infinity QX50 please," I said.

He looked at me perplexed. "This is Acura dealership," he replied.

"Yes, I want to see the QX50," I insisted.

"We don't carry the QX50, this is ACURA," he emphasized.

My husband shook his head, amused. I finally got it. "Oh!... Well, may I see that white car parked on the left in front?"

I test drove the RDX, a new model the Acura brand had just released that year – so new in fact that they did not have it online when I did my research. I loved the cream leather interior. It was fully loaded with back-up camera, side object alerts and a navigation system, and the ride proved to be satisfactory.

I still went across the highway to the Infinity dealer (the turn the GPS initially instructed me to take) to look at the QX50. The car rounded silhouette did not really appeal to me, not sleek enough. Then we proceeded to the Lexus lot, where the ride was too uncomfortable to be so expensive. I went back home and researched the RDX, compared prices and features with the other cars and settled on the RDX.

I have been enjoying its ride for going on four years now and it still catches my breath when I come up on it. I look at my car and think, "You sexy beast!" – Oh, yeah, I have a personal relationship with my car. – Thankful I was able to afford it and I am happy to still enjoy it.

It is somewhat like what one experiences in dating and in choosing a mate. When you least expect it, God, or the universe – depending on your belief – sends you this person that you were not looking at. At first you do not even think of them as a possibility. However, you catch something, enough to spark your interest. Then as you get to know them, examining the special features like in a car, you realize, "Wow, this did not come up in my research, but look at what it's offering!"

At the same time, one should be prepared that dating against type might also backfire. I tried dating people who were not necessarily my type before. Those relationships did not develop into anything, not because of the physical type, but rather because the internal type (character, values, etc.) did not match up.

A failed experience should not stop one from trying different, even though the tendency is to gravitate toward your type. Some wise souls have even advised that if one keeps trying one's type and is not successful, one should switch types.

Breaking away from established patterns can help you avoid repeating the same mistakes and might lead to a healthier, more successful relationship.

Often, we are very attracted to an ideal or a model that may not be right for us.

One example is the good looking, successful, charming man that every woman has their eye on. For a man, it might the beautiful, glamorous, sexy woman that all the guys are checking out. If these people are selfish and full of themselves because of their looks or their success, they are not wired to make someone else happy. They come first. Their needs and their wants supersede yours.

If you persist in always seeking that same type of person, it will always end up the same way. With you crying in your tea, beer, tub of Haagen-Daz ice cream (me) or your alcohol infused drink of choice.

As much as I love me some Haagen-Daz coffee flavored mixed with butter pecan, I would rather be scooping it up under different circumstances; same as the next person would prefer to enjoy their Mojito or Long Island Ice tea for a festive occasion. Nobody wants to have to cry over the demise of a relationship. Consequently, one must tread carefully in choosing what you want to retain for the long haul.

Yes, everyone should consult their heart in making the decision to engage in a relationship with another person. The heart wants what the heart wants. Your type touches something in you that is pleasurable. However, no one should be so fixated on a type – brand or model – that you miss the opportunity to experience something new that while different in packaging, may feature the most important things that you need or long for.

◊◊◊

Dating across cultural lines

Speaking of different packaging, a good segue is to touch on dating or marrying people of a culture that is different from your own.

I have personally never dated someone from a drastically different culture. I use the term "drastically" because I am of dual background: Haitian and American. While the languages, mannerism, and history of the two cultures differ, it so happens that my dating life was compartmentalized where I barely felt the small differences.

I recounted earlier how in my late teens, when I was living in New York, I was engaged to a young man who was in medical school in Haiti. We did the back-and-forth, long distance thing, then I got scared when he talked about doing his residency in Chicago or Africa. In addition, the girlfriend of his best friend, an aspiring dancer, got pregnant and their families married them up. At the time I wanted a career as a singer. I was not ready for marriage and a baby or moving to Africa. I broke off the engagement.

You already know my mama never forgave me the opportunity to have a doctor as a son-in-law.

I went on a few dates with Haitian men after that, but nothing serious. I had started to connect with African Americans more as I dived into music and modeling. By the time I met Joe, a southern born, fashion photographer and designer who would become my live-in partner for the next ten years, I had become fully immersed in Black America. We loved jazz and R & B music. We read books on black civilizations, the Moors' invasion of southern Europe, Queen Hatshepsut (who ruled as pharaoh in Egypt circa 1458), Malcom X and other Black historical figures. We talked about his life as a teenager in Philadelphia (gang member), his days as a Black Panther and his stint as a guitar player in an R & B group. With him I became "a sistah," an African American woman.

I was inexperienced when I fell hard for his charismatic charm, his creativity, and his sex appeal. A heterosexual male fashion photographer with a studio in New York City, the fashion capital, Joe was always surrounded by beautiful women. I saw signs of his womanizing, but was bamboozled by his affirmation of love and seduced by the promises of riches to come from what had then become a jointly owned fashion design business.

I was in my mid-thirties when I walked away from a relationship that had become toxic. Newly single and older, my dating pool was now strictly American.

My dating experience during that time was a mishmash of insecurity, confusion about what the men I met really wanted, and desperation that I would never meet the right person.

I had an epiphany when I was introduced to the group of Haitian American professionals who ran the non-profit community organization, the Haitian American Alliance, HAA. These were young men and women of Haitian descent around my age, who were either born on the island or in the States, but grew up and obtained their education here. They identified with both the Haitian culture and that of our adoptive country, the United States. I finally understood that I was a dual-cultured person, and how that reflected on who I am, and consequently, the type of person I was looking for, who would be compatible to me.

When I met Henri, a Haitian immigrant, at first I hesitated to accept his advances, since I was more Americanized. However, because of our shared background, there is an effortless comfort that has existed since the early days of our dating that is still present after over twenty years together. Nevertheless, as we got to know each other, I discovered that we were different in various ways, and I had to acknowledge those differences and decide whether they mattered.

I arrived in New York City at sixteen years old, went to school and became of age there in the 1980s, eventually immersed in African American culture. Henri, on the other hand is hard core Haitian, having come here as an adult. Consequently, there are cultural differences that have persisted over the years, some of which I have come to accept and others he is still trying to convince me to embrace.

Henri wakes up listening to Haitian radio. I do it with the *Get Up! Mornings* with Erica Campbell gospel show. He eats a boiled plantain (like a green banana) every single day. I prefer the occasional fried ones. That does not stop him from boiling one for me anyway, although I've requested that he asks me first whether I want one. Sometimes I welcome it, recognizing its nutritional value. Other times, I pass on it because a boiled plantain is kind of tasteless after it sits for a while. I used to get mad at him for "forcing" one on me. It's already cooked, right? Now I recognize that this is one of the ways he utilizes to take care of me, feeding me right. I still told him not to get mad if I decide not to eat his plantain, if that is not what I'm in the mood for. He also eats rice (a Haitian staple) every single day, except for the occasional times I can coax him to have some pasta or quinoa.

At first, I used to get upset at him. Rice again! – Eventually I came to understand that this is how he has eaten his entire life. *If this makes you happy baby, go for it!* Consequently, not surprisingly, there are the occasional days in my two-person household where two different meals are prepared.

Don't worry. Be happy!

Food choice is simple enough to address. It is a bit more challenging when it comes to the way you function or take care of business. Americans are trained to plan, while Haitians are reactive.

In the beginning Henri used to be offended when I offered suggestions on how to do certain things. He considered it a put down and would call me "Miss Know-it-all." Over the years, he has come to embrace the fact that we each have different strengths, and when it comes to certain things, I have been functioning in the American system longer and in a deeper capacity than he has.

In the same way, I had to relearn a lot of the Haitian cultural norms. The traditional way of greeting each other in a lot of our ancestral people of Africa, is a long exchange of asking about each other's relatives. I had gotten unused to that living in America. It caught me by surprise, when Henri who is very close to his family, would launch into the inquiry every time he talked to one of them, even when they had talked only a couple of days earlier.

"How is your wife? How are the children? How is your mother? And your father? Your sister? ..."

My American self is limited by the "How you doing?" and even a "What's up?" when communicating with family members before we launch into the business at hand. When interacting with Henri's family, I had to remember to inquire about everyone, at the risk of appearing rude.

Henri has picked up a lot of my tips and formulas for self-organization. But occasionally, he and I find ourselves butting heads because at the last minute he is pulling me into something that should have been in my view, planned or prepared for. I have learned to balance my over-planning tendencies and jump in to address his situations, but not without first voicing my offended opinion.

This is often met by his standard "Leave me alone" – a direct translation from the French *"Laisse-moi tranquille"* to say "don't bother me."

To which I reply, "You want me to help you or leave you alone?"

Cue the exasperated Haitian, "Ah!"

In situations where each party is truly from diverse cultures, they must each learn to identify what the differences are at the beginning of a relationship. They must objectively analyze their personal beliefs to gauge if they are compatible, whether they create issues, and decide whether they are a deal breaker.

If everything suggests that they proceed, they must recognize that there will be adjustments to be made to peacefully coexist. Most importantly, they must respect each person's right to observe his or her own traditions without impinging on the relationship.

So, sisters, do give that African brother a chance, but make sure if you are a true Westerner and believe in monogamy, he is not from a polygamist culture where you will find out two years into the relationship that he has another wife back home.

Brothers, if you find that exotic beauty who happens to be from a different culture, be prepared to deal with unusual customs that you may find unpleasant. Some of it may be as benign as the type of food they eat. Others may be more difficult to get used to, such as daily rituals, their personal beliefs or ways of functioning.

These are just examples of issues I am personally familiar with that could come up when dealing with someone from a different part of the world. The minor differences are easier to work with. The more serious ones should be given in depth consideration as they can severely challenge a relationship.

Dating across racial lines

Beyond type and culture, romantic explorations across racial lines can also offer potential mates. With other cultures, you must contend with cultural differences. Here in America, a place where the word "race" is fraught with the harshness of the history of an oppressed people, interactions between blacks and whites at times carry perils more severe than mere cultural. An interracial relationship often raises a host of issues.

I have never personally liked or dated a white person. I've on occasions admired a well-built Caucasian, but I have never been attracted to one, to the point of considering dating. I honestly cannot even remember ever being approached by one. Consequently, I can only speak of other's experiences.

In my research survey, some respondents indicated they dated across race. Some of the relationships worked or others did not for a variety of reasons. The question was:

"Have you ever dated outside of your race or culture? If so, what were the challenges or difficulties you experienced?"

I will provide you with some sample responses to illustrate the diverse challenges the participants reported.

"The challenge was them not understanding the social struggles that my group faces."   *Dom – Educator*

"Challenges faced were cultures clashing. Didn't fully understand viewpoints of my culture." *Cmillie* – Make-up Artist*

"I dated a Hispanic girl for 7 years from middle school all through high school graduation. The hardest thing was winning over her dad. He didn't like the fact that she was dating a "white boy" and worked his hardest to tear us apart." *Jake – Auto parts Sales*

"Their parents did not like me." *Yvonne* – Project Manager*

"It was challenging. At first, we were attracted to each other, but came to find out we had nothing in common."

Dee Wat – Benefits Coordinator

"Yes, I have dated someone outside of my race and culture before. It was a learning experience for both of us, but we faced challenges such as cultural differences and misunderstandings."

Emily – Nurse*

"It was sometimes difficult to relate to each other's experiences and perspectives, but we worked through it and learned from each other."

Ava – Psychologist

"One of the main challenges was dealing with cultural differences and trying to understand each other's backgrounds and traditions."

Isabella – Sociologist

"Some family members and friends were not accepting of our relationship, causing tension and strain." *Abigail – Educator*

"I found that I watched what I would say due to the racial difference which is why I would not marry outside of my race."

Jay – Customer service Manager

"I am mixed race so I find it kind of hard to date outside my race but I have talked to people of different cultures and I find that most of the challenges we face as a whole, are kind of the same. And for the challenges we face that seem different it is more of a lack of understanding of that culture and practices."

Rico – Maintenance Technician

"They were interested in dating, but not marrying a black woman."

Kayla – Writer

◊◊◊

Interracial coupling among celebrities is common place. There are various reasons for this that I choose not to discuss here. I will simply say that when you are involved in the arts or professional sports, you interact with a diverse group of people in the same industry or in related fields. In addition, when you are successful, you move around the same circles as others on your level, and those comprise people from various backgrounds. Consequently, this results in a lot of mixed couple relationships, not all of which remain successful.

Singer Idina Menzel who is Jewish, was married to actor Taye Diggs, an African American, and subsequently divorced. During an episode of Jesse Tyler Ferguson's *Dinner's on Me* podcast, Idina indicated the major cause of the split was the fact that the relationship was an interracial one. She explained that when they became very famous and in the public eye, there appeared to be disappointment in the black community that Diggs, an African American heartthrob, was "married to a white Jewish girl."

The closest I can come to a personal interracial experience is that of one of my nieces. Hers and her partner's relationship is an amalgam of cultures and race. My sister, her mother, a Haitian woman living in Canada, married a man from India. That makes my niece an exotic café au lait skin toned Haitian/Indian/Canadian. Her partner is Caucasian, Canadian born and raised.

Because they both were born and raised in Canada, their shared culture is Canadian. The parts of my niece's persona that are Haitian or Indian have little effect on who she is at the core. Her values and her personal outlook on life matched her partner's. They are both achievers (she lawyer, he military commander) who believe in family and building wealth.

They successfully co-habited, had three children, and built a life together for twenty years before they took the vows of marriage in a big wedding ceremony a few months before this writing. The relationship that grew and got better over time is so good for them that they "put a ring on it."

Theirs is the epitome of what shared values and genuine affection produces in a relationship!

No matter the type, culture, or race, if you have the components just stated – shared values and genuine affection – you are holding a great hand and are on your way to a win in this great game of love relationships.

Difficulties or challenges should not deter anyone from trying to achieve something meaningful. If an interracial relationship is the opportunity that presents itself to you, be bold and brave to try it. Just go in with your eyes wide open, cognizant of the complications that may come with it, but be willing to work together to render them insignificant, compared to the beauty of the strong bond and satisfying partnership that could develop.

◊◊◊

Let us conclude this segment on type the same way we began, with the car metaphor.

In my car story, I had my list of preferences and requirements.

- I already knew the type of car I wanted, a midsize SUV, preferably a semi-luxury brand.
- I had picked the colors – brown, red, or gold.
- I wanted an appealing silhouette and special features like rear camera and navigation.
- A good sound system was required, of course.
- I had budgeted a price range I could afford comfortably.

I was not even thinking about or looking for a white car – remember,

I've never liked black or white cars. But that RDX checked off so many of my requirements (unfortunately no Bose sound system), and it appealed to my aesthetics. I committed.

I happily signed on the dotted line for that five-year car note.

While it's perfectly normal to have preferences, expanding your horizons and being open to different types, looks and cultures can be greatly beneficial.

<u>Auntie Wisdom:</u> As in my car story, sometimes a very satisfactory ride can show up in an unexpected brand (cultural background), design (looks or type), or color (race).

Keep your options open.

INCREASE THE ODDS FOR SUCCESS

We navigated quite a bit of territory in the last few pages. Let us take a quick look back to see what we gathered through this exploration before we proceed further.

- We looked at various ways of identifying a possible mate based on your preferences.
- We determined whether the two of you are compatible based on beliefs and lifestyle.
- We analyzed hazardous red flags and beige flags you can tolerate.
- We investigated background history and financial profile.
- We discussed your position on sex before marriage.
- We reviewed how important it is to have shared beliefs and common aspirations.
- You are aware that all new relationships experience some sort of challenge or test that must be conquered for it to survive.
- You are opened to exploring a relationship outside of your regular type.
- You are cognizant of the challenges presented by dating outside of

your cultural or racial profile.

To continue with our voyage metaphor, some of you should leave that lovely island that proved to be short of your expectations. The more you discovered about it, the more you kept repeating to yourself, "This aint it!"

As you pull away, reflect on what worked and what did not, and take stock of why the relationship failed. Next time you land somewhere, that assessment will prevent you from repeating similar mistakes. You will be better prepared to ensure success in making a connection that endures.

Participants were asked:

"What are two things you would do differently in future relationships to ensure they are successful?"

The free responses provided covered the gamut from the common mantra of "communication" to more personal answers. Let us look at a few that relate to both sides of the communication spectrum, that is:

1) Active listening and 2) Sharing thoughts and feelings.

"Communicate my feelings, and dislikes in the beginning."

Yvonne* – Project Manager

"Listen better. Have more hope."

Kristen – Librarian

"Listen more, work less.   "

Charles Z* – Marketing Exec.

"Be patient and be a better communicator."

KP* – Barber

"Be more communicative. Open and honest. In the past did not want to hurt feelings but it made things worse."

Cmillie* - Make-up Artist

"Strive to maintain open and honest communication with the other person, sharing my thoughts and feelings while also listening to the other person's thoughts and feelings."

Brian – Accountant

"Communicate and express your thoughts and feelings frequently, so that both parties can understand each other's ideas and needs."

Sammie – Attorney

"Communicate openly and honestly with my partner, actively listening to their perspective and concerns. -- Maintain independence and self-care, while also making time for quality moments and shared experiences with my partner."

Olivia - Social Worker*

"Communicate openly and honestly with my partner about my needs, wants, and concerns. -- Set boundaries and maintain them to ensure mutual respect and understanding in the relationship."

Brian – Electrician

"Maintain my own individual hobbies, interests, and friendships to ensure a healthy balance in the relationship."

Sofia – Public health*

"Communication, honesty."   *Shaq – Medical Technician*

"Communicate with my mate vs friends and outside influence."

Metra – Finance

Other individuals shared what was more personal to them.

"Recognize red flags early, and be true to myself."

Ari – Public relations Manager

"Set boundaries right away."   Ashlyn – Sales Associate

"Make sure the family on both sides are ok with what we are and make sure I communicate when I feel something is wrong."

Jake – Auto parts Sales

"Operate on trust: Trust is the foundation for building strong relationships. I will respect the other person's privacy and boundaries, respect their decisions and choices, and at the same time make reliable commitments for the other person and keep them."

Walter – Architect

"Resolve conflicts in a healthy and respectful manner, rather than

avoiding or escalating them Support and encourage each other's personal goals and dreams."
Ava - Psychologist*

"Have my finances and lifestyle together. Be further along in my career."
Nick – Comedian/Actor

"Ask the right questions. Pay attention to character traits."
Justo – Dock Worker*

"Not let my insecurities get in the way of a good woman."
Romello – Coach

"Address and resolve conflicts in a healthy and respectful manner. Prioritize quality time and make an effort to keep the relationship exciting and fulfilling."
Robert – Doctor

"Stricter with expectations and giving less chances in dating phase."
Kayla - Writer

You just heard from the local experts. People like you and me who have gone through failed relationships and are now the wiser for it.

Our objective for this journey has been from the beginning to find a suitable mate. Regardless of what happened to you before, life is always ready to give you second, third and fourth chances, if only you believe and do the necessary work.

You can have a do over. Please follow the instructions carefully, I did not say "repeat cycle." I said "DO. OVER!"

Start with a new mindset and a new attitude. You are prepared and fully equipped to recognize the fantastic island of your dreams the moment you step foot onto that golden sand and are greeted by a native band, dancing joyfully while they sing a welcome song.

You see, they have been waiting for an illustrious VIP just like you!

THE FANTASTIC ISLAND

You take a deep breath as you pass by a fragrant bush. You crush a leaf and bring it to your nostrils. "Live, real plants. How refreshing." "Wow!" you exclaim as you pass a gentle stream. "This is gorgeous. Reminds me of this dream I had that still lives in my memory."

You step to the desk and are greeted with warmth and courtesy.

"We have been expecting you, **V**aluable, **I**ncredible, **P**erfect, YOU! We are blessed by your presence. We hope you find everything to your liking and stay a while."

"I am liking what I see so far," you reply as you survey the room. Great décor, clean and pleasant environment. The other patrons around the lobby appear to be your kind of people. Everyone seems relaxed and in great mood. *"Mmm! Looking good."*

You walk into a room on the third floor. High enough to be removed from the noise, but not too high that you cannot run down the stairs in an emergency. The view overlooks a beautiful, well-manicured garden, edged by a small lake with a quiet shoreline. A modern bathroom, gigantic bed and a well-appointed desk area offers more luxury. You sigh with satisfaction. "This is good stuff!"

By the time you wake up in the morning from a good night sleep and enjoyed a hearty breakfast made to your specifications, you have given this resort a five star. However, you still take time to review the fliers you picked up in the lobby to see the history of this place and what else it has to offer.

When you visit the concierge and show them your list of desired excursions, they pull out their custom brochure and it contains everything you wanted.

"This is what I was looking for!" you exclaim. "This is perfect! – No, wait. This is too good to be true. What am I missing?"

"No worries," the smiling concierge replies. "This island and this resort offer lots of amenities. But, my apologies, nothing is perfect. It rains really hard here a couple of times a month. When it does, everything stops. It is not safe to go anywhere. It only lasts a few hours, then things go back to normal."

"I can live with that," you say.

Every day that you are there, you are enjoying the atmosphere, a variety of home style meal and gourmet feast, the entertainment, and the relaxation. You extend your stay.

As the days go by and you fall more in love with the island, the resort, and its people, you are thinking that this could be a place to settle. So, when it does rain and you are cooked up in your room for eight hours with no internet, you are thinking you might go crazy. But then they call everyone down to the covered patio for an improvised barbecue. You run into a couple of people you met over your stay and enjoy the company and the food while the skies pour out their entire reserve around you. Then, one last thunder clap and the sun comes out! Everyone applauds and cheers.

"Even in a storm, this place wants to make sure I am taken care of. I am sold!"
You have found your fantastic island!

"Auntie. What does this made-up story have to do with relationships?" the young one asked.

"Everything, my dear. I am just being biblical. You know how most lessons in the bible are a story or a parable? Well, that is because it helps you understand a philosophical concept better when you can picture a tangible scenario."

We just observed all the components of initiating and securing a relationship that we previously discussed, but in the context of an island exploration.

- You have the initial attraction, (like what you see)
- You recognize genuine qualities (real plants that are fragrant)
- Felt validated by the immediate reception (you feel welcome and connected)
- You did your inquiry/investigation (check the grounds and review local fliers)
- You checked your list (Compare your list of desired excursions to resort's custom brochure offering)
- There is transparency from the onset (bad feature/storms is acknowledged).
- You identified the red/beige flags (Heavy rain means nothing to do)
- Common aspiration is present (you want to relax – this place provides you all the accommodation necessary to do that)
- You endured the initial challenge or test (Survived the rain storm)
- You feel taken care of in a style you enjoy (accommodations even in a storm).
- You feel relaxed and are in good spirit (you are with like-minded people).

If you were looking for an island to relocate to, you have found your new base. You can now take a quick trip back home to close out all other business, and transfer to this place that you enjoy, where they enjoy you, and you feel all your needs are met.

The closing of business I am referring to are those loose end connections you may have in your life: the in-the-meantime person, the on again-off again exes, the uncooperative co-parents, drama inducers, etc.

You must wipe the slate clean and start anew with this new life you have come into. You have observed, examined, tested, assessed, and evaluated.

You have decided that you want to commit to this situation: a long-term relationship, eventually to engagement, and possibly marriage.

◊◊◊

People usually recognize when they see potential in a relationship. How they proceed from there will determine whether this budding possibility can develop into a tangible partnership.

Participants were asked how they addressed the next step in dating. The responses show that women prefer to set the expectations early on, but a large percentage keep going without addressing the topic. Men on the other hand will more frequently formally state their intentions to going steady. Here is what the survey shows.

After dating someone for some time, do you?

	Men	**Women**
Formally state your intentions to Going steady, boyfriend/girlfriend	67%	41%
Set the expectations early on	33%	56%
Keep going without addressing the topic	7%	29%

I also asked the men this follow up question which could be a bonus for the ladies. "Do you mind if the woman initiates that conversation?"

Good news! 89% of the men said they did not mind. So, sisters, take a chance on love. If the brother is feeling you, this might be an opening that could facilitate that move up the ladder. But as always, I must remain the voice of reason. He might not be ready or willing to move up the next step and instead, he either declines or fakes a deeper interest. In the latter case, be careful. He may stay in the relationship in an attempt not to mess up his ongoing good thing, but not be genuine about a long-term situation.

Mon Dieu! My goodness! The assessment and evaluation never cease.

Oui mon amour. Yes, my love. It keeps going until you know for sure that you know, that you know.

◊◊◊

While you are in a committed phase, whether temporary long-term dating, or engagement, or, permanently co-habiting or married, your relationship checklist should always be in prominence. A relationship is tested all throughout its course. You must always keep in mind the positive reasons the two of you got together in the first place, and keep choosing each other again and again.

During the early stages of a committed relationship, there is still a lot to discover about each other. Especially for those who did not live together before marriage, little unknowns will pop up. If both parties did their homework before hand by having open communication or through pre-marital counseling, there won't be nasty surprises. However, you occasionally hear stories of people who thought they had done the work to learn everything they could about a prospective mate, only to discover that they don't really know this complete stranger they are involved or living with.

A May 2016 episode of *"This American Life,"* a public radio show hosted by Ira Glass, entitled *"The Perils of Intimacy,"* which was rebroadcasted in April 2024, recounts the story of Rachel R. whose identity was stolen. Credit cards, bank accounts; the works. Paranoid, she went off grid, using only all cash on financial transactions. She later found out that her live-in boyfriend of three years had been the one to withdraw her money, use her cards with no authorization to buy stuff, prompting her to believe she had been the victim of identity theft by some unknown scammer.

She also discovered that his job did not exist, although he left home every day and talked often about concocted co-workers and a boss.

Humph! Mercy!

He finally confessed to having been diagnosed with "an impulse control disorder," and that he was seeing a therapist. It still took Rachel some time to wean her emotions from the relationship and separate from the boyfriend.

You don't know someone until you know them. Sounds a bit moronic and redundant; but in essence, you only know for sure when you find out the truth.

◊◊◊

Sorry my loves! I may have just scared the dickens out of most of you. Not to fret. That was an extreme example of rare cases of the "expect the unexpected" doctrine. What you will encounter for sure are little idiosyncrasies or annoying habits that you may have to adjust to, to peacefully co-exist with your mate.

Those are the days your checklist will come in handy, even after years together when you no longer need to consult the physical list because it's seating right there in your brain and lounging around in your heart. When you find yourself asking the question: "Why am I with this person. Why did I get married?" you can do a quick retrospective.

Let me see. I like a, b, c, and d. Can tolerate f, g, and h. He or she brings me l, m, n, o, p. Oh, and I adore x, y, and z!

<u>Auntie Wisdom:</u> There you go! You got a good thing going, so work it out. Brood if you must, but keep accentuating the positives. When it comes to the negatives, tolerate if you can. If necessary, talk it out, preferably calmy. Apologize. Explain. Make up always!

◊◊◊

Alright my loves. This concludes our segment specifically addressed to the singles, whether you are currently dating or not. I hope that as we delved into the various topics we explored, it opened you up to:

- Understand yourself better
- Know what you desire for your heart and life

167

- What to expect in your search for a mate, and
- How to successfully connect with that life partner.

We will now begin examining coupled life in the next chapters. **You, singles are not off the hook, yet.**

- I am asking you to **STAY!** Till the very last page of this book.
- Gain the wisdom of the ones who have managed to jump the threshold into long-term, possibly forever domain.
- Most importantly, they successfully maintained that joint journey for years, through the ups and downs of life.

You can learn from their experience – and mine – to prepare you for what is to come. After all, why get into something when you have no idea what to expect? You want marriage; but do you know what it is? It may not be for you.

"Knowledge is power" is frequently quoted when it comes to education and politics. In regards to marriage, it is a key component in ensuring success. The more you know about how marriage or coupled life works, the better your chances to make yours function successfully.

So go grab a snack and some refreshment, and come right back here. You will see the beauty, witness the challenges, laugh at the funny, experience the triumphs of those of us who are blessed to have achieved the coveted state of being successfully married or coupled.

If you have been married or are currently coupled, the next chapters are of primary importance for you as well. Pay close attention to the stories coming up, especially if you feel that your relationship could use a refresher or a needed boost.

Gather around!

Let us tune in to see how to do this LOVE THANG!

Walking in to the tune of "I Gotta Feeling" that tonight's
gonna be a good night, by The Black Eyes Peas.
Henri and I married in an intimate civil ceremony in 2002, a week
after Valentine's Day. Then, for our tenth-year anniversary, we had the
party we couldn't afford originally, by renewing our wedding vows, with a
big celebration attended by family and friends.

PART IV

PARTNERING FOR LIFE

Marriage is one of the best things that could happen to two individuals. But when you marry someone, you are taking a chance on them and on love. There is no guarantee that it's going to work. The best that you can do is prepare seriously, go in with both eyes wide open, and be ready to work on the marriage because you feel strongly about the relationship, and see enough potential to propel you to take that leap of faith.

THE CHOSEN MATE

Marriage - it's a GO!

"*Here comes the bride!*" Congratulations! You did it! You walked down the aisle to that Wedding March. You stood at the altar, and in front of witnesses, professed your love for each other and pledged your devoted commitment for as long as you live. – That was 84% of the survey respondents who took the "Couples" survey. We will refer to them as "married couples." – Or, as 14% of the participants did, you moved in together and set up house without the pomp and circumstances. Those we are calling "established couples."

Either way, you are a couple, and the expectations as life partners are the exact same: caring, sharing, providing, nurturing, loving, etc. The only difference is that in an unmarried situation, there is this unspoken vibe floating in the air that either party could just impulsively pick up and leave at any time. In fact, sometimes one person may hold that over the other's head. "*If you bother me, I am out of here.*" The complications of dissolving a legal marriage sometimes serve as a much-needed deterrent, and consequently, considered a last resort strategy. Very often all that is needed is time to work out your differences.

For the purposes of the survey and this book, couples are considered those legally married as well as those in common law or co-habitation. So, even if you do not believe in legalistic, and opted for common law, these chapters on marriage apply to you as well.

On February 21, 2024 Benzinga.com published an article by Jeannine Mancini titled: "Warren Buffett Has Spent 70 Years of His Life Married – His Advice: 'If you Want A Marriage To Last, Look for Someone With Low Expectations."

I became familiar with the 93-year-old Buffett (as of 2024), when I worked in the financial industry, and always admired The Berkshire Hathaway's leader business and investment acumen. I wished I had the kind of capital to engage in his financial market strategies. Come to find out the "Oracle of Omaha" – his nickname as one of the world's most successful investors – also applies his wisdom to marriage and relationships.

I am sure Mr. Buffett was not suggesting that we settle for anyone just for the sake of having a partner or a spouse. Rather, I believe he was cautioning the romantic heart to be realistic in choosing someone to share your life with. Romance itself tends to foster fantasies about married life that are idealistic. Buffet's company, Berkshire Hathaway, is known in the financial world for successfully earning great returns based on a strategy of sticking to sensible and foundationally solid stocks.

A parallel can be drawn here as it relates to relationships. Are you easily seduced by the superficial, the flash and dash that looks or sounds good? Or, are you willing to identify the inherent values and solid qualities that a long-term investment requires to grow?

Marriage is one of the best things that could happen to two individuals. But as Mr. Buffett suggests, do keep your expectations in check.

You have taken some time to apply all the great advice I have been giving you. You have found that "fantastic island" we talked about before and made the decision to commit and stay there. You planned a big day where family and friends on both sides came out to celebrate with you and offer their blessing. Everything is perfect as you embark on this great adventure called married life. The wedding was fun! – But please note, **the wedding is not the marriage.** The wedding is just a party.

Aye! Miss Killjoy! Can I just bask in the moment?

Of course, sweetie! But I would be remiss if I didn't tell it to you like it is.

◊◊◊

The Honeymoon – Let the lessons begin

For most couples the honeymoon is the big highlight of the wedding night, especially if you held out based on your religious beliefs. Finally, you get to experience each other physically!

If you already live together, the excitement is lessened by the fact that you already know each other intimately. Nevertheless, it is still considered a special night, for everything that being married represents.

A wedding night is a highly romanticized event, but it can be unpredictable. There have been situations where somebody drank too much and passed out on the bed. My Jewish and Italian married friends in New York shared how a good portion of the night was spent counting the money received from relatives. If you know anything about these cultures, enough money is made at a wedding to put a sizable down payment on a home. Others were so tired from wedding planning followed by too much partying; they were not up to much.

My wedding night story highlighted from day one that marriage is not for the thin skinned or easily rattled, and the art of compromise is a learned skill and necessary attribute.

Henri had moved in with me when we got engaged, and we were planning a wedding when September 11, 2001 happened. He lost his job in the World Financial Center building, adjacent to the Towers. We decided to have a civil ceremony the following February, until things got better and we were able to afford a proper wedding. As we got closer to the date, I asked him who he was inviting.

"Nobody," he replied. "I'll wait until we have the wedding then invite everybody."

"Okay. But I am inviting my people," I said.

When we showed up at the courthouse with my brother who lived with us at the time, my friend Annie and her husband who were our witnesses were there with their baby, (my goddaughter) and her elderly mom. Then, my niece K. arrived, together with a girlfriend from down the street and another one from my job. I smiled, reassured that I was surrounded by representation of all the people who loved me: family, friends, and colleagues.

It was a simple but beautifully moving ceremony performed by an ordained pastor (bonus for the believer in me) and I got teary eyed when we exchanged our vows. Afterwards, we all went to a local restaurant where everyone toasted us. When we left, my brother went to the city – New York that is – to give us privacy for the night, and Henri and I returned home.

I was elated! My love and I were married. We took a vow to love each other for better or for worse, for richer or poorer, through sickness and in health. Forever! That is enough to make your head spin and intensify your desire for each other, right? I was bubbling with visions of a magic night of lovemaking to blow all records. *We is married now!*

Well. Don't think that's going to happen. Not when apparently, something is bothering somebody.

Already? This is supposed to be our "honeymoon."

I noticed Henri slumped in a chair, sulking. I asked him what was wrong.

"I didn't have any of my people there with me tonight," he said.

"But you were the one who said you didn't want to invite anybody until the wedding," I reminded him.

"Yeah, but you had your people there."

"Not my fault you decided to have no one there. No way was **I** gonna get married, and not have my family and my best friends represented there," I countered.

He just grunted in reply.

"You dumb butt," I silently added in my mind as I walked away, disappointed.

Henri proceeded to sulk the rest of the night. When we later got into bed, one person faced east, the other faced west, leaving a large gap in the middle of the bed.

By the time we woke up the next day, Henri's dark mood had dissipated. We resumed our morning routine and the subject was never brought up again. A couple of days later, our marriage was properly consummated.

That first night could have been disastrous had I chosen to pick an argument. I understood that Henri wasn't mad at me, but rather, at himself, for missing the opportunity to celebrate the occasion with his people. I learned three things on that very first day of marriage.

A committed partnership requires that you adjust on the fly.

If you have a point to make, state your case succinctly and calmly, then move on. Do not drag. Do not berate.

Give your partner a chance to cool off. Time is a healing balm.

I live by these rules to this day, twenty-two years after that "memorable, non-event night."

BLUEPRINT FOR
A SUCCESSFUL MARRIAGE

As I began writing these chapters on marriage, Pastor Jacqueline Martin, the lead pastor at my church – *Light of The World*, in Humble, Texas began a sermon series on marriage. I admit that I am biased as a Christian, but it always amazes me how the teachings of the bible provide concrete formulas for successful living. Our Creator knows what we humans need to function properly, and since He first put man and woman together, and gave them a mandate to "be fruitful and multiply," He knows what is required to make it all work.

Pastor Jackie, as she is affectionately called by the congregation, reminded us that God instituted the concept of companionship. *"It is not good for man to be alone,"* it says in Genesis, the first book of the bible. So, God made the woman and presented her to the first man Adam. That is probably why, human beings naturally crave genuine connections with others, and in the romantic context, a significant other.

Hey! I see you rolling them eyes. *"Here she goes again with that God thing."*

As you were. Eyes on the page. Remember I said a wise person seeks knowledge. I am quoting from THE book of knowledge and wisdom. So. Stop it! Keep reading and learn.

In her sermon "Biblical Foundation of the Family," Pastor Jackie, shared a template for "A Marriage According to God," that could have easily been titled "The Ten Commandments of Marriage." The list is based on biblical scriptures. I want you to pretend you didn't know where this information comes from, and look and assess its content for yourself, objectively.

- Love
- Unity
- Respect
- Commitment
- Forgiveness
- Servanthood
- Faith
- Discipleship
- Stewardship
- Grace

Wow! Right? It's all right there. If you want to hear the entire message for yourself, check out Pastor's message at the link provided in the "Referenced Sources" section in the back of this book. For our purpose here, I solely use her list and will discuss what each of those components may look like in a general context. To confirm, the following is my own interpretation of Pastor Jackie's list. For her biblical perspective, consult her sermon directly.

1. Love

"Love is a many splendored thing" as described in poems (William Waterway), in films (1955), and in Academy Award winning songs (lyrics Paul Francis Webster). – **"Love makes the world go round"** says 19th century dramatist, William S. Gilbert. – **"All you need is love"** sing The Beatles. – **"Faith, hope, and love abide … but the greatest of these is love,"** writes the apostle Paul in the book of 1 Corinthians.

We can all agree that love is considered the main ingredient in romantic relationships and "above all these" the thing quoted as the greatest by the bible. Of course, we must make the distinction that we are not talking about misguided or crazy love.

Rather, the kind we refer to here is one where, LOVE is "selfless, patient and kind; it does not envy, it does not boast, it is not proud. It does not dishonor others, it is not self-seeking, it is not easily angered, it keeps no record of wrongs. Love does not delight in evil but rejoices with the truth. It always protects, always trusts, always hopes, always perseveres." (1 Corinthians 13: 4 - 7)

Ladies and gentlemen of the jury, I rest my case! There is nothing I can add to that perfectly complete and profound statement.

2. Unity

Pastor Jackie referred to a couple being "united in purpose." In my view, this refers to you and your partner being a team. There is no "I" in that word. Rather, it begins with a "u" just like in "us." You and your mate become a unique unit, a family, that may later grow into more members, your children.

As such it is imperative that **you are both in agreement about how you want your life and what you want to achieve.**

Like the exercise we did in the dating phase, you are now going to: **Practice being on the same page regarding lifestyle choices, daily routines, financial decisions, the rearing of children, etc.**

You accomplish this by applying the three Cs of couple interaction:
- **Communication**
- **Cooperation**
- **Commitment.**

3. Respect

That word came up so many times in my survey participants' responses. **What is respect?**

The following list regarding "Respectful Relationships" was posted on the Queensland Government's (Australia) website as a resource for youth to "have healthy, respectful relationships and know what respectful behaviour looks like." I believe the strategies mentioned can be used by anyone, in all human interactions, including couples, as a guide for what respect looks like. Their list shows the following examples of how to show respect to others:

- *Be a good listener*
- *Understand someone's point of view*
- *Express your needs and wants in a direct, calm and respectful way*
- *Respond in a timely manner if someone requests something*
- *Acknowledge what others do well*
- *Let people know you appreciate them*
- *If someone shares something intimate and personal with you, keep it private*
- *Emphasise someone's strengths, not their weaknesses*
- *Ensure your humour is sensitive to others' feelings and avoid embarrassing them*
- *Speak directly with others, don't talk behind their back*
- *Allow someone space if they need it.*

I have expressed several of these viewpoints throughout this book, but it is helpful to see them together in this context. I will add to this list to always remember the adage, **"Do onto others as you would have them do onto you."**

Respect requires that you put yourself in the other person's shoes and ask yourself, "Would I like it if someone did or said that to me?"

<u>Auntie Wisdom:</u>

- **When you love someone, you want to see and bring out the best in them.**
- You maintain a positive cycle of energy between the two of you.
- You build each other up, allowing your relationship to thrive.

4. Commitment

I will not elaborate much on the topic here. We discussed it in depth in earlier chapters. Suffice it to say, that you both promised to do your utmost best to make this relationship work, through thick and thin, whether you publicly pledged "I dos" or simply agreed in private to commit in a common law arrangement.

- **You are bound by your contract.**
- **Honor its written or implied clauses.**

5. Forgiveness

Remember "love keeps no records of wrong" mentioned in 1 Corinthians? That is what it means to forgive. Humans are not perfect. Everyone makes mistakes. We often violate boundaries or intentionally or inadvertently offend. If forgiveness did not exist, you would have throngs of people walking around with gigantic gashes on their chest, carrying open wounds of unforgiven wrongs. Zombie invasion of sort...

To take it a step further, what if Jesus decided He did not want to forgive my sins? I would have never known the goodness of the Lord. I would not be in this blessed state where I am today.

In a marriage or coupled relationship, you excuse or overlook the minor issues and sometimes you must forgive more serious transgressions.

We will revisit this topic later when we talk about tests and challenges in a marriage.

Keep in mind that if the God of the universe forgives, who are we to withhold forgiveness? Especially when He explicitly directs us to do so. (… Forgive, and you will be forgiven. – Luke 6:37)

It may take time to forget, but if you love, you forgive!

6. Servanthood

Oh, oh! Servant? What do you mean Auntie?

Yep, servant. A couple must be willing to serve each other. What do I mean by that? You must be attentive to one another's needs and cater to each other. Traditionally the connotation of "serving" has been tainted with the common belief that a woman should serve her husband. In every way.

Welcome to the twenty-first century where role reversal is widely practiced. Better yet, what about adopting equal opportunity as it exists in my household. I believe that when it comes to serving, men and women are interchangeable pieces on the game board.

My husband is just as quick to fix me a cup of tea, place it on a tray with some crackers and deliver it to my desk, as I intuitively prepare his dinner plate and bring it to him in front of the television, if he happens to be engrossed in a movie or a game. We tag team each other with household duties, taking turns cooking, cleaning, or doing laundry. Yes, there is *King Henri the Great* and *Queen Danielle the Magnificent*, but neither one of us hesitates to care for each other.

In a March 2024 episode of the TV show, *"Today with Hoda & Jenna,"* referenced in a People.com article, co-host Jenna Bush Hager, former president George W. Bush's daughter, discusses with Hoda the little things partners sometimes do to demonstrate caring. She revealed that her father brings her mom her daily cup of coffee, fixed the way she likes it, every single morning.

Imagine this, the president of these mighty United States brings a cup of coffee to his wife, every single morning!

The objective in servanthood is the desire to please your partner and anticipate their needs. I like Google's *Oxford Languages* dictionary's definition on that one.

A servant is:
- a person who performs duties for others;
- a devoted and helpful follower or supporter.
- You are to perform the duties of your role for each other. (I hear *the snickering- get your mind out of the gutter.)*
- You are to be devoted to one another, and
- You are to be each other's greatest supporter.
- You are, Numero uno, fan club leader, cheerleader extraordinaire!

7. Faith

When one hears the word faith, one immediately thinks religion. Here again, I call on *Oxford's* expertise. Their number one definition is: *"Complete trust or confidence in someone or something."*

You hear that! Your relationship must be so solid that you completely trust your partner and have confidence in their commitment to you, your happiness, and the success of your relationship. How do you accomplish that?

Simply refer to numbers 1 through 6 above, and what will come in numbers 8 to 10. If you adhere to these precepts, you are almost guaranteed to be successful in your marriage journey.

8. Discipleship

The term discipleship is usually used in a Christian framework to refer to followers of Christ, who imitate his life, embrace his values, and adhere to his views on life.

When placed in the context of human relationships, I would interpret being a disciple of someone to be that individual's follower. You "follow" people on social media. You are interested in their viewpoints. You engage with information they disseminate. You share and invite others to join in. You build their numbers up.

Why not be that for your partner? Your relationship should focus on actively building a life together, embracing each other's values, and supporting one another.

Be each other's most devoted disciple and advocate. And for those of us who fervently follow Jesus, walk side by side with your partner, with Jesus at the helm.

9. Stewardship

One more time, good ole Oxford provided me with a definition for the word: "The job of supervising or taking care of something …"

You are one another's steward. You take care of each other and I would venture to say, you are **responsible** for each other. Are you your brother/

sister's keeper? A resounding "YES!" in this scenario. You are responsible for their wellbeing, both physical and emotional and in all circumstances. For richer and poorer, in sickness and in health, remember.

In case you, coward and selfish that you are, are thinking this is too much responsibility, look at it this way. What if you are the one who needs looking after?

Uhm! Looks more appealing now, doesn't it? Fool. The beauty of sharing a life together is the comfort of knowing that somebody has your back and you can depend on their support, their help, and their love AT ALL TIMES!

It is up to each partner, to make sure those feelings are consistently nurtured, so that your mate rests assured that you are one hundred percent for them and with them.

10. Grace

In a January 26, 2024 article that appeared on Christian.com, *"What is Grace? Bible Meaning and Importance,"* Bishop Justin Holcomb explores the meaning of the word in the biblical context. Here is a quote headlining the article that I thought was very insightful.

"Grace is the opposite of karma, which is all about getting what you deserve. Grace is getting what you don't deserve."

The writer goes on to define the word as: *"God's favor toward the unworthy"* or *"God's benevolence on the undeserving." In His grace, God is willing to forgive us and bless us, even though we fall short of living righteously."*

The God of the universe is willing to forgive us even when we mess up in grand fashion. We are expected to extend the same grace to others.

So, that knucklehead had the nerve to check out that woman's booty while you were strolling together at the mall. Head snapped all the way around.

"How could you disrespect me like that," you bemoan. You really want to smack him over his oversized noggin, right there in public.

"I am sorry babe. It was just reflex," he says sheepishly. "Damn, this was unreal."

You stifle a smile. You are a little upset, but you understand. Sister did look like she had a size 20x20 pillow attached to each cheek, when her waistline itself was barely a 24 contour. Was that nature's whimsy or an overestimated BBL?

Okay, that was a benign case requiring grace. What about when the causes of your anger are more severe? Financial irresponsibility? Infidelity? Ugh!

That is all part of the package. And the bible gives us the *modus operandi* for these situations in Romans 5:20. How should we act towards one another?

"…where sin abounded, grace abounded much more."

The more egregious your partner's infraction, the more you must find it within yourself to forgive and help both of you heal your hearts and the relationship.

Caveat added: I do not condone embracing someone walking all over you or taking advantage of your loving nature. If that is the way they operate, that is abuse. My view on that: Get. Out. Of. Town!

SUGGESTED TIPS FOR A SUCCESSFUL MARRIAGE

If you are married or coupled to the right partner, marriage or domestic partnership is one of the greatest blessings you could ever experience.

I remember the first time Henri referred to me as "my wife." How sweet the sound! Those two words rang like a melodious song. I heard love, caring, commitment and belonging, pride even. This woman who I love and apparently loves me enough to marry me, is mine! I felt elevated. This man wants the world to know we belong. I am esteemed.

In turn, the first time I uttered the words, "my husband," a secret smile filled my heart. I love this man. Now I am his and he is mine.

The first few months and even the full first year of marriage is spent learning more about your partner and establishing certain life routines. Assuming there are no babies yet, **you can and should focus on each other**. This is the time when you set the tone for how you will function daily, how you will run your life and handle your affairs. In a few pages, we will talk about some practical strategies you can put in place to ensure a successful partnership. For now, the primary thing to concentrate on is getting comfortable with each other and enjoying each other.

Just married should be viewed as an extension of dating, but with lots of fringe benefits. You two now have a partner, a best friend to talk to, to help shoulder life's burdens, a buddy to share and enjoy the simple things and marvel at life's grand events. And hey, hooray for consistent, guilt-free sex! You were thinking it, so I said it. Being real. Hundred percent.

Make each other a PRIORITY

<u>Auntie Wisdom</u>: I believe that couples should learn to manage their time and responsibilities and intentionally set aside time for each other.

In 2022 a comment singer and actress LeToya Luckett made on the podcast *Good Moms, Bad Choices* about her belief that her next husband should come before her kids, was met with pointed criticism. She referred to the sacrifices mothers make daily to ensure their children's wellbeing often take precedence over other things, even a husband. She indicated that in a future marriage she would go by the biblical order, where a wife puts the husband first.

Her comments sparked a fury with social media users and fans who believe that when it comes to being a mother, children come first.

I cannot personally speak on this because I do not have children. However, I have witnessed my share of mothers who were so focused on the children that they completely neglected giving attention to their partner.

In an ideal partnership, the man is as involved as the woman in the daily process of caring for the children. In most situations, however, the reality is that it is primarily the woman's responsibility. This can impede on devoting time to being a couple. There are cases where women complained of feeling so drained after caring for the children that they have no energy or desire left to cater to a husband's needs.

This should tell husbands that if they do their share of the chores and childcare, it will create openings for their wives to have some "me" time for themselves, as well as allowing them opportunities to spend personal time with the husbands.

Older generations were mostly set in the traditional roles of man as breadwinner and woman as the homemaker. It was then expected that the woman alone would do the child rearing and home care. Nowadays most women work as well. There are days when I work and come home tired and have no desire to cook or clean house. I have the luxury of no children to care for, and my husband is competent at self-care and sharing chores. I can just imagine what a busy working woman with a family must face.

It is imperative that couples have personal time together. At one time this might be a few minutes a week or a couple of hours a month, because there are small children that require constant daily attention. But it should preferably be a few minutes each day to connect with your partner.

◊◊◊

Action Steps that Nurture a Marriage/Domestic partnership

This book does not portend to be a how-to instructional on marriage specifically. There are plenty of texts written on the subject. However, I intend to give you an overview of what is expected, so that you have a better understanding of what marriage entails. Consequently, before we begin the serious discussions about married life, I offer you a few simple tips that if practiced consistently, will extend the life of your marriage or partnership.

Behaviors to Avoid

<u>Auntie Wisdom:</u> Adopt the motto from the bible verse: "Do unto others – your partner – as you would have them do onto you." Solidify

that with: "How would I feel if that were said or done to me?"

Very often, couples have a disagreement, but out of frustration or miscommunication, it turns into an argument. When that happens, refrain from using or participating in the corrosive behaviors that marriage counselors refer to as **"The Four Horsemen."** The phrase is a metaphor representing the end of times according to the New Testament of the bible, but in the context of relationships, those forebearers of doom can precipitate the apocalypse of a marriage. May Soo, a counseling psychologist, wrote an article posted on *RWA Psychology's* website, *The Four Horsemen Toxic Communication Styles and How to Rein Them In,* in which she references the work of relationship expert and author, Dr. John Gottman of The Gottman Institute. Dr. Gottman's concept is summarized as follows:

Criticism – put downs, attacks on personality/character rather than behavior, insults, derogatory remarks, fault finding, etc.

Contempt – toxic language or attacks meant to demean, being disrespectful

Defensiveness – blame game, "yes-but" answers, making excuses

Stonewalling – shut down, tune out, minimize, or ignore, failure to communicate authentically.

This destructive posse should be replaced with authentic and consistent communication for smoother interactions and harmonious interrelation.

DAILY/WEEKLY RELATIONSHIP
MAINTENANCE PRACTICES

Always greet each other in the morning. A simple "Good morning" or "Morning, babe!" sets the tone.

- You are acknowledging each other's presence.

Always say goodbye and wish your partner a good day as the last thing you do when leaving for the day.

- It prepares them for how they will face the world that day.

If possible, give your partner a quick call during the day.

- Another chance to say "I love you."
- A reminder that they are on your mind at all time.
- Sometimes also serves as a precursor of fun times to come later, if it includes flirtation.

Take a moment when you get home to ask your partner about their day.

- A simple "how was your day" opens the way for the person to unload if they experienced a bad day. Or, it may start a quick exchange about something funny you encountered and you can share a laugh.

End the day at night with a "Good night, baby!" (love, sweetheart, etc.)! to conclude the day with an emphasis on your love for each other.

Do not go to bed angry at each other! At least try.

- There will be times when one of you or both of you need to cool off for a few hours. Allow that time as calmly as possible. We will talk about that again later.

Be cognizant of what your partner likes, if you have not already learned during courtship or dating.

- Utilize that knowledge to keep the person happy.
- Incorporate that thing or gesture in your daily interactions.
- Use it for little surprises.

Develop the habit of transparency between the two of you.

- In the beginning there may be things you are not comfortable sharing. But little by little, build a "friendship" by sharing your dreams, your concerns, your challenges, and your successes.
- Remember, the objective is to become and remain each other's best friend.

Focus on each other. Make time for the two of you.

- Put down the phone!

- Connect daily with little conversations, confide about your day, share a laugh with a joke, a tease, something non-sensical or do something fun together.
- Engage in joint activities, like going to the gym, going for a walk, watching a TV show or movie, sitting down for dinner, etc.

Emphasize the pluses, the things that informed your decision to choose that person.

- There will always be minuses, the negative stuff.
- Work to minimize them - Do not let them over-power the positive.
- Accentuate the positive, give compliments, show appreciation.

Tread carefully when dealing with family members: parents, previous children, etc.

- You become each other's main priority when you join in marriage.
- However, family holds a special place in people's hearts and life.
- Learn how to interact with them respectfully and with love.
- Discuss with spouse the preferred approach and come to agreement.

Communicate, communicate, communicate! Discuss how things will be handled, including family visits, holidays, travel, emergencies.

- Agree on how you will take care of things before they happen, so you already know how to address them when they do.

Connect frequently and consistently, preferably every day.

- I repeat: put down the phone. Shut off the television.
- Talk face to face and give your partner your undivided attention for a few minutes each day.
- Showing stuff on your phone does not count, as it includes some third party.

Laugh every day. Laughter is good for the soul and sharing a laugh is a good way of remaining connected.

- Share a joke, tease each other (gently), watch a funny clip on your phone together. Report on a funny event witnessed earlier, etc.

Touch each other – Whoa! Let me clarify. Yes, share intimacies. We'll talk about that next. – You certainly don't need any prompting from me for carnal exploration. What I refer to here, is to make sure you are physical with each other in a non-sexual way.

- A gentle hug, a quick kiss, a pat on the shoulder or other places, a hip bump, running your fingers through their hair. Little gestures that say you are present and you see them.

LONG-TERM STRATEGIES FOR HARMONIOUS INTERACTIONS

Pick a day that is considered date day/night, at least once a month, if not weekly, even if you have children.

- Do something that is just for the two of you and that you will both enjoy – lunch, dinner, movie, a show, go for dessert, a game, bowling, etc.

Call a babysitter or ask grandma or auntie for back-up, if there are children.

Talk about your plans or schedule for the coming week and month.

- Everyone is aware of what is going on and how that will affect the other.

Review your household financial issues:

- Monthly bills, upcoming projects, vacations, or other expenses.

Share the tasks of cleaning, laundry and food shopping and cooking.

- Allocate based on individual preferences or availability, or

Do tasks together for a fun tag team moment. – I wash the dishes; you towel them dry.

Have pet names for each other, a sweet term of endearment (muffin, cutie patootie, baby cakes, bunny, sunshine); or a word that invokes an intimate or personal story (Tiger tail, Stevie Wonder, Hercules, Wonder Woman, Sexy Tina) – I am making these up as I write. Every time you hear that moniker, you smile internally. It's like a private joke. – Side note: could also be helpful if AI tries to fool you. Only the two of you know this special word.

Have a code word to diffuse situations. Teachers learn little tricks to take control of a class, including words, phrases, gestures that when used are a signal for quiet or attentiveness. On a recent Friday before a holiday, I witnessed an instructional coach (lead teacher) take complete command of a class of seventh graders. I was covering for the teacher and this woman came in to give them the assignment. The room was full of loud chatter as expected from middle schoolers with nothing to do. She raised her voice and said "Waterfalls!" The room immediately went completely silent.

Couples need a code word that when used lets the other party know to cool down during an argument. Talk about it and decide together what that word will be. Also agree on what is expected to happen when it's used: time out or postpone discussion, change your tone, pipe down, or lighten up? Maybe all of the above.

Make time for each other. Fit in time devoted to you two just being together on a regular basis.

- Stream a movie that you can both enjoy.
- Set the table and have a nice home cooked meal or order delivery; but still use the good plates and forks.
- Play your favorite song and dance.

Make time for intimacy. Sharing physical intimacy for a couple is like kids getting together with best friends for play. It is fun, and it's good for you. But here again, you cannot take anything for granted.

- Learn each other's style and preferences – ask, talk, communicate.
- Be flexible to accommodate your partner – within reason.
- Be spontaneous when you can, it creates excitement.
- Put on your schedule if necessary; especially if there are children.

Auntie Wisdom: You must be intentional in expressing love and

caring to your partner in concrete terms.

Some people are big on saying "I love you." The words are nice to hear, and the occasional grand gestures are great, but:

Every day, your interactions with each other must demonstrate

- Caring
- Respect
- A willingness to cooperate and
- The desire to please and uplift each other

◊◊◊

Financial discussions

I reserved the following discussion for the end of the suggested tips category, because it deserves focused attention. One of the main culprits and causes of disagreement between couples, is the area of finances. More specifically, how each party manages their affairs, who is bringing what to the table, and who is responsible for what. So let us address this elephant in the room.

When we discussed dating in the previous chapters, I suggested that a **<u>financial discussion was a must</u>** for individuals who are considering merging their lives, through committed cohabitation or marriage. Now that you two have become one unit, having a financial discussion is a healthy exercise that helps establish common ground and create a template for assets and expenses management. Financial status and philosophy should be discussed, and a lot of questions asked before effecting the merger or marriage. Some people go as far as preparing a pre-nuptial agreement.

I will caution women to tread lightly, because most men, especially those from previous generations, are touchy about the subject. Most men who were raised being told that they must be the providers, adhere to the model of them being the breadwinner. A lot of people also prefer to keep their income a secret from the other person as a mean of keeping control of their affairs or avoiding their partner "getting into their business."

I profess transparency. There are a lot of writing on the subject that provide distinct questions or a blueprint you can follow to address the topic of personal financial management. But it should always be an organic occurrence, weaved in between a related conversation or event.

The reality is that nowadays, a lot of women earn more than their partners. Some who want to lift themselves up and stabilize their lives, buy a home on their own and they are also self-sufficient financially. As a matter of fact, a January 16, 2024 article by Jacob Channel, *"Homeownership Gender Gap: Single Women Own More Homes Than Single Men"* was posted by Lending Tree, the online lending platform. It reported that single women who live by themselves are more likely to own a home than single men in 48 out of 50 states.

In my opinion, these ladies do not need a man to take care of them, to provide, but rather, they would desire a partner with whom to maintain or elevate a lifestyle.

Sadly, that becomes a problem in instances where a woman is not aware of the politics of handling such situations.

A woman in her late 30's found herself in that situation. In a discussion with a man she had been dating for a while, she expressed that she needed somebody on her level with similar aspirations, good job or career and who possibly owned property – (she owns her own home). There were other issues to be dealt with, but the fact that he did not own property made him feel that he could not give her what she wanted.

From my personal experience, man over thirty who have been in previous relationships most likely have children for whom they are paying child support. In those cases, their available income is reduced and not sufficient to spread to investments. In addition, they are spending to impress the woman they are currently pursuing. So even less serious money available for investing.

To be objective, a lot of single women find themselves with limited resources as well, when there are children to care for, and no partner to help shoulder the burden. In either case, unless the person is making a lot of money and is wise about how they spend it, they may not have a strong portfolio of assets to offer into a romantic partnership.

The issue of financial transparency must be constant and consistent. This is vital in maintaining a healthy marriage enterprise and help avoid nasty surprises. One of the issues that have reared an ugly head in relationships is what the experts are calling **"Financial Infidelity."**

A definition of the term was offered by Verner Brumley Mueller Parker PC, a Dallas, TX law firm that specializes in family law, in a blog posted on their site on August 9, 2023. It states:

Financial infidelity occurs when one partner hides or misrepresents financial information from the other, such as keeping secret bank accounts or hiding purchases.

Financial infidelity is a form of dishonesty that can have serious repercussions for a marriage, (even divorce). Though it does not involve physical cheating, the hidden spending or secret accounts can lead to feelings of betrayal and mistrust.

They added that according to a Harris Poll survey, this was a common deception. They found that over 50% of adults admitted to having committed financial infidelity in their relationships.

Years ago, I worked with a twenty-something young woman who had been married for a few years. She and her husband had a young son at the time. She occasionally came to me for professional or personal advice. One day I overheard her talking on the phone with great agitation. She slammed the phone down when she hung up.

"Is everything okay," I inquired.

"No," she replied. "Michael (her husband) and I were arguing about these unexpected expenses on the joint account. He bought himself a $250 pair of sneakers! The thing is, I just wrote a bunch of checks to pay the bills. Now some of those checks are gonna bounce."

"Then he had the nerve to tell me, "It's <u>my</u> money," she continued. "He's supposed to check with me first."

This husband had committed financial infidelity!

Two hundred and fifty dollars may not appear much for fancy sneakers in the 2020s, but in early 2000, that was a hefty sum.

Their arrangement was that they would both deposit their paychecks in the account and pay bills from there, as well as use it for personal expenses. Big mistake!

This young couple apparently did not have a proper plan in place for their finances. They functioned under the common belief that once married, you and your partner "become one" in every sense of the way, including your money.

No sir and no ma'am!

As adults, each person has obligations and desires of their own, based on lifestyle, past experiences, or aspirations. This is even more relevant in cases of mature adults who may have had previous marriages or relationships, and children.

There are several factors that can affect how one views and manages their money. For example, there is *the lifestyle I am accustomed to.* One also hears the: *"I earn X, I am entitled to spending X."* Also consider the *"I have child support that cuts into my earnings,"* or *"I have family that depend on me for support."*

The first example reflects my philosophy. The last two applied to my situation when Henri and I became serious. I had worked very hard to build a comfortable lifestyle for myself including living in a luxury condo and sustaining a social life that included nights out and travel. Although we earned about the same amount in salary, I was concerned whether my then boyfriend would be able to help me sustain the lifestyle I sought to maintain and even upgrade. He was paying child support for two underage children and had a slew of family back in Haiti that he supports to this day.

In dating there is a lot of "observe and learn" that is supposed to be followed by "communicate and plan."

From the beginning Henri demonstrated that he was responsible in meeting his obligations. At the time he was paying the child support directly to his ex-wife by mutual agreement. I observed how every two weeks he would religiously make a money drop in Brooklyn. I even dropped it off for him on occasions when he could not make the trip. - This was before Zelle and Cash App. - The regularity was also present when it came to sending money to his mom or other relatives back home.

Hum! I thought. *Dependable.* Observe and learn.

He maintained a nice apartment for himself and had been there a while. *Okay, consistency.* Observe and learn.

We eventually got to the point of knowing how much we each earned. I was pleased to note that although my salary at the time was slightly higher, that did not stop Henri from stepping up when it came to spending on dates or travel. At the same time, we had an understanding that these were shared experiences and since we were both able to, we would share the expenses in a practical way. He was then and still is an old school guy who likes to be "the man" by paying for stuff. Having slightly more disposable income, sometimes I treat or we share the cost.

What is important is the fluidity of our transactions. There is no showing off or hang up on either side. We learned to be a team, and in a team, whoever can score that goal or basket, does. It does not matter who, so long as you win the game.

We observed, we learned, communicated, and planned.

◇◇◇

"You're the man," she said. "It's your responsibility to pay the bills. My money is my money."

This was an older family member, who still believed in the man being the sole provider, talking to her husband. She lavished on her children (car paid for in cash) and put her money in a secret bank account with the purpose of leaving them an inheritance.

"I bought a new car," our young cousin said, but I let De'Andre keep it so he can take the baby to daycare."

Brianna had dated and broken off from this young man who had been her first love. During an on again, off again episode she had gotten pregnant. The adults, including me, could tell that the guy was not interested in the relationship, even with a baby on the way. But Brianna being young and inexperienced as I remember being once myself, thought she could win him over with the baby and by supporting him. He was living at home with his mother at the time and pursuing an unstable career in show business.

Both situations are the extremes of a pattern of not being on the same page with your partner. In one case, the older relative engaged in financial infidelity. She hid her assets, and left all responsibilities on the man's shoulder, regardless of how much he made or how much he could use her additional income for the household. On the other end of the spectrum, the young woman took it all on her shoulders, even buying the guy a car, failing to hold him accountable for any financial responsibilities.

How do you avoid creating a situation that can foster financial infidelity?

By the time you decide to become a couple, whether by cohabitation or by marriage, you better have a serious sit-down conversation about your finances that includes a plan on how you will operate. Remember I indicated in earlier discussions that dating and marriage are akin to a business partnership? Well, you do not want to run the risk of a breach of contract in the form of financial infidelity.

A company would not merge with another without first disclosing all financial information and outlining a plan of operation that details very specific terms or scenarios. The following table provides some guidelines by taking business questions or propositions, and connecting them to situations relevant to relationships.

Business questions or propositions (Business)

Answers based on personal situations (Personal)

Business: How much of an investment is each party bringing to the table?

Personal: Current salary/income or future earnings

Business: What are the assets being placed on this agreement?

Personal: Homes, cars, real estate, pensions, government benefits, investments, etc.

Business: What assets are being excluded from this agreement and will remain sole benefit of individual owner?

Personal: Personal savings, IRA, spousal support from previous marriage, previous homes, or cars, etc.

Business: What are the mutual obligations that this partnership will incur?

Personal: Rent/mortgage, utilities, food, insurance, school tuition, maintenance, vacations, etc.

Business: In what format will the partnership handle common expenses or obligations?

Personal: A common pool/joint account (best), or each party responsible for a set of expenses.

Business: What percentage of common expenses will each party be responsible for?

Personal: Split 50/50, 60/40, 70/30, etc. Based on income capacity or who can or wants to carry the heavier load?

Business: Who will handle or administer the processing?

Personal: Choose who will keep track of and pay the bills based on personal ability for management or preference.

Business: What are individual obligations?

Personal: School loan, child support, parent or spousal support, personal credit cards, car loans, previous mortgages, etc.

Business: What happens in case of decreased or increased revenues (income shift)?

Personal: Job loss, reduced salary, promotion, higher paid job, etc. Reevaluate percentages.

This may appear crude if you look at a relationship simply from the perspective of romance, but the truth is, all relationships are also business arrangements that require a level of objectivity.

Failing to prepare and plan for a successful financial partnership can lead to severe losses when financial infidelity comes into the picture.

In a February 16, 2024 *MoneyWise* article on Yahoo titled, "I'm Contemplating Bankruptcy…" writer Sabina Wex reports about a woman, K. R, who lost $500,000 worth of savings, a mortgage-free home and inherited a ton of debts, because of her husband's financial infidelity.

"A lack of openness around money may be a sign of financial infidelity," the writer said.

She noted that according to a Bread Financial survey, nearly half of people in relationships admitted to financial deceit, including hiding outstanding credit card balances and expensive purchases. The article also mentioned that 48% of respondents uncovered surprises when they started sharing one or more bank accounts with their partners – some of them were good ones, while others, such as frivolous spending habits and bad credit, were not so good.

A successful financial partnership boils down to three essential things: honesty, trust, and transparency.

In addition, a degree of vulnerability is also required, where one is willing to be open about everything concerning yourself, including your finances.

I will caution that everyone should always have their eyes wide open in all circumstances to protect themselves. Trust is not something you bestow on someone just because it is expected. **Trust is earned**. The recipient must prove themselves trustworthy and that takes a bit of time as you observe each other and experience circumstances that show you how a person handles situations and responds to crises. Are they open with you? Are they able to handle things responsibly? Have they demonstrated that they have your back? Do they take the time to run things by you or keep you apprised of what is going on? Do they show that they are in it for what is beneficial to both of you, even sometimes putting you first?

The woman referred to in the article let her husband handle everything and she never noticed that money was being siphoned out and credit cards, including those under her name, were not being paid. From my perspective, that is negligence on her part. Regardless of who is handling the financial administration, both parties should have regular reporting to be aware of what is going on.

Observe and learn. Communicate and plan.

Most of all, avoid costly surprises.

How my husband and I apply these concepts

I promised you from the onset that in addition to talking about others, I would also be candid with my own history. This then brings me to a personal analysis of how my husband and I handle our finances.

While Henri and I dated, we shared expenses in turn as the occasion called for. When he proposed after a few years into our relationship, we agreed that he could move in with me in the condo that I owned at the time so we could save money for a future wedding. One evening he asked me to have a talk about how we were going to handle the bills. I told him what the mortgage and other utilities ran monthly, and explained that the two roommates I had at the time helped me defray the cost of maintaining the household. He asked me to give him a couple of days to figure out his budget.

When we talked again, he offered that he took his other obligations and child support in consideration and would be able to contribute X amount to the household expenses monthly. He passed his apartment to his brother and moved in with me. I also discontinued my roommates. That amount was adjusted over time whenever necessary. We also both contributed to other expenses, taking turns paying for or sharing the cost for food shopping, home repairs and other incidentals.

To keep things simpler, we opened a joint account where we each deposit our portion of the household expenses every month. All household bills are paid from that account, leaving each of us the freedom to have and use our personal bank accounts to our liking. So, my dropping $300 on spring clothes at Burlington or buying a $150 French perfume at Macy's is not his concern. Likewise, him expediting a $200 Western Union to a distant cousin or buying yet another pair of sneakers when his closet is full of them, is none of my business.

After years of being together, we even have the passwords to each other's accounts – (complete trust). We are aware of the accounts' statuses; we see the statements; we occasionally log in to each other's accounts to process an emergency transaction for the other. But neither one of us finds it necessary to spy on what the other does with "their" money.

We sold the condo when we decided to relocate to Houston, Texas. I shared some of the proceeds of the sale with him because he had been instrumental in my being able to keep that property for several years. When we bought a new home in Texas, we went half and half on the down payment, as equal partners. We continue to share our common expenses and big house repairs (like a bathroom remodel) equally. However, we have no problem with the occasional solo projects that whoever wants it, pays for it.

Guess who is always spending on redecorating the house? Moi! This former designer has these flights of fancy where I am repainting a room, changing drapes, and redoing a whole décor. After all, everything must flow spectacularly for the Diva!

Henri and I have never had an argument or misunderstanding regarding finances. He will occasionally tell me I am spending too much.

My reply, "I am spending the inheritance, darling. My nieces and nephews are okay and I do not have children to leave it to. I worked hard for it, so I may as well enjoy it myself while God is giving me this time on the planet."

To which he acknowledges: "Do your thing, baby."

Henri and I from the very beginning applied the recipe I mentioned earlier, the **three essential things: honesty, trust, and transparency.** Throughout our years together, we cultivated the formula to attain the space of complete comfort and dependency where we are today, even while being independent.

MARRIED LIFE

I am on a mission to help as many people as possible reach that coveted goal of enjoying a loving, long-term, successful, committed relationship.

Danielle

From what I have observed, every relationship has three phases, starting with the beginning or developing period, followed by the maturity stage, then the fully established state. When you get married or set up house together, you start all over again with the process of learning about each other. Every day you discover things about the person, as they are now visible in a different light. They are no longer in the ephemeral, "we are dating." They are in the "we are doing life together" serious, and supposedly permanent category.

Yes, my love. It is not a done deal. Marriage is a continuous progression that becomes more intuitive as you learn about each other and become more responsive to one another. It takes time, like every good thing. You must be patient with the process and yourselves.

I am not a licensed professional who dispenses scientific facts or statistics regarding marriage. However, I am an observer of life who has been studying people over four decades of my adult life. I have been blessed with a successful marriage and I listen to and process other people's stories, including the couples who participated in the survey. Consequently, I have learned a thing or two about what it takes to make a romantic partnership work.

We will first review the composition of the population that completed the survey, to establish a general profile associated with the view or information they offered to the discussion. Then, we will analyze responses to ten of their questions that were like the ones asked of the singles. Their answers will help us compare and determine which steps and processes led to their successfully committing to their relationship.

The respondents were a diverse group, with 84% of them legally married and 16% in a common law established relationship.

Most of them (45%) have been together for between 11-20 years;

- 21% of them for 6-10 years;
- 16% for one to five years and
- 18% for more than 26 years.

The majority of them (73%) have between 1 and 3 children.

- 9% of them have 4+ children, and
- 18% have no children

The children's age ranged as follows:

- 67% are age 6 - 12 years old
- 28% are age 18+
- 11% are 13 – 17
- 8% are under age 5

The answers they provided to the first question will be helpful for the singles who are still searching, as this can be considered proven data.

<u>Question 1:</u>

The survey asked couples, "**Where did you meet each other?**"

Covid 19 may have affected the number one result: work, since a lot of individuals are now working from home. However, it is still a viable forum for meeting new people.

Work	22%
Social Event/Party	20%
Online Dating Apps	17%
Introduced by friends	12%
Public Place	12%
Other	10%
Church	7%
Bar	5%
Introduced by Family Members	5%
Random Meeting	5%
Membership Organization	2%

I chuckled when I noticed that bars, introduction by family members and random meetings fared equally at 5%. Nevertheless, these numbers indicate overall that you could meet a partner in various ways and at diverse places. One couple, Kerry, a divorcé who had almost given up on love, and Renea, a widow, met on the website Farmers.com. They confessed that neither one of them was a farmer.

Question 2:

When asked what were **the first three things that attracted them** to their partner, it was no surprise that looks were the number one factor for both sexes.

Category	Women	Men
Looks/Physical Appearance	83%	84%
Intellect	57%	35%
Personality/Creativity	51%	49%
Charm or self-confidence	34%	38%
Attentive/Caring	29%	32%
Instant Connection	9%	16%
Position/Title	9%	22%

The numbers run very similar for both sides, except for "Intellect" where there is a marked difference. This is one area where it mattered more for the women than it did for the men.

There is also a wider margin for "Instant Connection" where the men feel more strongly about it. The category for "Position/Title" is a bit of a puzzle to me, with men coming in at a much higher percentage than women.

Are men liking high achievers as well? I was under the impression that women looked at men's position. I am learning.

Question 3:

The next question asked was: **"Did you both feel ready for a long-term relationship or marriage when you met each other?"**
The responses were as follows:

Husband was, 49%   Wife was, 23%   Both of us were, 28%

This shows that a certain level of readiness is necessary to ensure the parties come together for that merger. In my opinion, it is even better when both parties are or the man is. If a man is ready, he will take the necessary steps and do what he must do to secure the relationship and initiate a partnership. When just the woman is, she will have to do some convincing to stir the man in the right direction.

Question 4:

Next, respondents were asked to **reflect on their desired preferences** in their pre-marital search for a partner.

Did you both have a specific list of requirements or preferences for your potential mate that included the desired traits and the deal breakers?

The responses were:

Both of us did -   49%   Neither of us did - 7%

Husband did -   26%   Wife did - 1   9%

<u>Question 5:</u>

We followed that question with one I am sure was a chuckle when the couple looked at it together.

On a scale of 5-10 how much of your list did your mate meet that lead to the decision to become an established couple or marry?

To soften its potential for bad feelings I added a note: *"Lovers rarely, if ever meet 100% of your list; we will assume that they hit at least half, since you did couple up or marry. No shade."* The scale given was from 5 to 10, accentuated with a smiley emoji.

	Women	**Men**
9 - 10	24%	23%
7 - 8	63%	65%
5 - 6	13%	13%

This table supports investment guru, Warren Buffett's suggestion to "lower your expectations" or in my view "<u>manage</u> your expectations." The results show most people do go with their list, but to varying degrees. The closer the match, we assume the better the odds for success. However, so long as the partners meet at least half their respective expectations, and they are willing to work at the relationship, everyone achieves success. Proof is in the pudding, most of the respondents have been married from six to twenty years, and a good number for over twenty-six.

<u>Question 6:</u>

The survey also asked: **"Did either of you need to adjust anything in your thinking or lifestyle to be more compatible with your mate once you confirmed a true interest or potential? If yes, who did and what?"**

CJ, an airline mechanic said he "had to let go of his lust for other women." That is one of the things the romance movies get right. When you meet someone who touches that button on your heart, everybody else fades away. At least, they should, if you want to make room for the true love relationship to grow.

Pastor Jackie, my church pastor, mentioned the age difference being one of the challenges she encountered in the early days of her connecting with her husband, who is a little over a decade older than she is. I have found that when you are in your twenties, and still young and growing, being with someone older may present some challenges, because you are from different generations and may enjoy different things. However, as you mature, you either draw closer if you are truly compatible, or grow apart as you develop into your true self, which may be a different person. Both being equally yoked, my pastors' marriage blossomed and thrived.

Harry* a contractor, confessed to him learning to pick up after himself and Sally* an underwriting assistant, practicing letting go of the small things.

I can absolutely relate to that last one. I am mildly OCD and prefer things in a designated space, in containers, in drawers, but not loitering around on the counter. Henri likes to leave things where he used it. *"Hello, didn't you take this out of the cabinet? Why is it still on the counter?"* Do I walk around the house, scoffing fifteen times a day? Absolutely! However, I have a mental lips pincher that I use frequently. I force myself to only address the egregious instances of disorder. Otherwise, I would be a nagging wife.

Brandon, an IT professional, indicated that he had to "learn to be more caring and compassionate." He explained that by nature he is "very dry" and his wife Erian, a Learning & Development specialist, is very sensitive. When you really want the relationship, you are willing to work at making it better.

Maurice, an interior designer who met his common law partner in college, said that he had to "Learn how to be comfortable with who I am and trust that I could be loved."

We talked about knowing yourself well in the dating process, and being cognizant of what you want.

The segue from that is, **loving yourself in an organic way that will allow you to love others authentically, and to fully embrace <u>accepting</u>**

love from others.

Question 7:

When it came to **how soon in the relationship the respondents knew that this was their person,** the answers varied from first date, to two weeks, or one month, one year, two years to five years. This shows that sometimes that instant connection is the real thing, but most often it is more like opening an overflowing gift bag. Each layer brings successive "Oohs" and "Aahs" and you realize that you love everything in that package. The love thing develops as you discover about each other. Then you just know.

Question 8:

How long were you dating before you decided to make a life together or became officially engaged?

The answers were as varied as the individual relationships.

5 – 7 years	38%
1 year or less	31%
2 – 4 years	19%
8 + years	12%

I am gauging that if two people are where they want to be in life and career, making the decision to become engaged happens quickly. They know what they want and they are ready to proceed. In religious circles, engagement periods are also shorter. If the parties are serious about a vow of celibacy, that eliminates a lot of the things couples enjoy together, including sex, sleep overs and traveling for leisure.

Most commonly, as the survey shows, people take time to get to know their partner, resolve troublesome issues and build a career before committing. That process can take several years.

In my case, within one year I knew Henri was someone I would like to marry. I had learned enough about him to recognize him as a suitable and desirable mate. However, several months into our dating, I discovered that he was still legally married to his ex. They had been living separately for a couple of years, but there had not been a divorce. I almost ended the relationship because at the time I had begun a more serious walk in my religious life. He vowed that he was working on it. I reasoned to myself that if God had sent me this man who was apparently an answer to my prayers, maybe I was to give him and the relationship a chance. It took some time till he finally told me one evening that his divorce was imminent, if the ex-wife did not contest it. By the time he finally proposed, it was almost four years after first meeting him. This was a case where unresolved issues had to be addressed first.

Full disclosure, originally Henri intended to wait until his daughters, who were eleven and thirteen at the time, reached eighteen years old. Like a lot of men prefer to do, he wanted to compartmentalize his relationships, perhaps thinking,

"Let me take care of the kids for now, to avoid drama, then once done with that, I will consider marriage."

I was vocal about my feelings. "No can do my dear. Your youngest daughter will be eighteen in seven years. Sorry, I am not waiting that long to be married."

I knew what I wanted, a married life with a compatible mate. Fortunately for me, Henri's feelings were strong enough that he decided if marriage was necessary to be with me, he was willing to take that chance.

Notice I use the term "take that chance." Because when you marry someone, you are taking a chance on them and on love. There is no guarantee that it's going to work. The best that you can do is prepare seriously, go in with both eyes wide open, and be ready to work on the marriage because you feel strongly about the relationship, and see enough potential to propel you to take that leap of faith.

Question 9:

Respondents were asked, when the couple decided to live together.

Most of the participants moved in together after engagement (52%), some lived together before engagement (29%) and a small group, (19%) waited until marriage. Henri sublet his apartment to his younger brother and moved in with me when we became engaged. He always jokes that he kept the apartment in case I kicked him out. Wise man that one.

Unfortunately, there have been situations where someone gave up their place or even moved to a different state, and the engagement did not work out. They found themselves homeless or in search of an abode. Like I said, it all boils down to taking a chance. One never knows. Do one?

Question 10:

The question was, "Is this a first marriage for you?"

The answers were:

First time for both 46%

First time for wife 42%

First time for husband   12%

If you are over the age of 35, the likelihood of one partner having been married before or having children is more of a possibility. If that is your situation, I want you to remember this.

Auntie Wisdom: Each relationship is unique, based on the dynamics between the two specific individuals. Do not compare. And do not expect that this person you are currently with is going to behave or be like your ex.

To be fair, you must take every person on his or her own merit. That is one of the reasons it is so important to really know your person. I am sure you're aware of what happens when you "ass-u-me." So, avoid speculation and instead, be wise and be transparent.

TESTS AND CRISES

In scientific circles testing is a required component of any process. New model cars are tested for their performance and safety. Vaccines and new medications go through trials of various sort to assess their effectiveness and identify possible side effects. Recipes are tried for compatibility and measurement of its ingredients. Even Christians speak of the tests of faith, when circumstances challenge us to rely on God's goodness and favor.

A relationship, especially a marriage, is a process that also experiences tests. Things happen that challenge its reliability, function, strength, and endurance. Sometimes they are minor inconveniences that can be resolved quickly, but often they are major crises that shake the foundation of the partnership.

My marriage, as well as that of most of the survey respondents, was tested in various ways.

The survey provided a few common issues or challenges that people might experience during their committed partnership or marriage. These are the percentages for the answers that they chose.

Affairs	15%
Major illness	15%
Job loss	29%
Loss of a child	5%

Loss of a parent	7%
Physical separation- long distance for job	7%
Other	22%

Where there are crises, there must be emergency measures to respond to what is affecting the health of the relationship. A couple must decide together what processes they will use to address or resolve their crises. Open communication is key, always. Talk about how whatever happened is affecting you and enlist your partner's cooperation and support in dealing with it.

For example, "job loss" garnered the highest percentage as a challenge couples may face. Losing one's earning is a huge deal for anyone who is used to bringing in their own money and the ability to spend as they please. It is an even bigger issue for men, as they are supposed to be the provider. In my experience, men who went through a layoff while I was involved with them went through a kind of depression. It was as though they had been demoted from Vice President of Corporate Affairs to Member of the Janitorial Staff. A woman must be patient, supportive and encouraging in those times. You must become stronger to shoulder the emotional and possibly the financial load, and by the same token, keep building your mate up to reassure him that he's still the VP in charge.

I did say that relationship is work, right?

The survey also asked, "How did you survive the crisis?"

The participants obviously used more than one method to correct their situation, based on the numbers shown.

Communication and re-commitment	63%
Therapy/counseling	29%
Prayers	53%
Re-set expectation	37%

| Patience and work it out | 29% |
| Other | 8% |

No relationship or marriage is immune from trouble. It happens to regular folks like you and me and to celebrities and rich people. **Trouble is one of those things that connects all humans in that it is irrespective of race, financial status, or education.**

America Got Talent host Terry Crews and his wife Rebecca are reported to have overcome years of cheating and addiction. These challenges could have ruined their marriage. Fortunately for them, they worked it out and have been together for thirty-five years as of this writing.

Rapper Ja Rule and his wife Aisha celebrated 23 years of marriage in 2024. The Atkins experienced a tough challenge when the rapper spent two years in prison due to a conviction of gun possession and tax evasion back in 2011. The couple made it through the crisis and are still going strong.

Couples take the blows together and sustain each other through the assaults. Rock*, a facilities director and Faith*, a nurse, survived Faith's cancer battle, which brought them closer. Charles F.* and Shannon, an entertainer (*Let the Music Play*) went through the loss of a child and other family members. They all indicated that using the recovery methods listed a few paragraphs back, helped them survive the crisis and even strengthened their bond.

One couple Harry* and Sally* mentioned struggling through drug addiction. They are still determined to keep going, citing "We can handle anything with The Lord."

<u>Auntie Wisdom:</u> Significant changes that you go through can either break a relationship or secure the bond. When you face life's challenges and discover that this person supports you and stands by you, you know you have a true partner.

◊◊◊

My marriage experienced a challenge that lasted longer than I would have preferred.

My husband and I lived in a commuter marriage for a period of ten years, with him living and working in New York and me in Houston, Texas. We had decided to relocate from New Jersey to Houston, where the cost of living was cheaper and my closest sister resides. We had purchased a house there in preparation for our eventual move and rented it out while we both continued working up north. I eventually resigned from my compliance job in New York and moved down to Houston. Henri was supposed to follow in a year or two, but realized later that the salaries down south were much lower than up north. He was also a few years away from retirement and a lower salary would have meant reduced social security benefits.

While we saw each other every other month, it was different from living together on a day-to-day basis. We joked about him being on a "tourist visa" when he visited me and looked forward to him signing up for a "permanent visa." That is an immigrant joke that might resonate with some of you more readily than others. The point is that when we saw each other during our bi-monthly visits, it was a honeymoon of sort. We both wanted to make the best of the few days we had together.

As time went on, I became more and more agitated about us living separate lives. I was married but felt like a single woman. I did not have my husband on the pillow next to me in the bed. *Well, some people don't have a husband at all,* I reasoned. I was socializing by myself, to the point where some people did not even realize I was married. Any little crisis, like a problem with plumbing, would send me into an "I'm all by myself" pity party. I was tired of the physical separation.

Several years in, my husband started going through a strange episode, where he appeared unsure of where he wanted to live. One moment he was building on his family property in Haiti; next time he talked about visiting

Cuba to buy a piece of land. Houston did not appear to be a destination of choice. Then every year that I thought would be the last of us being separated, he'd announce that "next year..." I felt like we were disconnecting, as if we were just going through the motions. I began to get depressed and prayed about it.

God, is this the end of us? Does he want an out? I accept your will for me on this. You gave me this husband, but if this is supposed to end here, your will be done.

What happens next is nothing short of God's sense of humor demonstrated in his mighty power. I had a Facebook account for years, but in the early days of the platform, I rarely checked my Messenger, to limit the junk contacts. One day I decided to open it and found a four months old message from my ex-fiancé, the young medical student in Haiti, who was now a renown surgeon in New York. He had been living on Long Island, New York for years and since I had stepped away from the Haitian circle when I was with Joe, we never ran into each other or reconnected.

In his message, he expressed how overjoyed he was to find me. He had been heart-broken when I broke off our engagement and looked for me for years. He was thrilled I was still singing – he listened to my CD. We first met when I was 16 and he was 20. I was preparing for a concert with a pianist who was his best friend's father and he became attracted to me when he heard me sing. We reconnected when I was 19 and began a long-distance courtship that led to our engagement.

I was shocked! I had looked for him as well, but this was before social media and the sophistication of internet searches. I thought maybe he had gone to Africa, as this was one of his post-graduation options. I was glad for the opportunity to apologize for ending the relationship. I confessed to being scared. *"I was too young and wasn't sure the life offered was what I wanted,"* I said.

I took my time scripting my response. I knew this was something I would have to share with my husband; and I did not want anything to appear inappropriate. After all, this was an ex-lover. I made a point to mention that I was happily married, no kids.

He replied to my message and shared that he was married to a doctor (psychiatrist) and had a daughter who was a lawyer and a son at NYU (New York University) earning an MBA. – A quintessential professional family, in true middle class Haitian fashion. In response to my not having children, he said something about "the kids we could have had." I kept my message generic with a "Nice hearing from you."

A few days later Henri and I had a conversation in which the topic of exes came up. I seize the opportunity to share my news.

"By the way," I said. "You'll never guess who reached out to me on Facebook."

I told him about the Facebook message. Henri did not flinch. He just said, "Mm-hmm." But when I showed up in New Jersey for my conjugal visit a month later, out of the blue he asked:

"Let me see that message your ex-boyfriend sent you?"

"You sure you want to see it?" I confirmed.

"Yes. I want to see it."

"Okay," I said. I turned on my laptop, signed on to Facebook and brought up the message. I handed him the device and walked away.

Several minutes later, he came and handed me the laptop. He said nothing. I asked nothing. He had been satisfied that I conducted myself properly.

Let me tell you how God works! From that day on Henri became the model husband. Solicitous, attentive, loving. What happened? We had been going through such a choppy, rough patch. What caused this reversal?

I surmise that Henri saw this "successful New York surgeon" who could have been my husband, who spoke to me with such high regards and enthusiasm; and there he was, the one who had me, and he was taking me for granted.

The funny thing is, this message sat in my inbox for months. God had me open it at precisely the moment when I was feeling shaky about my marriage and most needed a boost to my ego. This incident turned out to be the thing that turned my husband around to start appreciating me again and demonstrating it.

This crisis was averted and Henri and I continued our long-distance marriage, but I was getting tired of being separated. In the beginning it had felt like an adventure and there were times when we even met at a vacation destination, like lovers. But as the years dragged on, the fun of it wore off. I wanted my husband with me.

My husband is old-fashioned in that he believes a man should be able to take care of a family's financial situation. I wish he would have won the lotto. Unfortunately, the salaries offered in Houston could not match what he was making in New York as a fire safety manager, a position that became plentiful and in demand after September 11, 2001, in New York where you have a lot of high-rise buildings.

He had a financial plan to earn a high salary to boost his social security retirement benefits. He also wanted to save some money and pay down his debts before retirement. Sound and wise plan. That did nothing to alleviate my discomfort at being separated. So, I prayed. I got on my knees and prayed for strength, for wisdom and for patience.

I resigned myself to giving him the time that he needed to make the decision to move. I did not want to be responsible for any deviations in his plans if I pushed for it when he was not ready.

The sudden death of a teacher friend I collaborated with on a daily basis was the final blow that accelerated my feelings on the matter of our separation. I could not take it anymore! I even stopped flying to New York on alternate visits. I no longer wanted a "tourist visa." I wrote a long letter to Henri (forever a writer) and expressed what I was going through: too many years apart, life is unpredictable, we are both getting old, this uncertainty is unbearable, should I move back to New York, do you want to move somewhere else, do you still want us together…

Henri reassured me that the plan was still the same, just on delayed timing. He would definitely make the move to Houston by the end of the year. "I'll believe it when I see it," I replied. At that point I was prepared that a full separation might be imminent. I was done!

A few months later he told me that he was turning over his apartment and would stay with one of his friends a couple of weeks to finish closing out his affairs before he came down.

When he called to give me his flight information for the trip that would be his permanent move to Houston, I just said, "Okay." When I got off the phone however, I bounced around the room in a joyous praise dance as I shouted: "Halleluiah! Thank you, Jesus!"

◊◊◊
Adjusting after the storm

In the same way that re-building and repairs are necessary after a storm, adjustments may be required after a crisis is averted or a status quo is upended. Things may be different. Expectations may have to change. Be willing and be prepared to adjust.

Parents who become empty nesters for example may have to re-learn their mates in the absence of children. What do you have in common, what do you enjoy? Who is this person you are waking up to everyday? Your conversations and your activities are now related to the two of you, not the children. How do you re-connect as a couple, instead of parents? Take time to re-discover each other on a personal level and extend yourself as in courtship, to rekindle the personal relationship.

When Henri and I finally reunited as a cohabitating couple, if was as though we had to learn about each other all over again. My need to be organized annoyed him as it appeared I was constantly nitpicking. In turn, his little quirks, and the way he did things got on my nerves and I was often vocal about it to express my frustration.

One day I was yapping away and the dear man looked at me and said, "Why are you screaming at me?"

I stammered, "Huh..." stumped for an answer.

"I am so sorry," I finally came up with.

I realized right then and there that we needed to address the elephant in the room. We had gotten unused to each other's quirks and mannerism. I am a methodical freak who organizes stuff in categories and have a system for everything. This will come in handy, if God forbid, I should ever have memory lapses. Dear hubby on the other hand is leave-everything-where-it-is, as though, if he doesn't see it, he won't know where it is. I am always fixing and moving and re-arranging. This prompts a frequent refrain, "Dani, where is my x, y and z?"

"Baby, we need to talk about this," I told my husband.

"We have both forgotten about each other's ways. We have been living separately for a while and need to re-learn how to adjust to each other. But I am concerned about the way I responded to you because you got on my nerves. In the future, if you see me flying off the handle on nonsense, can you please crack a joke to bring me down?"

He agreed.

The first time he used that technique, it took me a while to catch on. I was carrying on about some nonsense, all flustered and voice elevated. He replied deadpan with something totally unrelated that made absolutely no sense. Can't even remember what now. But it was as silly as "The weather forecast predicted snow today," while we were in the middle of a Houston perpetual heat wave.

I looked at him puzzled. "Huh?"

He broke into a mischievous grin and I recognized that whatever he said was the clue for me to bring it down a couple of notches.

Since then, our arguments are less frequent and less severe. If the matter is inconsequential (as domestic matters usually are, i.e., unwashed dishes, socks on the floor), we turn it into a joke, resulting in a lot of laughter in our household. If it is a serious issue, we sit down and analyze it with cool heads to determine what is in our best interest as a couple.

◊◊◊

Inevitable Arguments and Disagreements

<u>Auntie Wisdom</u>: Arguments are inevitable. The key to keeping the peace is how you handle a misunderstanding or disagreement during, and after.

"F@x#*^?!" He snarled.

"Hey. You know I hate cussing" I snapped.

"Well, I am mad! F@x#*^?!" He retorted and proceeded to spew a heap of expletives in French and in Creole. *"Merde. Foutre. Tonnere.!"*

"Okay then, F@x#*^?!" I screamed and stomped off.

What? No! …Yes. Cool heads my foot! My darling husband and I were having an argument. One of those "I'm mad-you're-unreasonable, I don't care-go dive in a pile of manure" kind of moments. Thankfully for us, those only happen about once a year and are short-lived.

I am not one to cuss, but my husband is very vocal when upset. This man, who often struggles with the English language, suddenly becomes so fluent when anger prompts him, with cuss words spilling out of him, like vomit from a churned stomach. So, Ms. Thang sometimes loses her restraint and tosses them right back, careful not to add any seasonings, as my wordsmith brain suggests.

I could very well come back with, "You calling me ugly? You. Are. UGLY!

A monkey sees you coming, looks at itself in the mirror, and starts singing, *"I feel pretty!"*

Additional commentaries would for sure fan the flames and prolong the argument. I force myself to be an echo, repeating back to you only the exact thing you spat at me. Wisdom prevails.

News flash! **Happy couples have arguments all the time,** some benign, some more severe. Remember you are two different species (man/woman) trying to co-exist on the same planet (a relationship or home). As author John Gray confirmed in his book, *"Men Are from Mars, Women Are from Venus,"* we are different.

Further, you are two individuals working to maintain commonality in a working relationship. Very often, each of you is going to see, process or receive things differently, resulting in clashes that are at times hostile. Henri is fond of referring to this Haitian proverb for these situations:

"The tongue and teeth reside in the same mouth, but every once in a while, the teeth will accidently bite the tongue."

The full story? Hubby and I had an awesome Valentine the weekend before and were marking a twenty-plus years anniversary in two days. Earlier that morning, I had made what I assumed would be a funny comment about a habit of his. He blew up in response, taking it to be a put down. He was so incensed he mentioned the word separation. I am one of those who measures my words even when I am angry, and only say what I mean. I was shocked.

"Do you realize what you just said? I told him. "What was so serious that you had to go that far?" I continued.

In my native culture of Haiti, people go back and forth in an argument, intent on winning their side of it. My personal preference is a succinct discussion, where we alternate giving viewpoints and evidences and come to a quick meeting of the minds.

In true form, Henri kept on and on, even after I explained myself and offered an apology. Finally, I announced I was walking away. I had to go to work.

I thought about the incident the rest of the afternoon. Is this how couples end up separating, over stupid, insignificant stuff that get blown out of proportion?

Later, when I got home, I tried to re-open the conversation to add what I had meditated on all afternoon.

"You want to talk about what happened this morning. Maybe there is an underlying issue that we need to address."

I proposed a solution to his apprehension about something he had mentioned earlier. Pouf! Gasoline on the fire.

The exchange you saw a few lines back, was him slinging it and me trying to avoid fueling it further.

I am of the belief that what is said in anger, is usually something festering in the heart, that one can no longer hold in at that moment. Once it comes out, it cannot be taken back. The consequences can be mild or severe, depending on the seriousness of the issue. Therefore, be wise and know your person.

My husband is the sweetest guy, in general. When he is upset however, he is a beast with words. It is a learned skill with Haitians, how to give a "*jouman*" – hurl insults that hurt. I don't have it and never cared to acquire it, because I hate arguments. I am of the "let's discuss this and come to a solution" school of thought.

In March 2023, rapper Ice-T appeared on an E! News interview with Francesca Amiker where he revealed secrets to his successful twenty plus years marriage to model Coco Austin. He compared marriage to a movie that includes a variety of scene: fun ones, sad ones, though ones and even fights. He observed that unfortunately, a lot of people sign up for the enjoyable parts only, not the whole movie.

Ice-T hit the nail on its head. Relationships and marriage encompass all the literary genres. There is romance that can at times transfer to romantic comedy, there are tragedies and sad scenes, there is plenty of drama, you will experience exciting adventures, fun times, and yes, sometimes go through "quasi" fight scenes. I buffer my comment with "quasi," when it comes to fight, because I do not believe one should ever get physical or verbally abusive with a partner.

"Okay Auntie, how do you handle a disagreement?" You may ask.

Glad you asked darling!

It is a refined art that requires all parties to be fully committed. That means when this partner gets on your last freaking nerve, **you are willing to keep in mind the good stuff to buffer your reaction.** Let's take a look at how this might play out.

First you must establish a blueprint, a mode of operation for arguments, based on personalities and or strength. This can be informal – a note to self, or a casual conversation between the two of you where you agree to some simple rules of engagement that will work for both of you.

- Identify who is most likely to fly off the handle, – my husband.
- Who is more tempered and willing to keep things on a leveled tone, me.

Consequently, whenever something flares up, I immediately go into diffuse mode. I state my concern calmly. If that doesn't work, I shit gear. I will make my point later. Right then, the important thing is to de-escalate.

De-escalating a situation may take various forms and necessitate quick thinking, something that is very hard to do when you are upset.

- Be quick to say "I am sorry." - "I am sorry you misunderstood."
- Remind the other person that you care. "I am sorry you feel hurt. I did not mean to hurt you."
- Request to be heard. "I just want you to be aware that…" "I feel that "
- Be willing to listen. "I hear what you are saying. What can I do to make things better."

If a calmer approach does not work to bring the other party down, postpone the discussion.

- Maybe we can discuss this later when we have both cooled down.
- Can we postpone this discussion for another time when I can really listen to you.

Full disclosure. What usually comes out of my mouth is more like:

- Let's talk about this later when you can act more civilized.

You get my point. It is important to show your partner a willingness to listen to their side and reach common ground to resolve a disagreement.

Auntie Wisdom: Everyone seeks to be heard and to be understood. Your willingness to be flexible and listen is a vital component in providing a safe space for your partner.

After that screaming match and toe-to-toe repartee, we both went on about our business in different parts of the house and barely exchanged a word. At bedtime Henri gathered his pajamas and headed for the guest bedroom. I turned off my lamp and went to sleep.

The next morning when we crossed path in the kitchen, he tossed a sheepish *"Bonjour voisine!"* – Good morning good neighbor!

"Good morning," I replied in a neutral tone.

"I already boiled water for our morning tea," he said.

"Thank you." I acknowledged.

And that was it. His offer to resume our domesticated routine was a peace offering. I accepted it. We could now move on.

Henri had needed time to cool off the previous night, and judging by how soundly I slept in the bed <u>alone</u>, so did I. That morning, not a word of the argument. It was done and gone.

Forgiveness! How much couples must practice that skill. It applies when it relates to the big stuff, but is even more imperative when the cause of disagreement is something benign. God knew we would need to take this seriously when He taught us to forgive as He has forgiven us. When you truly love someone, you should not hold a grudge. That is a dark specter threatening to tint every interaction. And Lord knows how negative vibes can spiral into discontent and disconnect.

<u>Auntie Wisdom</u>: Be quick to forgive! Make peace and get back to the good stuff!

In this specific disagreement, forgiveness had been organic. I understood why Henri got upset and gave him time to cool off. His *"bonjour voisine"* had been his way of testing that we were cool. My resuming our morning exchange was a sign that I forgave his outburst. We had moved on.

There are times when forgiveness needs to be more direct in the seeking and the getting. We have had occasions where a discussion caused an outburst from one of us that felt unmerited. I have snapped at him unnecessarily if I am stressed or overwhelmed with something and had to be quick with the "I am sorry" when I saw the hurt in his eyes. Henri is one to stew in his misery for a while and needs time to come down. But I can always count on him coming to me later to apologize and explain, sometimes on the pillow at bed time. I forgive and we move on.

The night after the incident, I went to bed before him. When I woke up in the middle of the night to use the bathroom, I found him snoring next to me. I thought to myself, *"Oh, you are back."*

Next morning, no comment from me. Zip.

As we marked our twenty-second anniversary, I contemplated how important it is to keep learning about your partner and adjusting to each other.

The topic of the argument had been a habit that Henri has that I was aware of since we first met. It is a harmless mannerism that annoys me sometimes, but happens to be who he is. If I would change him, that would also mean that all the great things I admire and love about him would also disappear. He would no longer be my Henri. Consequently, I must accept the entire package. After all, I committed to love and cherish all of him, as is.

When the whole thing began that morning, I had apologized and acknowledged that I realized my mentioning this thing bothers him to the core.

"I will never bring this up again." I promised.

It occurred to me then, that my husband gets upset not just because I am annoying him when I bring attention to that habit. He is angry that I talk about it when this is something he cannot change about himself. It is part of his upbringing, it is his culture, it is him. His anger is his way of voicing:

"You say you love me. This is who I am. Accept me as I am."

<u>Auntie Wisdom</u>: Loving someone and committing to a relationship with them, requires that you accept them for who they are. While adjustments or improvements can be suggested or fostered where necessary, it is essential that you allow your partner to be their authentic self. You must do that for each other, to maintain that safe and loving environment.

It also helps when that authentic self is so easy to love.

When I got home from work that afternoon, my husband was in the kitchen. I noticed through the laundry room's open door, that the washing machine green light was on, indicating that a load of laundry had just been completed. I put down my bags and put the load in the dryer, – we are a tag team. When I came around to the kitchen, Henri greeted me with a cheerful, "Hey, baby!" He was standing in front of the stove, wearing an apron, and stirring a steaming pot of "legumes" – a mixed vegetables stew, while chicken legs sizzled in another pan.

Ice-T was right, marriage is like a movie. In my epic narrative, I am happy to share all the scenes with my leading man; the good, the bad, the happy and sad, the ridiculous and the sublime. I am enjoying this great adventure too much to let little squabbles get in the way. Especially when it includes laundry service and coming home to a delicious freshly cooked meal.

Yep! Blessed me. I am keeping this one for another twenty years!

◊◊◊

The Sex Thing

Whoa! Slow down. I am not about to become a sex therapist here, nor am I launching into a raunchy romp. However, you cannot talk about romantic relationships and marriage without mentioning sex.

Referencing the first couple in the Bible, it says in Genesis 1:28 that, "God bless them (the man and the woman) and said to them, 'Be fruitful and increase in numbers'…"

One could interpret this to mean that sex was originally intended for procreation. Reproduce. Multiply. God made it to feel good because He knew that were it to be like what a woman experiences during childbirth; procreation would not take place. But human being, an intellectual creature, realized *"This feels good! Let's do it for fun!"*

Contrary to humans, animal species are direct and efficient when it comes to reproduction. I have witnessed domestic animals copulating since I was a kid. First, they only do it when nature requires it, that is when the female is ovulating. Second, no preliminaries or feelings are involved. They just engage in the act, do the deed and part ways without a goodbye or a kiss.

Unfortunately, some of our human counterparts act the same way: *Wham! Bam! Thank you, ma'am!* With modern day woman empowerment, it could also be *"Thank you, sir!"*

This kind of sex reminds me of the dilemma of prescription drugs that become addictive. Originally intended to treat a certain health condition, people discover that it also makes them feel good, it gives them a high. That medication then becomes a recreational drug.

That is sex in its simplistic form.

Fully engaged sex is so much more in the human context.

I personally believe that sex, when it takes the form of making love, is one of the most profound experiences two human beings can share.

It is recommended that a couple seeks pre-marital counseling before they say their I do's. I believe one of the questions that is commonly asked is each person's view on sex and its frequency. Whatever someone responds is most likely their expected norm. Whether you use formal counseling or have a private discussion between the two of you, it is up to you to jointly come to some manageable ground. If no agreement can be reached, that may be a red flag to future problems.

◊◊◊

There are three camps when it comes to how people respond to the topic of sex. The first is the prudish kind that firmly believes that the topic has no place in a social discussion. In that group are also the people who view it as a personal item that belongs only to the two people involved. Those are the people who started to fill out my survey *Dating and Relationships,* and stopped short after the identification information when they noticed the questions relating to sex within their marriage. *"What kind of questions are these?"* some voiced to me. I did not push them to complete the survey.

The third group (I know, I'll come back to number 2) – are the freakish ones who have some lewd remarks to blast every chance they get. Everything is described as "sexy" and their analogies frequently run along the lines of some bedroom act. They love to brag and engage in the topic.

The second group is where I and a lot of the survey respondents are. We are clear that sex is a normal part of being a couple, whether it is frequent or infrequent, ordinary, or sublime.

I will reiterate what social scientists elaborate on in books and television shows. SEX AND INTIMACY ARE IMPORTANT TO A MARRIAGE! This is something the Creator put in place not just to procreate. It is also a tool to remain connected to your partner, to experience the human touch and explore intimacy together. However, it is a practice that is best handled by mutual agreement, especially since it all depends on your age, physical and medical health, or personal appetite.

The survey asked couples whether sex was an important component in their relationship. 52% of the respondents chose "yes" and 48% said "no". It also asked if they still engaged in regular sex. I specified that "regular" could mean anywhere from once a week to once a month, which 41% responded "yes." The category identified as "occasionally" referred to a few times a year or special occasions, which came in at 34%. The rest selected "no" because of health issues, children, age or one partner no longer being interested.

The principal components in maintaining a healthy relationship are commitment and communication. These two factors both came in at 60% when couples were asked to recommend the top five things that make a relationship successful. Just like couples must be committed to the journey, and communicate about finances, children, and lifestyle among others issues, sex should also be an open conversation. Ultimately, the decision to have sex is one that both partners must mutually agree upon, ensuring they are on the same page.

While physical interaction is important in a relationship, in some circumstances a couple may still be able to maintain a healthy unit although they no longer engage in physical intimacy. I know of middle-aged and older couples who are there because of any of the reasons previously stated. Nevertheless, they still enjoy being together and remain together as a couple and family.

In October 2023, AARP published an article *"Are You Adrift in a Sexless Relationship?"* written by Ken Budd, which talked about how a great number of people in their 50s were having less sex than they would like. Among the causes cited for this reduction in sexual activity were: physical changes, health issues, medications or depression that lowered libido.

The article referenced a couple the author interviewed, who had been married for twenty years and had three children. Several challenges including a major illness experienced by the wife and subsequent depression killed their sex life. They were getting a divorce. It was mentioned that they both shared a deep Christian faith, and the husband appeared to have remained faithful throughout. He was quoted as *"nervous about dating yet eager to end 10 years of agonizing celibacy." "I want so badly to have that closeness with someone,"* he says. *"I dream about it."*

A couple of years ago, my pastors at The Light of the World Christian Fellowship in Humble, Texas, took the bold initiative of hosting a seminar on sexual health for the married couples. The guest speakers included a therapist who spoke on the psychological implications of sex, a doctor who reported on case studies of couples experiencing physical challenges and medical treatments available, and other pastors who reviewed biblical principles of intimacy. The audience was of various age groups. During certain discussions that were very "real," I could tell some of the older members became uncomfortable.

My church leaders must have felt the need for this program based on their counseling experiences. Couples sometimes encounter difficulties in intimacy, but often, individuals are not open enough to be transparent with each other about their issues. Knowing and understanding your partner is of primary importance in this domain as it is in others.

My personal belief is that there is nothing more satisfying than "righteous sex," that is where two people who are married physically demonstrate love to each other. There is no guilt or shame, no guess work or afterthought. The Christians among us will understand what I am talking about. The belief of the faith is that there is no sex before marriage. Consequently, even when one of us decides to engage in it without the benefit of marriage, there is frequently a sense of "We shouldn't be doing this." Once married however, no holds bar! It is legal, certified, and righteous! Have you ever noticed how some church couples have large families? Say no more.

In all seriousness, working together is the key. What is at the beginning of an era in a marriage is not what is in the middle or in later years. Things change, life happens and everything is in a constant state of flux. One must be realistic and manage one's expectations as well as make the effort to keep the flames going regardless of circumstances. There are so many factors that can affect a couple's love life.

In the early stages of marriage, the level of passion is usually high. There is the newness and if the partners are young, plenty of the right hormones and stamina. A few years in, children come into the picture. 73% of the respondents had 1-3 children, 67% of which were ages 6 to 12 and 8% under the age of 5. That is one status where a lot of time and energy devoted to the care of children is required, leaving little for couple time. This illustrates a situation where **couples need to be intentional about their intimate life.** Schedule intimacy if you must, just like you do playdates for your children, doctor appointments, trips to the supermarket, workout time at the gym, etc.

Men, share the household duties and help with caring for the children (feeding, cleaning, homework, etc.) so that your partner can have some energy left to give you some quality time.

Ladies, every so often, use that scented shower gel or lotion and slip into something lacy to rev up his motor. Men are visual, remember! That works even when there are more bulges and stretch marks to cover. They do not mind. The only thing they notice is that you just ignited the signal for seduction and fun times. Cue the strip tease drum roll. *Laissez les bons temps rouler!* – Let the good times roll, like they say in New Orleans.

Also note that what is good for the goose is also good for the gander. Fun time is a reciprocal activity where both parties benefit.

By the time most couples reach middle-aged, or have been married for a good number of years, the pop may fizzle out a bit or go flat altogether. If both parties are cool with that it is a non-issue. If, however, one person or both are still interested, it behooves you to talk about it, and adjust with the circumstances.

- See a doctor if it is a medical issue.
- See a therapist or counselor if there are psychological stressors.
- Lose weight if too many pounds make things difficult.
- Work out and possibly lose weight if it affects physical attraction.
- Give each other massages.
- Engage in game play and flirtation.
- Be intentional (make time, use seduction, activate turn on).

Again, I am no sex therapist. My suggestions are merely to offer some tools you can use. You own this. Research books and articles on the subject to help you out if you are serious about fixing your intimacy issues.

As for me, in my house, we believe in going for as long as we can. We organically adjusted with time, being both fully committed to keeping each other happy in every way. As of this writing I am in my late sixties and my husband just hit his seventies. The frequency and the intensity of our physical interactions have greatly diminished over the years, but our enthusiasm for intimacy hasn't dimmed. In fact, at our age, we look at the demise of our ability to engage as imminent, so our philosophy is: enjoy today while we still can.

We are both incredibly blessed to be two goofy individuals. We approach physical intimacy like child play. If you've ever watched the glee on children's faces when they run around chasing each other on the playground or are tossing a ball around, or playing hop scotch or pretending with their dolls, that is what happens when one of us gives the other "the signal." It could be a hug that lasts too long, a come-hither or appreciative look, a purposeful embrace or a direct, "time to come out and play." If one of us initiates, the other one is game for it.

Auntie Wisdom: Every couple should have their code that a partner can pick up on to act accordingly. Learn to read each other's signals.

Further: DON'T DENY PARTNER, willy nilly! If you can help it.

This is an attitude I recommend. There are times when medical problems – fake headaches notwithstanding – or other issues may affect a partner's mood and hamper their response to physical advances. Outside of physical engagement, one might be reaching for emotional connection. Handle rejection carefully and gently, whether on the giving or receiving end. If there is an imbalance in sexual appetite, pre-marital counseling and candid conversations would have helped. In any event, you will have to find a way to work it out.

Henri and I have always functioned with that understanding of no denial, except when medically or emotionally warranted. In our twenty-two years of marriage, I can barely recount incidents where one of us pushed back the other's advances.

On one such occasion where I was feeling frisky, Henri declined. I felt rejected and pulled back with an exasperated, "Well, excuse me!"

Sensing my hurt, he came back with, "I am sorry. I have a lot on my mind."

"What's going on?" I asked gently. – Time to switch mode. He was obviously going through something.

He proceeded to share about a family crisis that weighed heavily on his mind. I lay next to him and listened, empathizing when necessary. My husband needed intimacy of a different kind.

We continue to adjust as we both age. Having good genes and maintaining a health-conscious lifestyle helped to keep us well preserved. **But we are old!** Our bodies have changed, there are health issues and challenges on both sides that we address with a sense of humor. In my younger days I had a nice round booty. Now I have a bump in the front as well, my belly. Henri often teases me by patting me on my stomach and inquiring, "How many months?" In turn, I slap his disappearing fanny with a solicitous, "How is my Nasatol?" – a moniker for "no-ass-at-all."

Receding hairlines (both of us), big bellies (ditto) diabetes, blood pressure, prostate issues have slowed us down, but have not completely stopped us. The objective is to have fun with each other and to enjoy each other physically. And where there is a will, there will be a way. Intimacy is good for the soul and it does wonders for the body.

We have talked about the day that will inevitably come when one of us or both of us will be completely unwilling or unable to engage in the activity. And we agreed. Let us enjoy it while we can, and when it is no more, it is no more. We will still have each other and we will still love one another.

That is when you reach the point of such complete harmony, in a wholesome, transcendental kind of way, that sex is no longer an important factor in the relationship.

I completely understand the participants who answered "No" to the survey question about the importance of sex. You are no longer engaging in it, but its absence does not affect the fullness of your relationship. All is well with everyone.

Henri and I will be there someday, but not today.

Sleeping Apart

This topic is a good segue from talking about the married sex life, so I will touch on it briefly.

Carson Daly, host of the early morning show Today, reported in an interview with People magazine in 2024, that he and his wife Siri Pinter, a food blogger and author, sometimes sleep in separate beds. The actor explained that they do this by mutual agreement, whenever their schedules or events in their lives necessitated them being apart together, which they jokingly refer to as "sleep divorce." In their case, these voluntary moments of separation do not affect their relationship. They are reported as being "happy as ever together."

Momentary apartness occurs in couples. Someone is feeling sick and needs to isolate. A pregnant body is taking more space in the bed and neither partner can get comfortable. Someone works the late-night shift and does not want to awaken the partner who rises early for a morning shift, etc.

I personally know of older couples who do not share the same bedroom. In one case, the wife's loud snoring impedes on the husband's sleep pattern. In another, the man has health issues that prompted him to move to a separate bedroom. My take on this: do what works for you.

However, I do caution that intimacy is not only about sex. There is something about conversations in bed, waking up in the middle of the night and seeing your person's silhouette next to you, finding your partner's face half way on your pillow (flip them over), waking up in the morning and cuddling for a bit. All things that keep you close and feeling connected.

There have been times when I woke up to an empty space next to me when Henri relocated himself to the guest bedroom because sinus issues caused my snoring to be too intrusive. In addition, whenever one of us has symptoms of an oncoming cold, he is quick to claim that guest room. I gather he enjoys spending time in the only space in the house that feels masculine among the various shades of beige and peach that is the house décor. When I designed the room, I painted it a dark blue and accessorized it in various shades of the same color. I believe Henri secretly relishes being in a room that feels like a bachelor pad. He even jokes as such when he is spending the night there. "I am going to my *'chambre de garçon'* – my bachelor pad" – he would announce.

<u>Auntie Wisdom</u>: Do what works for you, but do not take your partner for granted. Make sure that whatever it is, is working for the both of you.

September 2023 - interview with actor and comedian Cedric the Entertainer, while he was on tour in Houston to promote his book, *Flipping Boxcars: A Novel.*

HOW TO KEEP IT GOING

In September 2023, I had a chance to interview actor and comedian Cedric the Entertainer, while he was on tour in Houston to promote his book, *Flipping Boxcars: A Novel.*

My question to him was, "You mentioned that you have been happily married for twenty-four years. What is something you can tell us that you really like about being married?"

"My wife is just really a great mate for me" he said. "We are evenly yoked. The main thing I like, is that my wife makes sure my house is my home. And when I come home, I feel comfortable. – I travel a lot. That is where her energy is: there is no static, no nonsense going on at the house. It's all about love and respect when we are with each other. It actually makes me want to be at home, out of any place that I could be. That's the place where I feel most myself, chill and loved.

Kids, everybody is super respectful. My wife makes sure it's all out of love. Not like a sergeant, but with respect, love, and adoration. That's how it is at home."

Men need to be and feel nurtured

Before you chop my head off for labeling this section "Men need…" let me clarify that ALL human beings have a need to feel nurtured. That is part of our DNA. We all want to feel taken care of.

It is generally believed that women are the more nurturing gender. Something in a woman's genetic makeup predisposes her to give care, a necessary requirement when there is an offspring. That same capacity is present in females of other species as well.

I recently watched the transformation in my eighteen-year-old niece who gave birth to a baby boy. She was always considered a most immature, dazed teenager who was not very expressive. I visited her when the baby was three weeks old. The little guy was whimpering as she held him in her arms. She instinctively started rocking him and cooing in a soft voice. "What's wrong baby? Are you hungry? Are you wet?"

She had never been around a family member who had just given birth. No one told her what to do.

In the same way, my sister's female Rottweiler had a litter of puppies. She was exhausted after pushing out eight of them. Still, she laid on her side and accommodated them breast feeding. No one taught her how to do that. Instinct kicked in for her as it did for my niece to feed, hold, care for.

Women often crave nurturing, but they are so accustomed to providing it that they frequently put others' needs above their own, denying themselves the care they desire. While receiving nurturing is beneficial for women, it may not be essential. Perhaps the act of *giving* nurture satisfies that emotional need in a fulfilling way.

Men on the other hand, from the creation of mankind to more recent centuries, have been expected to provide and protect. They hunted for meat, worked the fields, defended their homes and encampments from invasive wild animals, fought territorial wars, etc., while the women kept the home and the babies.

Less than a hundred years ago in the western world, a modified version of that system was still in effect; with men working outside the home and women filling the role of homemakers. Those roles, along with a lot of other things, have changed in the 2020s. Today, most women are part of the workforce, and most of them work outside the home.

I have worked all my adult life. I did not have to tend to children, except for a handful of times I cared for my nieces while my sister was stationed overseas in the military. Children use an extraordinary amount of a caregiver's energy, especially when they are still young.

This makes it difficult sometimes for a woman to find time and energy to dispense on their mate. <u>But it is something that you must do!</u> It is vital to the health of a relationship, including marriage.

Our personality and early experiences with nurturing shape how we expect to receive care and how we show it to a partner.

There is a need for men to be nurtured that is even more prevalent among Black men, when it is coupled with a desire to be respected. Some women may feel, "Well, I am not your mama!"

No, you are not. But a man's need for nurturing seeks it in you, his partner. He also craves receiving respect, which for him is an indication that he is valued. While I do not condone spoiling a partner by excessively catering to them hands and foot, a woman must learn to care for and cater to her mate and create a safe space for him to be vulnerable.

Like Cedric said, he wants to be where he "feel comfortable… It's all about love and respect." Home is the place where he "feels most myself, chill and loved" because his wife is intentional about creating that atmosphere for him.

Women need to feel loved and supported

On occasions where I publicly acknowledged how well Henri took care of something, I could see the pride in his eyes. I am showing respect for who he is. I am building him up to others. I am demonstrating his value to me and the relationship.

Likewise, I also crave appreciation.

While the woman is busy nurturing her mate, she also needs to feel loved and experience his support in its various forms. She must be able to rely on her partner shouldering financial responsibilities. She needs to feel safe, protected and supported, physically and emotionally. She will extend herself if she knows she is valued and appreciated.

Henri frequently uses the expression, "I just want to please you, baby." Realistically, that is sometimes a cope out when he doesn't feel like making a decision about something. But most often, he genuinely wants me to be happy with whatever it is I desire. Consequently, he will do whatever he can to help me accomplish what I seek.

I in return relish it when he shows gratitude and speaks of me in flattering terms. Henri is quick to announce, "What would I do without you" and mean it.

Men, make it your duty to acknowledge, compliment, and commuicate Women need your tangible appreciation and the occasional ego boost as well. You can be so easily critical when things are not the way you like it. How about building her up when she is taking great care of you and the family. Let her know it. Let the world know it. Cedric publicly gave his wife her flowers.

Ms. Lorna Wells, keep up the good work. Mr. Cedric is a very happy man, because of you.

◊◊◊

A woman wants to be loved and feel it, but she also needs to feel supported by her mate in every aspect: career, dreams, and goals.

A man who feels respected while being loved will give his woman the moon.

So, love your mate for real. Give them what they need emotionally.

TRICKS AND TOOLS
FOR SUCCESS

In October 2023 news outlets reported the 20th wedding anniversary of Dame Joan Collins of television show *Dynasty* fame and Percy Sutton, a theater and film producer. For a generation that was not around when that glamorous show was on television, Ms. Collins is the quintessential femme fatale. She was married four times before uniting with Sutton.

Collins gave insight to their successful union, when she posted a picture of their wedding on Instagram with the caption "#togetherness, #happilymarried #separatebathrooms."

Yours truly will add to that, "#separateclosets." We are fortunate to have a master bedroom with separate closets and separate vanities, which was a huge selling point for me when we bought our home. While some things can be viewed as luxuries, they in fact represent the opportunity to have your own space and be your own person, even while in a union.

A lot of people mistakenly view being a couple as a complete assimilation into each other, as if one person could melt into the other and disappear. To the contrary, who one is as an individual always remains. The key is accommodation.

When I was teaching, I learned about accommodations as a tool to assist students with special needs. An accommodation was something that would help that student be successful in your class. Some required additional time to turn assignments in. Others needed reading instructions aloud. Some benefited from a quiet area to do their work. Sometime around the first few weeks of the school year, the counselors would send teachers a report on which ones of your students needed accommodations and specify what those were. Most of the time, an experienced teacher like myself, would recognize flags or issues with students even before we received the report.

Well, a relationship needs accommodations too. **Some people are not in a relationship because one or the other person was not willing to bend.** Now, don't get me wrong. One should never have to go out of your character or against your values to accommodate someone. That would mean losing yourself and ultimately build resentment. Once that festers, it would eventually lead to the demise of the relationship.

What I speak of here are the little things that allow each person to be themselves comfortably.

Let's look at something as mundane as the closets. When we first got married, our bedroom in New Jersey had one large walk-in closet where I occupied the larger side – of course – and Henri, the other. I happen to like sturdy, even velvet hangers, hung with the hook facing back and color coordinating sections so it's easy for me to select my daily wardrobe. My husband is attached to dry cleaner wire hangers, (he says they take less space), hook facing forward. His sections are full of empty dry cleaner plastic bags. *Quelle horreure*! – The horror!

While I can always count on finding a plastic bag if I need to store clothes away, the disorganization on his side of the closet drove me bananas. I bought him beautiful polished wood hangers for his suits that were left unused. When I mentioned this to him, his reply was, "Leave me alone." I had to make a conscious effort to disregard my preferences and allow him to do things his way. To him, so long as his clothes were hung, that was enough.

Our different way of managing our closet space can be irritating, but in the grand scheme of things, is that a deal breaker? No.

While a lot of you might not be as fortunate as I was to end up in a house with separate closets, you must identify what your pet peeves are in a relationship and find a way to either address them or accommodate them. For the time we were in our first home, I learned to live with my side of the closet looking organized and his being… *"I can't find my grey pants."*

Cue in eye roll from me or a clever retort: *"I am wearing them."*

When you are committed, while seriously dating or in an established relationship, you must understand that there is a lot of give and take. There is this fantasy that "happily ever after" exists. It does if you are willing to do the work to ensure it remains present.

Ask any married person whether their partner occasionally gets on their nerves. The answer will be a resounding "Yes!" Mine does, at least five times a day. Those are the times I use his Spanish surname: Mr. Panendiaz. Translate to "pain in the a…" The funny thing is, I get on his nerves at least as often. He'll retort with calling me "little Miss Perfect" or use his standard "Leave me alone."

The key to addressing slight differences of opinion or the way we do things is to leave room for the other to function the way they feel most comfortable. So long as it doesn't set the house on fire.

Most of all, you must always keep LOVE present. This pronouncement may sound elementary, but love is the glue that keeps it all together.

Tips:

You should never be so mad at your partner that you forget that you love them and they love you.

You should not want to hurt someone you love, and words are a sharp weapon that can cut to the core when they are mean and angry.

In a piece she wrote for The Mail Sunday in February 2018, "Dame

Joan Collins: After four divorces I finally worked out the secret of a happy marriage: separate bathrooms, banishment for snoring and a fit young husband," iconic actress Dame Joan Collins commented on accepting your partner for who they are. She said: "I'm not a Stepford wife and he's an alpha-male Peruvian-Scot, so sometimes we clash but it doesn't last long and we are quick to say sorry."

My husband and I have purposed to not stay angry at each other. We call it out if one of us says something hurtful and the other is quick to say "I'm sorry." The important thing is I know he loves me, and he knows I love him. We say it often enough and demonstrate it daily. So, when a little snag pops up, we look at it as just that and address it to resolve it quickly.

We are all guilty of a temporary lapse in judgement when we find something to be annoying. It does not justify saying or doing something hurtful or malicious. When we love someone and know their triggers, we should be very careful not to activate negative emotions in them. Love protects, love forgives.

The bible says it best in 1 Corinthians 13:

"Love is patient, love is kind. It does not envy, it does not boast, it is not proud. It does not dishonor others, it is not self-seeking, it is not easily angered, it keeps no record of wrongs."

Even if you do not subscribe to Christian beliefs, you must admit that this perfectly describes how love should be conducted and reflected in your interactions with your life partner.

Since none of us is a perfect being, and we are all different from one another, with our idiosyncrasies and particularities, we function in our own unique way. Consequently, there will be some snags in co-habiting with other people, especially a romantic partner or spouse. Do not ignore whatever that is. Address the issue and hopefully you don't have to confront a beast. If it is as severe as a beast, maybe there is a more serious problem and you should not even be together.

As I said before, the snags are usually the little things that fray your nerves. They are not lethal, but surely annoying. It is like when you are about to cook dry beans to make a pot of chili or to use for a Haitian rice and bean. You need to sift through and remove the damaged ones. In that case you end up with only the best beans.

In relationships however, it is more like you buy this beautiful wood table from a thrift shop. It has a little scratch in the left corner. You knew the table was not new, it had a life before you and was used by others. So, expect a little damage. But the design, the wood, the shape; you fell in love with it. Had to have it. You tried everything to remove that little scratch. Nothing. Are you going to let that prevent you from enjoying beautiful meals on your table? I hope not. You get used to that little scratch and call it "character." A relationship deserves that same grace. You cannot remove the damaged goods as in the beans, but you can accept the little scratch as with the table.

Remember that no romantic match is 100 percent or ten out of ten. If you think you have one, somebody is faking something. It is totally unrealistic to profess "all or nothing" when choosing a mate. No one can fill all the requirements of your crazy list. So, take your 7 or 8 out of ten and deal with the missing digits.

Acknowledge your mate's quirks and adjust accordingly, WITH LOVE! If you are really lucky, you would have found someone who would do the same for your crazy a… self.

Embrace the crazy in your partner

To take our discussion of accommodating your partner's personality a step further, I would also say that you must "embrace the crazy" in each other. What I mean is stepping out of your comfort zone to join your partner in activities they enjoy, even if that's not necessarily your cup of tea. Let me share a little story with you.

My husband and I were taking our exercise walk through the neighborhood one evening. As we turned a corner, we came upon a breathtaking view of the rising moon in a generous clearing between the rooftops. I am an incorrigible romantic, fascinated with nature's displays. I marvel at sprouting seeds, a butterfly's elegant flutter, or a fiery sunset.

"Hold on, babe," I told my husband. "Let me admire this beautiful moon." He paused his gait a moment as I gazed at the skies. George Benson's song *"Kisses in the Moonlight"* played in my head. I tugged at his sleeves. "Hey, kiss me under the moon," I said.

"You're crazy," he replied, then leaned in and planted a quick kiss on my lips. I giggled, feeling like a thirty-year-old for a brief instant, before he stepped off with a command, "Okay, let's go!"

As we continued on our walk, I caught glimpses of the perfect moon and realized, *my husband thinks I'm crazy but he still loves me enough to indulge my crazy.* I am a lucky girl! Okay, we were both in our late sixties. That's what made it fun!

People erroneously think that partners must be exactly alike to have a good relationship. *Au contraire!* While both partners should have similar values, a well-balanced relationship requires the awareness that you and your partner are different people. The key thing is to learn to accept each other's respective quirks and idiosyncrasies.

I am creative and adventurous. My husband joins in my adventures, but he has no creative bones in his body. I am a meticulous planner, he is not.

To maintain a good relationship with a partner, one must learn to embrace who they are, even indulging their whims, within limits. That's what made me smile during the moonlight experience. It barely lasted a minute, but I appreciated that hubby cared enough to let me have my moment.

Similarly, the previous week, the World Cup was on television and I was keeping him company watching Haiti play Mexico in a soccer match. I am not into soccer per se, but I don't mind watching a good game. Few minutes into the second half, however, I got up and walked away. "Where you going?" Henri asked. "I've watched enough," I replied. "Going back to my writing."

A few nights later, cooling down from my exercises, I sat on the floor mat and flipped the television to the Jane Fonda/Diane Keaton movie, *The Book Club*. "Come watch a chick flick with me," I called out to my husband. He plopped down next to me, stretched out, put his head on my lap… and promptly fell asleep. I shook my head but smiled.

I felt such a strong affection for this man as I watched his relaxed face laying across my thighs. He looked so at peace.

This is harmony, I thought. Like most men, my husband prefers action movies but will sometimes watch a romantic comedy with me. This time, he was willing, but a long days' worth of fatigue got the best of him. No hard feelings. I accepted his meeting me halfway by just staying with me. He didn't argue when I stepped away midway through the soccer match, the same way I wasn't bothered that he only stood a minute with me admiring the moon – my thing, not his.

Sometimes a partner imposes their ways and wants in a relationship and the other person suffocates. Conversely, one person might be so unwilling to accommodate the other that a chasm is created that grows wider and unbridgeable.

My husband and I are in a good place where we provide a safe space for each other. A 2023 Yahoo article by Ossiana Tepfenhart, *My Ex Taught Me What Men Truly Want in a Wife* quoted, "We all just want someone who can be our peace…"

I will add, we also need someone who gets us, "someone who embraces our crazy," those quirky, funny, peculiar, singular characteristics that make someone who they are.

When you find that someone you enjoy being with, where both parties can be their authentic selves, baby! You are blessed beyond measure.

Nurturing that ebb and flow, dancing in step with your partner, that's a successful relationship to last a lifetime.

Do you embrace your partner's crazy? Even when it involves kissing in the moonlight!

Do they embrace yours?

Their quirks may be sometimes annoying, but if you are able to find the charm or the humor in it, then you have found a safe place where you can both flourish.

◊◊◊

What is working for couples

In March 2022, actor Samuel L. Jackson celebrated 41 years of marriage with his wife LaTanya Richardson Jackson. During an interview with Vanity Fair's Emily Kirkpatrick, the actor and his wife both acknowledged that a shared vision of commitment was the secret to their lasting union. LaTanya explained, "… we made a decision to say, 'We are going to stay together no matter what. We'll figure it out.' "

Samuel added, "It's two people who respect each other, love each other and look out for each other."

July 2024 – Henri and I pose with King Kong in Times Square,
New York City, when I have a Marilyn Monroe moment with
my dress blowing up from the air coming out of the subway vents.
See link to TikTok video: "Silly Romantics in New York City" in back pages
Referenced Sources.

PART V

FOREVER IS A GOOD THING

You want to keep your relationship thriving? Strive to please your partner and remain connected. Invest emotional energy into it, as if you were in a continuous dating situation, one with plenty of fringe benefits, of course!

MAKE IT LAST A LIFETIME

Auntie Wisdom: **Marriage is not a destination. The love expedition doesn't stop there. Rather, it is an extended journey that continues throughout your lives together and should be filled with adventures and excitement daily, like a happy cruise.**

One of the perils of a long-term relationship is that it may become stale due to stagnation. Remember I compared relationships to a living plant that needs continuous feeding to remain vibrant. A culprit I can readily point to is when a partner is taken for granted.

Parents often tell their children, "You know I love you. I take care of you." Well, the child needs to hear and feel the love. The caring may come from a feeling of obligation, more so than love. A trained nurse cares for her patients, but does she love them? I doubt it. With the love of God, maybe, but that's it, caring out of obligation or duty.

Likewise in a partnership or marriage, you function daily with established routines: the household, the meals, the bills, the children, etc. You interact constantly on those terms. But what about the personal relationship? What are you doing to maintain the spice, the zest, the vibrancy of your romantic life?

The survey *Dating and Relationships in the 2020s* asked the coupled participants to identify the approaches they used to express love to their mate on an ongoing basis. The strategies listed were loosely based on the model popularized by Gary Chapman's 2015 book, *"The 5 Love Languages: The Secret To Love That Lasts.* Here are what the participants pointed to, choosing more than one method.

Do things for them/acts of service	65%
Quality time	55%
With words of affirmation	55%
Physical touch/Affection	43%
With small gifts	40%
With big gifts	35%
Other	3%

An act of service may be like President Bush getting his wife her cup of coffee every morning or Rock* who is married to Faith*, a nurse, taking her car to the carwash once a week.

Quality time involves those special date day or night we talked about earlier. Time dedicated to just the two of you being together, whether it is just to sit and talk, take a walk, or go out to dinner together.

Words of affirmation are the "I love you" stated genuinely, not just as a routine word. Showing appreciation is also included in this category. "You mean the world to me." "I am so glad we're together." "I would be lost without you."

Physical touch/Affection are those non-sexual touches we discussed earlier. I am big on hugs, and Henri readily embraces me whenever I lean in. He will frequently squeeze my shoulders or pat my backside randomly while I often tug on his ears or rub the back of his head. Those simple gestures demonstrate genuine affection.

Small gifts are those little mementos that let the person know you were thinking about them. It could be as simple as going to the supermarket and surprising your partner when you get home with a "They had those chocolate croissants that you like. I got you a box."

With Henri and I, whenever one of us goes somewhere without the other, a small token brought home is like saying, "Hey, I wish you had been there to share the experience with me." A cookie or a piece of cake from the dessert, if it was a meal. A small trinket or souvenir if it was a trip to the mall or travel to a different city.

Big gifts involve thoughtful execution. They usually are the things the person really wanted or desperately needed. You are happy to be the one to provide that for them. It's like that time my car broke down, and Henri gave me his entire income tax return to put with what I had to purchase a new car. And this was before we even got to the point of being engaged!

It could be something of a modest cost, like taking the person's broken heirloom watch to the jeweler, and presenting them with the repaired item. Another example may be a grand announcement of "Pack your bags. I am taking you to Paris!"

Keeping the flames burning

In addition to using love language to express your feelings of affection, you must also fan the flames of attraction between you and your partner to keep the spark alive. Here are the responses the participants chose.

Sharing and communicating	75%
Date Night	65%
Making time for each other	53%
Intimacy & flirtation	50%
Fun activities together	50%
Taking care of each other	40%
Other	3%

Keeping a relationship alive is dynamic. Both partners must actively and consistently do things to stimulate positive energy and allow it to radiate and circulate through the relationship. It's like fertilizing the plant.

You want to keep your relationship thriving? Strive to please your partner and remain connected. Invest emotional energy into it, as if you were in a continuous dating situation, one with plenty of fringe benefits, of course.

◊◊◊

Primary components that ensure a successful relationship

The last question asked of the participants was the following:

"If you had to give advice to a single person or to a young couple about what the top five most important things in a successful relationship are, what would they be?"

Here is how they answered:

Commitment	60%
Communication	60%
Selfless love	53%
Trust	53%
Shared values	48%
Respect	40%
Physical compatibility	23%
Compatible character	18%
Compatible lifestyle	13%

Some of the participants provided additional comments that give us more clarity on the topic.

Brandon and Erian offered:

"Personally, my best relationship that ultimately led to marriage was one based on friendship."

Harry* and Sally* said:

"Marriage is hard. So many people quit when things get hard. But we made a commitment to each other in front of God. We can handle anything with the Lord. Also, words hurt. Think before you speak."

My church pastor, Pastor Jackie concurs with that thought:

"It is important to keep God at the center of your relationships. Marriage is work and it takes a lot of commitment to have a successful, thriving relationship."

Other testimonies

People find their happily ever after when they marry that compatible mate and they both work at building a strong foundation. In addition, they do the ongoing maintenance work necessary to keep their edifice strong and in solid shape for years to come.

Social media is full of posts by regular folks and celebrities alike who celebrate their partners and share their formula for what works for them.

In my D'Auntie podcast, *Rekindle The Flames*, posted in June 2024, I share one of the things that my husband and I do to keep the fires burning. We dance. Slow dance. At home.

People give shout outs to their partners, especially for birthdays or anniversary. In August 2021, Stephen Curry's (Golden State Warrior) wife Ayesha Curry, posted a message on Instagram for their tenth anniversary that read in part: "My love! My adventure partner! My best friend! My confidant! My everything!

Steph also posted on his page how much he is thankful for his wife and concludes by saying: "You are the key to everything that I do… Lucky I'm (still) in love with my best friend."

Both Curry's refer to the other as "best friend." We should all be so lucky and **so blessed to <u>marry our best friend!</u>**

2023 - Blessed to be living our best life!
We "limo "ride into the sunset together…
Touring the Christmas Lights Festival in Houston.
In grand style!

ALWAYS AND FOREVER

Henri and I celebrated our tenth anniversary with a big shindig of a vow renewal. We had the public wedding we couldn't afford when we originally said I do. We went all out. We enlisted a wedding venue with full catering, had a jazz saxophonist play before the ceremony, hired a DJ for the party, traveled in a limousine, the works. This time, Henri had a chance to invite all of his family and friends to celebrate with us. A friend of mine from church, who is an ordained minister, officiated the exchange of vows.

I was elated that all my family and friends were able to be with us this time as well. There had not been a wedding in the family for a long time, and there was an entire generation of young people who had never been to a wedding. I wanted them to witness not only the pageantry of the ceremony, a beautiful event, but also the enduring love that had thus far lasted for ten years. I also desired that they experience the coming together of two families in a joyous occasion where love was celebrated and supported.

Henri and I were living proof that love stories can happen to ordinary people. Beyond just love, we demonstrated that true commitment – where two people pledge their lives to each other before God, and dedicate themselves to making the union work – creates a lifelong partnership that blesses both partners and their respective families.

◊◊◊

My husband is not comfortable writing in the English language. But every Valentine's Day, he will visit Walmart and spend some time at the greeting cards section, choosing the perfect card to express his feelings for me. He always manages to find a Hallmark or American Greetings product that provides flowery and poetic language that says exactly what he feels.

This past Valentine's, he chose an American Greetings card that contained a poem, to which he added his own prose. Reading it made me teary eyed and pumped my heart so full of love I would marry him all over again.

Here is the poem:
For My Wife
We share this love
That's meant to be –
I'm made for you,
You're made for me!

We share a home,
Our happy place –
Our cozy, warm,
And special space.
We share ideas
And conversations,
Plans and dreams
And celebrations.

We share a love
That's strong and true –
And I love sharing
Life with you!

Now get ready for it! Even writing this, I get emotional. Here are my Henri's own simple words coming from his heart:

You still make me laugh.
You still give me butterflies.
And I am still falling for you
Every single day.
Happy Valentines' Day!
I Love You Today, Tomorrow
And All the Days after that.
Henri

All the days after that! THAT IS LOVE FOREVER!

I am a blessed and highly favored woman! Despite our age (late sixties) and many years together, this man makes me feel thirty-five again, rekindling the love and excitement we felt when we first fell for each other.

I agree with the married survey participants: with God at the helm, the right tools at your disposal, and possessing a willingness to use them, partnered and married life is a great blessing!

The secret formula: Conquer the maze!

When two partners navigate life's ups and downs together, conquering challenges and celebrating victories while fully supporting each other, and honoring their vows of "for richer or poorer, for better or worse," they create a safe, sacred, and joyful space where love is authentic and both partners feel genuinely valued.

I married my best friend, my Prince Henri, and we are living our (mostly) happily ever after. – Hey! Manage your expectations, remember. It may not be 100 percent. But Thank God Almighty, in my humble opinion, 95 percent is A+ for AWESOME! The absent 5 percent keeps us grounded.

My prayer for you, if you are single, is that you cross path with the one designed just for you, under the perfect circumstances, where you can connect, and join each other as partners to walk this life journey together.

If you are currently in a relationship, I hope the stories and the insights shared here inspire you to explore new possibilities for deepening your connection and enhancing satisfaction in your romantic partnership.

Here is to: **Finding and loving A BEST FRIEND!** Forever!

Cheers!

God bless and God speed.

Auntie

ACKNOWLEDGEMENTS

I have been blessed to have many wonderful people support me and help bring this book together. However, this project would not exist if God hadn't put it upon my heart to write a book about relationships. For his many blessings, his consistent guidance, and Him trusting me to speak to others about LOVE, the universal truth that originated with Him, I am filled with gratitude. Always, in my life, to God be the glory!

To my darling husband, my best friend, I can't thank you enough for your consistent support and you loving me above one hundred percent. I am grateful you keep me grounded while allowing me room to be who God created me to be. Yes! I do love you forever.

My loving family – sisters, nieces, nephews, daughters-in-love and godchildren. Our reciprocal love feeds my soul. You have always supported me in my various endeavors and encourage me to pursue my dreams no matter my age. I love you all and am thankful for you.

A special thank you to Karen Anglade and Danielle Isles, my editors. Karen, your suggestion to use a labyrinth for the cover design was truly an inspiration. I am forever indebted to you both for your insightful comments and revisions that helped make this a better book. I can always count on you to give it to me straight and stir me in the direction that even I, could barely identify as the correct one. I am privileged to have you in my life.

My deepest gratitude to my pastors, Jacqueline and Jerry Martin of Light of the World Christian Fellowship in Humble, TX. You always cover me with your prayers and encourage me to seek God's purpose for my life.

Special thanks to the network of individuals I am privileged to call friends, especially my sisters at Light of the World. You provided words of encouragement, prayers and leads to fruitful connections.

Pat D., little did you know that our brunch conversation about divorce and the challenges of dating would inspire this book. You ignited sparks of motivation when you texted me later to say, "Danielle, you are truly a JEWEL! Thank you for being you." I recognized that God was speaking through you. He reminded me that I had wisdom and truth to share with those seeking a relationship or aspiring to strengthen the ones they were in. So, I listened to the prompting, and here is the final product.

Thank you to all the individuals, singles and married couples who so graciously completed my survey *Dating and Relationships in the 2020s.* You allowed yourselves the vulnerability to share with me your challenges, your concerns, and your success stories regarding relationships. And in so doing, you provided me a platform to support my theories on what works and what doesn't in romantic relationships.

Chasity – (Declared Marketing), my marketing guru, I appreciate your patience and guidance grooming this "seasoned lady" into a social media savvy content creator.

Thank you to Ellie at Starbuck store #11297 in Atascocita for your generous contribution of gift items for my survey.

Shout out to Ken and Kendrick Jones of Level One Fitness in Houston for so graciously facilitating my survey drive at your location.

A huge thank you to all the authors, publications and organizations listed in Referenced Sources, for granting me permission to use your published quotes and material. I am much obliged.

I pray that each and every one of you who contributed to this book and my creative endeavors in any way, be blessed with your "mostly happily ever after" love story, in a successful, enduring relationship with your special someone.

Thank you ALL from a heart overflowing with gratitude.

Here is to You and here is to LOVE!

Danielle

MY BELOVED Part 1 - My Inspiration

2015 - Danielle celebrates a milestone birthday surrounded by
a few of her beloved: husband, sister, nieces, nephews, grand-niece and
grand-nephew.

MY BELOVED Part 2

First Niece

Nieces

Nephew & niece-in-love

Niece

Goddaughter & grand-nephew

Daughter-in-love

Goddaughter
College Grad – 2024

Grand-nephew

REFERENCED SOURCES

PAGE   QUOTE

PART I

4   *"Look At me! – The Perils of Self-Absorption,"* Danielle Coulanges, blog post, October 2023 - https://butterflypublication.com/f/look-at-me---the-perils-of-self-absorption

4   *"Woman downs 48 oysters. Date heads for the door..."* – October 2023 – https://www.reddit.com/r/TikTokCringe/comments/1775qra/date_escapes_after_she_ate_48_oysters_and_an/?rdt=39578

8   *"A Therapist shares the 9 things people want most in life...,"* article by Charlotte Fox Weber – July 24, 2023 – https://www.cnbc.com/2023/07/24/therapist-shares-the-things-people-want-most-in-life-and-how-to-get-them.html

12   *'Abbott Elementary' Star Sheryl Lee Ralph at 66: 'My Life Has Been About Preparing For Longevity'* - AARP article by Harriette Cole – July 25, 2023 https://www.aarp.org/entertainment/celebrities/info-2023/sheryl-lee-ralph-interview.html

16   *"Five Reasons It Is Not Good for Man to Be Alone,"* – *LaPierre*, Scott, *Your Marriage God's Way*, Charis Publishing, 2016, page 40

17   Divorce statistics https://www.census.gov/library/stories/2023/07/marriage-divorce-rates.html

https://www.bgsu.edu/ncfmr/resources/data/family-profiles/loo-divorce-rate-US-geographicvariation2022fp2324.html#:~:text=After%20 reaching%20a%2040%2Dyear,increase%20from%202021%20to%202022.

22   *The Pivot Podcast.* Media Queen Gayle King Bond w/Oprah, Dating After Divorce, Her Favorite 4 Letter Word - January 2024 – https://www. youtube.com/watch?v=AhT58mUFhEQ

25   *CDC National Center for Disease Control.* 2005 Report – https://www. cdc.gov/nchs/data/nvsr/nvsr55/nvsr55_11.pdf

28   *"I Wish I Knew How It Would Feel To Be Free"* – 1967 song by Nina Simone - Originally written by Billy Taylor, with lyrics by Dick Dallas.

"Free," 1976 song by Deniece Williams – Columbia Records, Songwriters Deniece Williams, Hank Redd, Nathan Watts, Susaye Greene

"Free" 2008 song by Ultra Naté - Written by John Ciafone, Lem Springsteen & Ultra Naté.

"Soar" – song by Christina Aguilera, 2012 – Songwriters: Christina Aguilera / Heather Noelle Holley / Rob Hoffman

"Free" by John Legend 2022- Songwriters: John Roger Stephens

47   *"Jake's Insurance commercial"* – State Farm Insurance

57   *"What is courting? Why every relationship needs courtship"* – Thriveworks article by Jon Negroni, September 30, 2013 -https://thriveworks.com/blog/ every-relationshipneedscourtship/#:~:text=Courtship%20is%20the%20 slow%2C%20systematic,before%20becoming%20an%20intimate%20lover

57   *"Courting vs Dating: The vintage way of finding happily ever after",* by eHarmony Editorial Team – November 22, 2023 - https://www.eharmony. com/dating-advice/dating/courting-vs-dating/

PART II

67   *"Don't let him waste your time,"* Call Her Daddy podcast with Ciara – October 2023 – https://open.spotify.com/ episode/4viL9tit04Udd1qCv2BydB

73   KG Smooth – actor, radio host, *Magic After Dark, Quiet Storm.* - https://myhoustonmajic.com/author/kgsmooth/

84   *"Confidence is key"* – Herriman Telegraph website – Kendall Stables – November 12, 2021 – https://herrimantelegraph.org/3366/uncategorized/confidence-is-key/

84   *"The Importance of self-awareness in Emotional Intelligence,"* by Andrew Wallbridge – tsw.co.uk – February 27, 2023 – https://www.tsw.co.uk/blog/leadership-and-management/self-awareness-in-emotionalintelligence/#:~:text=Home%20%C2%BB%20The%20TSW%20Blog%20%C2%BB%20Leadership,thoughts%2C%20feelings%

92   *"Jumping the Broom"* – 2011 romantic comedy-drama film directed by Salim Akil

94   *"Maid in Manhattan"* – 2002 American romantic comedy film directed by Wayne Wang

95   *"Daddy's Little Girls"* – 2007 American romantic comedy-drama film written and directed by Tyler Perry

PART III

114   *"Who is Simone Biles Husband..."* by Bryan Murphy – Sporting News.com -https://www.sportingnews.com/us/nfl/news/simone-biles-husband-jonathan-owens-relationship-timeline/38637d941eaaf30507a1f9d4#:~:text=Simon%20Biles%20and%20Jonathan%20Owens,to%20the%20Wall%20Street%20Journal.

114   *"WNBA Star Chiney Ogwumike is married!"* by Sarah Hanlon. The Knot – November 2023 - https://www.theknot.com/content/chiney-ogwumike-relationship

115   *"Just Wright"* is a 2010 romantic comedy-drama film directed by Sanaa Hamri.

118   *"Queen Charlotte – A Bridgerton Story"* is a historical television drama

limited series created by Shonda Rhimes for Netflix.

120	*"Signs and Wonders,"* sermon by Pastor Jerry Martin – May 20, 2024 - https://www.youtube.com/watch?v=-mgKd-Cs7Wo

125	*"Singleness: The Journey"* by Pastor Jasmine Berry – May 30, 2024 https://www.youtube.com/watch?v=WOG7tpM7JJI

130	*"How Gen Z is challenging the taboo of talking about salaries…"* Yahoo.com article by Donnavan Smoot – March 15, 2024 - https://www.yahoo.com/news/how-gen-z-is-challenging-the-taboo-of-talking-about-salaries-its-important-to-showcase-my-finances-in-a-transparent-way-230652337.html

138	*"Suits"*1980s television series starring Meaghan Markle, picked up by Netflix in 2023.

154	*"Idina Menzel Dinner's on Me"* with Jesse Tyler Ferguson https://podcasts.apple.com/us/podcast/idinamenzel/id1683905652?i=1000630763064

165	*"The Perils of Intimacy"* – This American Life, public radio broadcast hosted by Ira Glass – May 2016 – rebroadcasted April 2024 - https://www.thisamericanlife.org/587/the-perils-of-intimacy

PART IV

172	*"Warren Buffett Has Spent 70 Years of His Life Married…"* by Jeannine Mancini Benzinga.com article – February 21, 2024 https://www.benzinga.com/general/24/02/37237342/warren-buffett-has-spent-70-years-of-his-life-married-his-advice-if-you-want-a-marriage-to-last-look

177	*"Biblical foundation of the family"* – Pastor Jackie Martin – LOWCF, sermon of April 21, 2024 – https://www.youtube.com/watch?v=MJikgYXviQo

179	*"Respectful Relationships"* posted on Queensland Government's website - https://www.qld.gov.au/youth/relationships-safety-sexuality/relationships-sexuality/respectful-relationships

181   *"Jenna Bush Hager Reveals the 'Sweet' Gesture Geoge W. Bush Does 'Every Single Morning' for Wife Laura Bush"* – People magazine article by Ingrid Vasquez – March 21, 2024 – https://people.com/george-w-bush-sweet-morning-gesture-laura-bush-8612984

183   *"What is Grace? Bible Meaning and Importance"* by Justin Holcomb – January 26, 2024 – https://www.christianity.com/wiki/christian-terms/what-is-grace.html#google_vignette

186   *"Shift Happens feat. LeToya Luckett"*- Good Moms Bad Choices podcast 2022

https://www.youtube.com/watch?v=UCF4oVqjD00

188   *"The Four Horsemen Toxic Communication Styles and How To Rein Them in"* article by May Soo, posted on RWA Psychology – https://www.rwapsych.com.au/blog/the-four-horsemen-toxic-communication-styles-and-how-to-rein-them-in/

194   *"Homeownership Gender Gap: Single Women Own More Homes Than Single Men"* article on Lending Tree.com By Jacob Channel – January 16, 2021

https://www.lendingtree.com/home/mortgage/single-women-own-more-homes-than-single-men-do/

195   *"What is financial infidelity"* – Verner Brumley Mueller Parker PC website – August 9, 2023 – https://www.vernerbrumley.com/blog/2023/august/what-is-financial-infidelity-/

200   *"Contemplating bankruptcy': This Florida woman had $500K in the bank and a mortgage-free home. Now she's broke — thanks to her husband — and joining a surge of Americans facing bankruptcy,"* by Sabina Wex , posted on Yahoo! Finance – March 8, 2024

https://finance.yahoo.com/news/m-contemplating-bankruptcy-florida-woman-110300154.html

215   *"American Got Talent' host Terry Crews and his wife Rebecca Have Overcome So Much"* by Kayla Keegan – Good Housekeeping - February 2022 https://www.goodhousekeeping.com/life/entertainment/a25605681/americas-got-talent-terry-crews-wife/

215   *"Ja Rule and Aisha Atkins, the WAGS of These Rappers Are Outshining Their Partners,"* by Patricia Rodriguez - Choices May 2024 --- https://www.daily-choices.com/the-wags-of-these-rappers-are-outshining-their-partners/2?xcmg=1&_d=d

223   *"I Feel Pretty"* 1961 song from the musical *Westside Story* – Songwriters: Stephen Sondheim/Leonard Bernstein

223   *"Men Are from Mars, Women Are from Venus,"* book by author John Gray

224   *"Ice-T Shares his Steamy Secrets to Successful Marriage with Coco Austin"* by Lindsay Weinberg – March 25, 2023 -https://www.eonline.com/news/1369299/ice-t-shares-his-steamy-secrets-to-successful-marriage-with-coco-austin

231   *"Are You Adrift in a Sexless Relationship?"* AARP article by Ken Budd – October 4, 2023 – https://www.aarp.org/home-family/friends-family/info-2023/sexless-relationship-after-50.html

236   *"Carson Daly Says Sleeping in Separate Bed from Wife Siri Helps Them 'Stay Together"* People magazine article, by Julia Moore and Dory Jackson – April 9, 2024 – https://people.com/carson-daly-says-sleeping-in-separate-bed-from-wife-siri-helps-them-stay-together-exclusive-8628808#:~:text=At%20the%20Today%20show's%20Solar,object%20is%20to%20stay%20together.

244   *"Dame Joan Collins: After four divorces I finally worked out the secret of a happy marriage: separate bathrooms, banishment for snoring and a fit young husband"* by Dame Joan Collins for The Mail Sunday – February 24, 2018 -   https://www.dailymail.co.uk/news/article-5430917/DAME-JOAN-

COLLINS-secret-happy-marriage.html

249 *"Kisses in the Moonlight,"* 1986 song by George Benson https://www.youtube.com/watch?v=oYb4lhgnfIw

250 *"My Ex Taught Me What Men Truly Want in a Wife,"* Yahoo.com article by Ossiana Tepfenhart – June 10, 2023 - https://www.yahoo.com/lifestyle/ex-taught-men-truly-want-000000180.html?a20

251 *"Samuel L. Jackson Shares the Secret to His 41-Year-Long Marriage to LaTanya Richardson"* – Vanity Fair by Emily Kirkpatrick – March 16, 2022 https://www.vanityfair.com/style/2022/03/samuel-l-jackson-latanya-richardson-marriage-advice-pace-stay-together-black-love

PART V

252 *"Silly Romantics in New York"* – a D'Auntie TikTok video: https://www.tiktok.com/@oneagingdiva/video/7401225990258642219

255 *"The 5 Love Languages – The Secrets to Love that Lasts"* book by Gary Chapman – https://5lovelanguages.com/learn

258 *"Rekindle The Flames"* – *D'Auntie Podcast Ep. 4*: https://youtu.be/x-7Bdfz-vDA

258 *"Ayesha and Stephen Curry Celebrated Their 10-Year Wedding Anniversary"* – Instagram @ayeshacurry and @stephencurry30

SPECIAL GIFT GIVEAWAY

<u>My gift to you</u>

Singles: receive a FREE copy of the *Relationship Profile Template, Ten Questions to Ask Yourself,* a personal questionnaire that is based on the survey questions.

That questionnaire is a self-analysis tool, to assist single individuals desiring a mate, in figuring out their preferences and building a profile for the person they wish to connect with.

Coupled/married: receive a FREE copy of the one-page handy *Daily/Weekly Relationship Maintenance Practices,* a personal checklist to help couples remain connected.

Go to my website: www.butterflypublication.com

Join/subscribe to my email list by entering your email address.

Request the template by name.

The template will be forwarded to you in response.

<u>Note: Pay it forward</u> – If you are already in a committed relationship and feel you don't need this template, request it, and share it with a single or coupled person who could use it.

SCAN THE QR CODE
TO TAKE YOU DIRECTLY TO WEBSITE

ABOUT THE AUTHOR

Danielle Coulanges, born in Haiti and a longtime New Yorker before relocating to Houston, Texas, is a multi-talented writer known for her vibrant presence in various fields. With a background as a former model and fashion designer, the quintessential diva penned several published articles and short stories. She made her mark in the literary world with her memoir, *Cads, Princes & Best Friends: A Tale of Lust, Love & Redemption*. Her engaging blog, "One Aging Diva," and the entertaining "D'Auntie Podcast" on YouTube showcase her insights on life, faith, and relationships.

Danielle's diverse experiences enrich her work: a degree in Economics and English Literature from New Jersey City University, a brief music career, a fashion design business, a compliance role on Wall Street, and teaching French to teenagers at a Houston high school, where daily she got to be teacher, mentor, counselor, and auntie. She also realized her dream of recording music with her album "I Live by Faith," reflecting her life motto.

Now, living with her husband in Houston, Texas, she balances her busy life with gardening, crossword puzzles, karaoke, and romantic movies on Netflix.

For updates on her projects and to participate in monthly giveaways, readers can join her mailing list through her website.

Website: www.butterflypublication.com
Email: danielle@butterflypublication.com
Instagram: https://www.instagram.com/dauntie1
TikTok: @oneagingdiva
YouTube: https://www.youtube.com/@ByFaithMusic

Other book by Danielle Coulanges:

Cads, Princes and Best Friends, A Tale of Lust, Love & Redemption, 2010